Germany 1989

Turning Points Series List

General Editor: Keith Robbins
Vice–Chancellor, University of Wales Lampeter

Germany 1989

In the aftermath of the Cold War

Lothar Kettenacker

PEARSON
Longman

Harlow, England • London • New York • Boston • San Francisco • Toronto
Sydney • Tokyo • Singapore • Hong Kong • Seoul • Taipei • New Delhi
Cape Town • Madrid • Mexico City • Amsterdam • Munich • Paris • Milan

PEARSON EDUCATION LIMITED

Edinburgh Gate
Harlow CM20 2JE
United Kingdom
Tel: +44 (0)1279 623623
Fax: +44 (0)1279 431059
Website: www.pearsoned.co.uk

_____

First edition published in Great Britain in 2009

ISBN: 978-0-582-41897-4

British Library Cataloguing in Publication Data
A CIP catalogue record for this book can be obtained from the British Library

Library of Congress Cataloging-in-Publication Data
Kettenacker, Lothar.
  Germany 1989 : in the aftermath of the Cold War / Lothar Kettenacker. — 1st ed.
    p. cm.
  Includes bibliographical references and index.
  ISBN 978-0-582-41897-4 (pbk.)
  1. Germany—History—Unification, 1990. I. Title.
  DD290.25.K488 2009
  943.087'8—dc22

                                                    2009001846

10 9 8 7 6 5 4 3 2 1
13 12 11 10 09

Set in 9/13.5pt Stone serif by 35
Printed in Malaysia (CTP-KHL)

The Publisher's policy is to use paper manufactured from sustainable forests.

Contents

Chronology of German Unification

I. The Period of Détente (1970–1989)

1970

19 March	Chancellor Willy Brandt and GDR Prime Minister Willi Stoph meet in Erfurt (East Germany)
21 May	Meeting of Brandt and Stoph in Kassel (West Germany)
12 August	Treaty between FRG and USSR, signed in Moscow

1971

3 May	Erich Honecker succeeds Walter Ulbricht as leader of the SED
3 September	Quadripartite Agreement on Berlin
17 December	Agreement between the FRG and the GDR on transit traffic between FRG and Berlin (West)

1972

26 May	Treaty between the FRG and the GDR on traffic questions
21 December	Treaty on the Basis of Relations between the FRG and the GDR (*Grundlagenvertrag*)

1973

18 September	The FRG and the GDR join the United Nations

1974

2 May	The FRG and the GDR set up "Permanent Representations" (kind of embassies) in each other's capital

12 December	Trade agreement between the two states on "Swing", i.e. an upper limit for import credits of the GDR, which will be extended in the future
20 December	Old age pensioners from the West to be freed from obligatory currency exchange as well as further easing of travel restrictions

1975

1 August	Both states sign Helsinki Final Act (CSCE), with "Basket III" on human rights

1976

16 November	Critical song-writer Wolf Biermann expelled

1977

26 September	Honecker defends Intershops because of the need for DM

1978

6 March	Crucial meeting between Honecker and leadership of GDR Protestant Church (*Bund der Evangelischen Kirchen*)
1 June	SED informs Protestant Church about introduction of *Sozialistische Wehrerziehung* (Socialist military education)
16 November	Agreement on motorway Berlin–Hamburg and transit payments

1979

12 December	NATO Council decides to deploy new range of nuclear missiles ("dual track decision")

1980

3 July	West German minister Egon Franke tells public about freedom bought for 13,000 political prisoners of the GDR

| 13 October | Honecker's "Gera Demands" (*inter alia* recognition of GDR citizenship which meets refusal by FRG) |
| 9 November | First "Peace Decade" of young members of the Protestant Church |

1981

| 12–13 December | Chancellor Helmut Schmidt meets Honecker at Lake Werbellin |

1982

15 February	Further easing of travel restrictions for East Germans visiting relations in the West on important family occasions
18 March	First official meeting between *Volkskammer* MPs and SPD deputies
1 October	Helmut Kohl succeeds Schmidt as chancellor following a vote in the *Bundestag*

1983

29 June	Federal government guarantees billion DM credit to GDR
24 July	Bavarian Prime Minister Franz Josef Strauss meets Honecker
22 November	*Bundestag*'s vote for stationing of intermediate-range missiles

1984

15 March	Kohl refers in state of nation speech to German Question still "being open"
25 July	FRG guarantees further credit to GDR
30 November	GDR dismantles automatic shooting devices along the border

1985

| 11 March | Mikhail Gorbachev new General-Secretary of CPSU |

1986

19 February	Horst Sindermann, President of East German parliament, visits Bonn
25 April	First town-twinning between two cities in West and East Germany (Saarlouis–Eisenhüttenstadt)
6 May	Cultural agreement between the two German states
11–12 December	Crucial meeting between US President Ronald Reagan and Gorbachev in Reykjavik and agreement to eliminate all nuclear missiles over time
10 November	Gorbachev announces liberalisation of Soviet policy in Eastern Europe

1987

12 June	Reagan visits West Berlin asking Gorbachev to pull down Wall
27 August	Publication of joint SPD–SED paper on the debate of ideologies and common security
5–6 September	GDR tolerates first unofficial demonstration of independent peace groups in East Berlin
7–11 September	Official state visit of Honecker in the FRG after several failed attempts in the past due to Soviet intervention
12 October	Honecker rejects Soviet reform programme as model for GDR

1988

17 January	Arrests and expulsion of civil rights activists demonstrating in the name of Rosa Luxemburg
15 August	GDR and EEC take up official relations
24–27 October	Kohl visits Moscow and achieves break-through in relations
14 December	Further lifting of travel restrictions

II. The Process of German Unification (1989–90)

1989

6 February	Chris Gueffroy shot while trying to cross the border from East Berlin – last victim along the Wall

2 May	Hungary starts to dismantle fortifications along the border with Austria
7 May	Local government elections in the GDR checked by independent observers and proved to be manipulated
12–15 June	Gorbachev visits FRG
July/August	Growing number of GDR citizens escape during holiday season via Hungary and FRG embassies in Eastern Europe
9 September	Civil rights movements sets up *Neues Forum*, declared to be illegal
11 September	Hungary opens the border with Austria for 6,500 East Germans waiting to cross
12 September	Foundation of the civil rights movement *Demokratie Jetzt (DJ)*
30 September	Nearly 7,000 migrants are allowed to leave for the West via the GDR (6,000 from Prague and 800 from Warsaw)
1 October	Egon Krenz visits China and approves of Tiananmen Square massacre (as had *Volkskammer*, including CDU, on 8.6.1989)
6–7 October	East Berlin celebrations of 40th anniversary of the GDR – hostile demonstrators being arrested. Gorbachev warns Honecker not to delay necessary reforms and says famous sentence that life will punish the latecomer
9 October	Largest, non-violent demonstration in the GDR (Leipzig) since popular uprising on 17 June 1953 (approx. 70,000)
18 October	Erich Honecker resigns from all his functions "for health reasons" and is succeeded by Egon Krenz
30 October	Party *Demokratischer Aufbruch (DA)* formed: Pastor Rainer Eppelmann and Angela Merkel in the forefront
4 November	East Berlin experiences largest mass gathering in the history of the GDR (more than half a million)
6 November	Front page of *Neues Deutschland*: draft of new travel law
8 November	SED Politburo resigns on occasion of tenth meeting of Central Committee
9 November	Berlin Wall comes down
13 November	Hans Modrow, SED chief of the Dresden district, new Prime Minister. – 4.5 *mio* visas since 9/11 for visits to the West
17 November	Modrow's government statement advocates separation of state and party

21 November	Nikolai Portugalov informs Horst Teltschik (Federal Chancery) of advanced Soviet thinking about German Question
26 November	200,000 party members have left the SED since October. East German intellectuals and artists publish appeal "For Our Country" demanding GDR be socialist alternative to FRG
27 November	Slogan "We are one people" dominates Leipzig demonstrations
28 November	Kohl announces "Ten Point Programme" for solving German Question (confederation for transitional period)
1 December	*Volkskammer* deletes leading role of SED from constitution
2 December	President Bush and Gorbachev meet in Malta
6 December	Following the resignation of Politburo and SED Central Committee Egon Krenz steps down as well
7 December	First session of the newly formed "Round Table" (15 government seats, 19 for oppositions, 4 independent)
11 December	Ambassadors of Four Powers meet at former West Berlin Control Council building, Bonn being excluded and upset
14 December	Under pressure from "Round Table" Modrow dissolves "Office of State Security" (the renamed Stasi ministry)
15 December	Special SED Conference votes for renaming party *Partei des Demokratischen Sozialismus* (PDS) with Gregor Gysi as new chairman
18–19 December	Party Conference of SPD in Berlin recognises East German sister party
19 December	Kohl visits Dresden, overwhelmed by cheering crowds, and is now convinced of unification in near future
22 December	Opening of Brandenburg Gate, symbol of the old capital, in presence of both Kohl and Modrow and the two Lord Mayors of West and East Berlin

1990

15 January	Crowds storm headquarters of Stasi in East Berlin
1 February	Modrow presents plan for German unification in stages. Kohl rejects neutrality of united Germany

5 February	"Alliance for Germany" formed, on the initiative of Kohl, consisting of CDU (East), DA and newly founded DSU (*Deutsche Soziale Union*)
7 February	Bonn decides to offer GDR "Monetary and Economic Union". Cabinet sets up Committee *Deutsche Einheit*
10 February	Kohl visits Moscow. Gorbachev gives green light for German unification to be worked out between the two states
13 February	East German PM Modrow comes to Bonn with newly appointed ministers of "Round Table" opposition asking for financial assistance
22–25 February	Party congress of SPD (East) passes timetable for unification and elects Ibrahim Böhme as chairman (soon to be uncovered as Stasi informer)
6 March	"Alliance for Germany" opts for fast track to unification according to § 23 (Basic Law)
18 March	First free elections in GDR won by Alliance against all forecasts
12 April	Lothar de Maiziere elected Prime Minister of a coalition government including SPD and Liberals
24 April	Agreement between Bonn and East Berlin on "Monetary, Economic and Social Union" by 1 July
5 May	"Two-plus-Four" negotiations begin in Bonn
6 May	Local government elections in East Germany confirm result of previous *Volkskammer* elections
18 May	West and East German ministers of finance, Theo Waigel and Walter Romberg, sign state treaty on monetary union
17 June	East German parliament passes new law concerning privatisation of industry and commerce by *Treuhand*
21 June	Two-third majority in both German parliaments for "Monetary, Economic and Social Union" (in force on 1 July)
6 July	Unity Treaty negotiations begin
20 July	Soviet–German summit in the Caucasus achieves breakthrough: united Germany can choose its alliance and remain in NATO
22 July	*Volkskammer* passes laws allowing for reintroduction of East German Länder and for regulating elections

22–23 August	A two-third majority of *Volkskammer* votes for accession of GDR to the area of Basic Law according to § 23 by 3 October
24 August	Parliament passes a law securing all files and data of the Stasi
12 September	Conclusion of "Two-plus-Four" negotiations and signing of agreement in Moscow (i.e. in lieu of a peace treaty)
3 October	GDR joins the Federal Republic of Germany at zero hour
9 November	FRG and Soviet Union sign treaty on "good neighbourliness"
2 December	First all-German elections in FRG and former GDR confirm Chancellor Helmut Kohl in office

Publisher's acknowledgements

We are grateful to the following for permission to reproduce copyright material:

Cartoons

Cartoons 1, 2, 3, 4, 6, 9 and 10 by Walter Hanel; Cartoon 5 from Foundation Haus der Geschichte, Zeitgeschichtliches Forum Leipzig, artist: Fritz Behrendt; Cartoons 7 and 8 by Egon Kaiser; Cartoon 11 Horst Haitzinger.

Maps

Map 2 adapted from *Die Demografische Lage der Nation*, Berlin-Institut für Bevölkerung und Entwicklung (2006) p. 39; Map 3 adapted from *Die Demografische Lage der Nation*, Berlin-Institut für Bevölkerung und Entwicklung (2006) p. 36; Map 4 adapted from *Die Demografische Lage der Nation*, Berlin-Institut für Bevölkerung und Entwicklung (2006) p. 23.

Photographs

Photograph on p. 261 by Andreas Schoelzel (www.schoelzel.net).

In some instances we have been unable to trace the owners of copyright material, and we would appreciate any information that would enable us to do so.

Author's acknowledgements

To my teacher Paul Kluke (1908–1990) who rejected both German dictatorships and never lost hope in a democratic and united Germany.

I would like to thank my daughter Polly who undertook the initial copy-editing. Thanks also to Marjorie Leith for her copy-editing work. I feel the need to express my thanks and gratitude to Keith Robbins who invited me to write this book, checked the manuscript and saw to it that I finished it. I have never experienced as close a relationship with any German publisher during the final phase of publication.

Glossary

Basic Law This is the Constitution of the Federal Republic of Germany, introduced on 23 May 1949 and still in force (with several amendments). Since West Germany saw itself as a provisional state, the term constitution (*Verfassung*) was thought to be inappropriate.

Blockade running/airlift As a reaction to the currency reform in the Western zones and West Berlin, the Soviets blocked all access routes to Berlin in the summer of 1948. The city had to be supplied from the air with all essentials (including coal), a task not thought to be feasible. The blockade was abandoned by the Russians in the spring of 1949.

Checkpoint Charlie Well-known transition point from the US to the Soviet Sector in Berlin, famous for confrontation of American and Russian tanks during the Berlin Wall crisis.

Hallstein doctrine Named by the Permanent Under-Secretary of State (*Staatssekretär*) Walter Hallstein in the German Foreign Office (*Auswärtiges Amt*), later first head of the European Commission. It laid down that diplomatic relations should be severed with all states that recognized the GDR (except the Soviet Union because it was one of the occupying powers). Introduced in 1955 after Chancellor Adenauer had visited Moscow in 1955 and established diplomatic relations with the Soviet Union and valid until the FR recognised the GDR in the early 1970s.

Helsinki Process The first attempt to overcome the Cold War through the Conference on Security and Cooperation in Europe (CSCE), opened in Helsinki in July 1973 and is famous for the signing of the final act in August 1975, by 35 European states as well as the USA and Canada. It recognized both the borders in Europe and certain human rights (so-called basket III) such as the right to travel freely. Human rights activists in the GDR and elsewhere kept appealing to it in following years.

July Plot Assassination attempt by Colonel Claus Schenk Graf von Stauffenberg on Hitler in his headquarters in East Prussia (now Poland) on 20 July 1944 in order to end the war. New US film due with Tom Cruise as Stauffenberg.

Stasi Popular name for the notorious GDR Ministry for State Security headed by Erich Mielke, whose character is explained in detail in the book.

"Trabant" (popularly "Trabi") was the name of the cheaply built East German car for which people had to wait years. It compared badly with West German cars and thus became the symbol of East Germany's quality of life. When the Wall came down on 9 November 1989 the picture of long queues (trek) of "Trabis" moving westwards implanted itself as an iconographic image of what had happened.

Introduction

The accommodation of the German people, or rather the German speaking peoples, within the modern nation state has plagued Europe for nearly two centuries and has been referred to by historians as the "German Question".[1] The Germanic tribes (*Stämme*) who settled in the centre of Europe could easily have evolved into different nation states the size of the Netherlands, Switzerland or modern Austria. Instead, late in the day and on the battlefield, a single nation state had been forged. In retrospect, German unification under Bismarck in 1871 takes on the character of a delayed nuclear reaction that was to release its destructive energy in two world wars. The second catastrophe ended with Germany's unconditional surrender followed by total occupation. The victorious allies made sure that the "German volcano" (Winston Churchill),[2] territorial expansionism fuelled by power-politics, would have no chance to erupt once again. And this is where the story of German unification mark II begins.

The first chapter will show in some detail how the division of Germany came about in the first place. There was one war aim on which all Allies could easily agree: emasculating Germany to the extent that she should never be able to start another war. One way seemed to be to undo the work of Bismarck. During the war the idea of dismembering the German Reich had been discussed at length among the Allies only to be rejected as unmanageable and historically retrograde. Reason triumphed over revenge. In the end partition re-entered the scene through the back door: as the unintended outcome of the zoning of Germany for the purpose of Allied occupation. As a result of the Cold War the Western demarcation line of the Soviet zone was to be transformed into the highly fortified border splitting the country into two states affiliated to the two hostile camps: the Federal Republic of Germany (FRG) and the German Democratic Republic (GDR). Various plans to overcome the division by neutralising Germany did not succeed. Soon Europe got used to the idea of two Germanys. After all, Austria had shown the way by establishing itself as another German-speaking nation in post-war Europe. But the division of Germany, so much the expression of the Cold War rather than the previous World War, did not foster peace in Europe. What had been the result of the war, a war fought for the extension of German *Lebensraum*, was the loss of the Eastern territories, one-fourth of the Reich, which is indeed irreversible. History is not without a sense of punitive logic.

Chapter 2 demonstrates that the confrontation of the two chief antagonists of the Cold War, the United States and Soviet Russia, on German soil was the cause of many dangerous conflicts in Europe, mainly centred on the fate of Berlin and fuelled by the growing build-up of German armies and a nuclear arsenal on both sides. The second Berlin crisis was not resolved until the East German régime closed the last loophole for escape by building the Berlin Wall in August 1961. The horrendous Wall, which cut all contacts between the Berlin population on both sides, as well as Bonn's stubborn policy of non-recognition (Hallstein doctrine), made the need for détente all the more apparent.

The answer was Willy Brandt's *Ostpolitik* (Chapter 3), which in the long run proved to be as crucial as Konrad Adenauer's *Westpolitik* in the 1950s. While the latter put the Western Allies at ease and laid the foundation for the European Economic Community, and thus West Germany's economic prosperity, *Ostpolitik* gave both the Soviet Government and the East German leadership an equal though false sense of security. At the time, the deal seemed to benefit the East more than the West: Bonn's recognition of the GDR and of the post-war borders in Europe that would not be violated by force, against a guarantee of West Berlin's long-term security and the hope for an improvement in human rights in Eastern Europe through the so-called Helsinki process. The various treaties, including the recognition of the Oder-Neisse border with Poland, seemed to confirm the mistaken view that the division of Germany was the eventual outcome of the war and as such an immutable historical fact. Today it is difficult to determine whether the chief architects of *Ostpolitik* – Willy Brandt and Egon Bahr – did mean to foster the conditions for German reunification or whether they just wished to ban the use of force and thereby improve human contacts between the two Germanys. The magic words were *"Wandel durch Annäherung"* ("change through rapprochement"). Whatever their motives and final intentions, this move did indeed prepare the ground for unification in 1990: the increasing influx of oxygen from the West helped to erode the rigid foundations of the East German dictatorship.

Ostpolitik brought about a change of political climate that, in turn, produced a fermentation process within Eastern bloc countries, notably Poland and Hungary and to a lesser extent in the GDR. While elsewhere governments tried to accommodate public grievances, the geriatric East German Politburo held on to its Stalinist approach to politics. The fundamental improvement in relations with Bonn, as indicated by the rapid increase of visits from West German politicians and businessmen, reassured Erich Honecker, the East German leader, that the GDR had no reason to fear Bonn any more. His own people had been kept in check through mass organisations and a most sophisticated surveillance system set up by the Ministry for State Security. Their many spies in West German government offices could only report what had been a standard news item during the First World War: "*Im Westen nichts Neues*" (i.e. no new danger emanating from West Germany) However, unknown to participants, the cunning of history made steady progress. The human rights activists who were to spearhead the revolution of 1989 seemed to be a manageable nuisance, no real threat because they did not question the GDR or Socialism.

In retrospect, the historian can clearly see which developments, by reinforcing each other, contributed to the eruption of 1989/90 (Chapter 4). However, at the time, their interconnectedness could not be discerned: the surge of free trade unions in Poland; the reformer Mikhail Gorbachev rising to the top of the Soviet government; the East German economy declining rapidly due to higher prices for Russian oil and gas deliveries; foreign credits propping up East German living standards; the subsequent rescue of East Berlin on the international money market through West German loans that brought, in return, the lifting of travel restrictions for East German pensioners and relatives and the dismantling of firing devices along the border; the peace movement in East and West Germany; Kohl insisting on the cultural entity and unity of the German nation and his refusal to recognise a separate GDR citizenship, and the Soviet leader relaxing his grip on East Germany by abandoning the Brezhnev doctrine.

In the end, an otherwise unimportant event such as the wire-cutting along the Hungarian border with Austria sufficed to set off a peaceful chain reaction that was to bring down the fragile nature of Europe's post-war structure (Chapter 5). As never before in the twentieth century, democratic self-determination proved to be the driving force for change: first, the unstoppable exodus of East Germans, mostly of the younger generation, via Hungary and Czechoslovakia, then the rapidly increasing demonstrations at home and mounting pressure for change leading first to the collapse of the one-party régime and then of the GDR as a separate state. All this will be described in some detail, including all unforeseen turns and twists such as the bankruptcy of the East German economy and the popular vote for a fast-track solution against the advice of human rights activists, the diplomatic accommodation of German unification (Chapter 6), and Bonn's economic take-over (Chapter 7) in the course of only a few months. This story has been told many times since 1990 and will therefore constitute only one-third of the book. Its heroes are all those ordinary East German citizens who had had enough of being bossed around by an unelected government. In the end, the high and mighty, leaders like Mikhail Gorbachev, Chancellor Helmut Kohl and US President George Bush, came to the conclusion that the situation would get out of control unless they tried to make the best of the inevitable. Thus, no Russian tanks were brought in as in Berlin (1953), in Budapest (1956) or Prague (1968). Thanks to common sense prevailing in Moscow, the revolutionary transformation of 1989/90 was brought about without a single shot or casualty. German unification mark II had been the outcome of crisis management both on the domestic and the international level. Contrary to 1871, it had not been anticipated. Nor was it the result of any kind of national yearning in the larger part of Germany. If the idea of national identity did come into play it was due to an uncanny union between the West German political establishment and the mass of the East German population. In the last consequence it was the East Germans then, less guilt-ridden about the common past, who reminded their fellow countrymen that they belonged to one and the same nation. The Left in both parts of Germany had been misled by the Zeitgeist which questioned the idea of a German nation state. Most of the leading intellectuals had persuaded themselves that the *status quo* was a necessary precondition for peace in Europe. More than elsewhere, historians in Germany tended to interpret the existing state of affairs as the definite verdict of history. When the chance of German unification arose, they misjudged the latent power of national consciousness. It is a curious phenomenon that Germany's neighbours seemed to be have been better informed about the significance of the nation state and the unnatural conditions in central Europe than the Germans themselves. This is one reason why their governments abandoned their reservations when the silent majority in East Germany indicated their wish to speak.

While the acceptance of German unification by the four wartime allies responsible for Germany as a whole, especially the integration of the enlarged Federal Republic into NATO, has been hailed as one of the greatest triumphs of diplomacy in the twentieth century, the subsequent process of actually merging the two estranged societies has been fraught with obstacles and difficulties. The celebrations when the Wall was breached in November 1989 and the new enlarged Germany came into being a year later (3 October 1990) were short-lived. The transformation process (Chapter 8) produced a crisis of identity in East Germany (Chapter 9) which still lingers on.

It has to be said, though, that the task of fusing two totally different economies, one capitalist and market driven, the other socialist and planned to the last button, as well as two societies of the same nation, which had been separated for more then 40 years, has been without precedent. German politicians could look nowhere for guidance. The collapse of Communist régimes all over Eastern Europe seemed to suggest that the state had failed to manage the economy since it was unable to provide decent living conditions for its peoples. Bonn had no clue what else to do except to bail out the economy and superimpose its own social, judicial and economic system upon a society totally unprepared for such an experience. Kohl went out of his way and out of his depth when he predicted "blossoming landscapes in the East within five years". It was unfortunate that all this happened in an election year. The last reliable election results in East Germany, though out of date by 60 years, suggested that a triumph of Social Democracy was a near certainty. Cynics may say that in order to undo this prediction Kohl turned 1990 into one huge election campaign: the votes of the East Germans were bought by fast-track unification and parity of the two unequal currencies while West Germans were told that all this could be achieved without raising taxes. In later years Kohl would be charged with not living up to the unique challenge by confronting the German nation with stark reality and asking for real sacrifices.

In his defence, it could be argued that few if any experts in the West had a clear picture of the state of the East German economy once exposed to market forces. Official statistics ranking the GDR as number ten among the world's strongest economies had been as misleading as the annual industrial showpiece of the Leipzig Trade Fair which attracted many West Germany businessmen and politicians. On the whole, Western correspondents and academics did nothing to correct the general impression that the political and economic stability of the GDR was unassailable. To some extent this blindness towards the real state of affairs was due to the overall desire in the West not to jeopardise the policy of détente (Chapter 4). There was no single secret office in Bonn that could prepare the country for day-X-plus-one in the unlikely event of a sudden collapse of the GDR. It was simply not expected to happen in one's lifetime. But it was a fortunate constellation that it happened in the lifetime of a German chancellor whose background and interests were that of a historian and who was driven by a sense of history. In the decisions he actually took Helmut Kohl would not be held back by short-term problems or reservations due to the prevailing *Zeitgeist*. However, in his rhetoric, he shrank from appealing more forcefully to national solidarity and a sense of burden-sharing. Like Adenauer, he had his doubts about the political maturity of his own people, once hyper-nationalistic and now in large parts in denial of its national responsibility. Yet, all in all, he was the creator of German unification mark II – though in a totally different historical context from Bismarck's mark I. Kohl was not founder of another German Reich but of a re-invented nation at peace with itself and safely embedded in the European Union.

The final chapter (Chapter 10) deals with the public debate on how the second German dictatorship should be remembered in relation to that of Hitler. In a global historical perspective it makes sense to argue that in the last resort German unification was due to the Soviet Union's loss of faith in its imperial mission rather than to the people's revolution in the autumn of 1989 or Chancellor Kohl's determination to make the best of it. On their own, without the protection of their Soviet masters and the Red Army, the East German leaders could not stay in power for any length of time. The intrinsic instability of the SED's rule had been exposed most clearly at the very end. In spite of frantic efforts over the years, a kind of *"plébiscite de tous les jours"* (Ernest Renan), to vindicate its existence, the GDR never succeeded in establishing lasting legitimacy. Right from the beginning up to the end it had been a state without democratic substance, a régime which had to resort to prison walls, barbed wire, border guards with shooting orders and a host of spies to prevent its people from running away. Given half a chance East Germans turned their back on the GDR, which they perceived to be neither German nor democratic.

The uprising of the people ("We are the people") in the autumn of 1989 had all the hallmarks of a genuine revolution: the demonstration of formidable defiance for the sake of political self-determination. Nothing like it had occurred in German history before. The hopes of the human rights activists for a symbiosis of democracy and socialism were not fulfilled. A second wave of demonstrations demanding German unification drowned all such utopian ideas. East Germans having suffered years of deprivation had enough common sense not to fall for the promises of another socialist experiment advocated by new paragons of virtue who assailed them with warnings against the consumer society. Thus a government, a political system and finally a state were swept away within a few months. Historians will forever debate how totalitarian the second German dictatorship had been or whether the uprising of 1989 met all the criteria of a genuine revolution.

Frankly speaking, this is of only academic interest. What matters is, as has been briefly outlined in this introduction, that the division of Germany and the Cold War have been seen off into history. Perhaps more importantly, the "German Question" has been put to rest as well.

Notes and references

1 See Peter Alter, *The German Question and Europe. A History* (London, 2000).

2 Winston S. Churchill, *The World Crisis 1916–1918*, vol. III/2 (London, 1927), p. 543. He concludes by writing: "Surely, Germans, for history it is enough!" Most unfortunately, it was not.

CHAPTER 1

Division through zoning

The story of German unification mark II in 1989/90 cannot be fully understood without a detailed examination of how the division of the country came about in the first place. Division and unification, neither of which had been anticipated by the former Allies when they occurred, are closely linked. No doubt, the Allies were in agreement about the demise of Prussia, founder state of the Second German Empire and alleged source of all evil: the Control Council issued its death certificate in March 1947.[1] The division of Germany into two separate and opposing states was a different matter. It was entirely due to the partitioning of Germany into zones of occupation and the ensuing Cold War, which froze provisional demarcation lines into solid borders, eventually creating frontiers between two antagonistic camps. No wonder, therefore, that unification should coincide with the end of the Cold War. The latter did not grow out of some avoidable misunderstanding between friends after fighting a common enemy. Rather it was the logical outcome of ideas about the future that were fundamentally different and in the end irreconcilable.

For some time, the heads of states had discussed the idea of emasculating Germany for good by dismembering the Reich. But this plan remained controversial to the end and had never been accepted as official policy. As a result of this inherent ambivalence there was, right from the beginning, no clear resolve to avert the eventual division of Germany, first into zones of occupation and then into separate states. The attitude of the Allies towards the so-called German Question showed an uncanny resemblance both during and after the war. The pragmatic position was: As long as we cannot control the whole of the country we should accept the situation as it develops. In the course of this development Germany changed from the trophy of a common victory and joint responsibility to a bone of contention.

The British Government, from July 1942, was the first to make detailed preparations for the post-war period.[2] The chief lesson of the past was not to repeat the mistakes made at Versailles after the First World War. All those leaders who had experienced the First World War and its aftermath, like Winston Churchill and Anthony Eden, now felt they were called upon to bring about a more lasting peace. These terms of reference constituted such a powerful influence on the decision-makers that John Maynard Keynes was concerned that they might deflect from future challenges.[3]

It was Great Britain that forged the grand alliance against Nazi Germany by conducting a joint strategy with the United States since January 1942 and concluding a formal alliance with Soviet Russia at the end of May 1942. For that reason, when preparing for the future, British planners had to take account of the security interests of their new allies. The most constructive and far-reaching American contribution to achieving lasting peace in Europe was Sumner Welles' suggestion that there should be a "cooling-off period" before any treaty was signed.[4] Again Versailles, where the passions of war had been allowed to overflow and to compromise the future, served as a warning of how not to proceed. All this pointed to the Reich being subjected to a joint post-war occupation régime of the Allies until the time for a definite peace treaty had come.

Unknown to his Western allies, Stalin pursued a different agenda: Soviet security required the installation of "friendly" governments in Eastern Europe, not least in Germany, that is to say either Communist or Popular Front governments preferably headed by exiled leaders who had been briefed in Moscow during the war. Stalin trusted his own agents more than any agreement reached with his Western Allies: for ideological reasons and given half a chance, they would leave him in the lurch. However, until the Wehrmacht had been defeated he was dependant on their goodwill and their promise to establish a Second Front in the West to relieve German pressure in the East. But he was not to share their view of the post-war world and commit himself to an open door policy.

All available evidence seems to indicate that both the British government and the Soviet leadership felt it wise to make plans for a worst-case scenario. For Stalin this meant that Anglo-Saxon forces once established on the continent might conquer the whole of Germany because the Wehrmacht would be tempted to invite them to do so. From Stalin's point of view it would have made perfect sense for Field Marshal Rommel to open the Western front to Eisenhower's armies.[5] Always open to conspiracy theories, the suspicion of some kind of collusion between the West and anti-Hitler elements in Germany was to torment him up to the end of the war.[6] As for the British, their greatest fear, especially after Stalingrad, was that the Red Army would reach the Rhine first and take possession of Germany's industrial heartland. Thus their chief concern was to commit Moscow to a binding post-war settlement based on joint occupation before it was too late.

British and American post-war planning for Germany was informed by two underlying assumptions: unconditional surrender and total occupation. While the removal of the Nazi Party from power was virtually a foregone conclusion, the demilitarisation of Germany was regarded as the more demanding task. Both in Britain and the United States there were powerful voices, including those of Churchill and Roosevelt, who felt strongly that the best way of emasculating Germany was to undo Bismarck's work and carve up the Reich into its constituent parts. At the conference of Teheran the Big Three seemed to favour this solution, though without reaching any final and binding decision. As a matter of fact the Western leaders had no brief from their advisers to discuss this matter, since both the Foreign Office and the State Department opposed the idea of "dismemberment" (UK term) or "partition" (US term). A vengeful policy such as dismemberment was regarded as historically and economically retrograde and bound to rekindle German nationalism. In the long run it could not be forced upon an unwilling German people and against public opinion at home. These views, which were shared by the British quality press,[7] would explain why reunification, pushed by popular pressure in 1989/90, could not be stopped. The Foreign Office kept this controversial issue in abeyance while proceeding with post-war planning on the basis of a unitary state. The reasons for this approach are self-evident: for planning to make sense, certain assumptions had to be made, one of which was that Germany would be dealt with in its entirety. Moreover, joint control of the whole of Germany would keep the wartime alliance in existence.

Military occupation was regarded as a technical problem best left to the experts at the War Office. The first draft, worked out by a Military Sub-Committee of the British Chiefs of Staff, reached the Foreign Office as early as mid-March 1943, only weeks after the decisive German defeat at Stalingrad. Naturally, by that time the British wished to satisfy Russian security interests *vis-à-vis* Germany and also to commit the Soviet Government to a joint approach to the German problem, in case they won the war before the Western Allies had had a chance to show their mettle. The first proposals were based on two assumptions that were to predetermine the future: occupation by zones or "areas," as they were then called, and the principle of "joint United Nations occupation". British planning staffs were keen to ensure that each of the three powers received an equal share of Germany.

Right from the beginning a special status was assigned to Berlin as the capital from which the whole of the country was to be supervised by some sort of Allied control machinery. Establishing an international zone of occupation was intended to demonstrate the principle of joint supervision.

In March 1943 Eden and his advisers visited Washington. They found out that American planning for Germany had not yet crystallised into an agreed policy. "The President appeared to favour the dismemberment of Germany as the only wholly satisfactory solution", Eden wrote to Churchill.[8] Sumner Welles, Roosevelt's chief adviser on foreign policy, went one step further and suggested that the areas into which the country was divided for the purposes of military occupation should broadly correspond to the separate states into which Germany would eventually be broken up. However, Secretary of State Cordell Hull and the Joint Chiefs of Staff were not at all convinced that the partition of Germany would solve all problems. US General George W. Strong pleaded for a mixed occupation. One British official, Gladwyn Jebb, noted: "It was thought, on the American side, that the allotment of large areas to any one Power would only result in the creation of zones of influence and that this, in the long run, would not promote harmony among the Big Three". Since the Russians were likely to treat the Germans much more brutally than either the British or the Americans the application of the "mixing-up theory" would ensure even-handed treatment. If this line of thinking had prevailed the division of Germany might well have been averted provided Stalin had been compensated by large-scale reparations. The State Department had first class experts on Germany but not the authority of the Foreign Office within Whitehall. The decision-making élite in London was ultra cautious if not outright defeatist. It is characteristic of this attitude that Lord Gladwyn should argue in his memoirs: "We might have had local Russian authorities established in the Rhineland or the Ruhr".[9] As far as the future was concerned he did not reflect for a moment what it would have meant for Germany and Poland if US troops had been garrisoned along the Oder. The fear of a Communist Germany was uppermost in the official mind.

British planners were perfectly aware that separate zones would lead to different spheres of influence that were bound to hamper a common policy. Thus they turned to Berlin as the focal point of joint responsibility for Germany as a whole. The German capital took on the character of an alibi to deflect from the fact that occupation by zones was basically incompatible with the idea of joint occupation. The Military Sub-Committee recommended a solution "which retains the principle of United Nations occupation but which in fact is primarily an occupation in British, Russian and USA zones". The Chiefs of Staff had their way. On 5 October 1943 the Cabinet, aware of the need to save manpower, accepted the principle of zonal occupation ("key areas") though not without issuing a last warning: "It would be important that the zones should be so arranged as to avoid creating for any of the occupying Powers special 'spheres of influence' within the occupied territories". This was just a way of appeasing those members of the cabinet with forebodings about occupation by zones.

For the military experts in charge of post-war planning safeguarding the unity of Germany was not a priority while saving British manpower certainly was. It was not until summer 1944, months after the Soviet and American governments had agreed in principle to the zoning of Germany, that the Chiefs of Staff were officially asked for their views on the question of dismemberment. Only then did the clash over the treatment of Germany rise to the surface. The military establishment, probably including Churchill, made no bones about their preference for dismembering Germany along the zones of occupation. A north-western state, the size of the Low Countries and completely under British control, was not only a more manageable unit, it was also a more appealing option than running the show in Germany as a whole along with the Russians once the Americans had withdrawn their forces . "We conclude that dismemberment would at least reduce the likelihood of the whole of Germany combining with the U.S.S.R. against us, and that, as an insurance against a hostile U.S.S.R. it would be to our long-term strategic advantage."[10] After all, Britain could supervise the demilitarisation of the Ruhr or else utilise Germany's industrial capacities in case of any future confrontation with the Soviet Union. The Foreign Office would have none of this. The Chiefs of Staff's approach to the German problem was inviting trouble rather than furthering peace. Eden emphatically rejected any idea "that the Germans may serve as part of an anti-Soviet bloc". He felt that "any such conception should be avoided like the plague in our consideration of German problems". He stated categorically: "This is not only a matter of strategy. It is a matter of high policy . . . to preserve the unity and collaboration of the United Nations". Since Soviet spies had infiltrated the Foreign Office[11] we can assume that this exchange of views must have been brought to Stalin's attention and that, with his instinctive preference for Realpolitik, he favoured the scenario sketched out by the Chiefs of Staff. After all, at Teheran he had agreed to the carving up of Germany. Later on he rejected the idea with a view to giving a helping hand to his German Communist agents.

By September 1943 British plans for the occupation of Germany had reached their final stage. One of the chief aims was "to bring home to every

German the realisation that Germany had suffered complete military defeat".[12] It was important "that at this time no room should be left for the legend of German military invincibility, and that the military 'caste' should be discredited in the eyes of every German". The military experts stressed the disadvantages of mixed occupation. Apart from administrative problems – logistics, different pay and provisions, etc. – it might "lead to Russia securing an undue preponderance owing to her superior man-power resources and to the fact that she alone of the great powers is not at war with Japan". The shortage of man-power was one of the political establishment's greatest worries and therefore one of the most powerful arguments in any debate. Only "key areas" were to be occupied and historical boundaries to be left intact to allow for German administration. The exception was Prussia which would be divided among two of the three Allies. "The undue preponderance of Prussia in the past has been one of the chief causes of the growth of the aggressive spirit in Germany, and we feel that the division of this State in two halves during the period of occupation is likely to discourage the rebirth of the Prussian military spirit." The partition of Prussia served as a perfect alibi for the dismemberment of the Reich, apparently still favoured by the Big Three.

The Western Allies had no clue about Soviet political intentions following the defeat of the common enemy. In order to avoid a scramble for Germany by the conquering armies it was essential to come to an understanding about the most immediate and most important requirements at the moment of German surrender:

1   the armistice terms which the Americans preferred to call "instrument of surrender", to be unilaterally imposed on Germany;

2   the form of Allied occupation: total or partial, mixed or by zone;

3   some kind of inter-Allied control machinery, if not outright military government, for the duration of occupation.

What Britain lacked in terms of manpower and military capacity in relation to her two chief Allies she now tried to make up for by diplomacy, in this case by being the first to submit sophisticated draft agreements. At the Moscow conference at the end of 1943, Allied foreign ministers decided to set up an inter-governmental body in London – the European Advisory Commission (EAC) – consisting of the ambassadors of the USA and the Soviet Union and a British delegate. By mid-January 1944, half a year before D-Day and one year before Yalta, the Foreign Office submitted draft agreements on all three requirements mentioned above. Some elements of these plans were to have far-reaching repercussions, i.e. shaping the future of Germany up to 1990. The chosen procedure was highly technocratic and, so it seemed, devoid of politics so as not to elicit controversy among the three Allies.

The draft proposal for the occupation of Germany submitted to the EAC on 15 January was an impressive document consisting of ten printed pages and divided into four parts:

1   Assumptions and Definitions;

2   The Case for and against Total Occupation;

3   Mixed Allied Forces or Occupation by Zones;

4   Zone Boundaries.

On the one hand Stalin must have been furious, indeed contemptuous, that the British should start dividing up the spoils of war before crossing the Channel. On the other hand, his response seems to indicate that he was positively surprised at the Western Allies' willingness to hand over half of Germany up to the River Elbe to the Red Army. Yet the boundaries of the occupation zones were not described in detail. Instead reference was made to an annexed map with the proviso that these boundaries were "put forward tentatively and may have to be reviewed in the light of any examination of this question by the military staffs". These reservations were mainly due to disagreement among the British and American military about who should have the coveted North-Western zone. Yet Stalin might well have suspected that not everybody in the West was happy about the size of the Russian zone. Moreover, part III of this document suggested that controversy was still raging among the Western Allies about the best form of occupation. Like the British Chiefs of Staff he disliked the mixing-up theory: close contacts between Allied troops over a period of time were bound to undermine Red Army morale. The sooner the Soviets agreed to what was on offer the better the chance of securing their interests in Germany. After all, the German capital, the seat of the Allied control machinery, was situated in their zone. Right from the beginning Stalin had thus been given the option of playing the all-German card and, if this did not work, of turning his own zone into a Communist bulwark, thereby bringing about the actual division of Germany. So with hindsight it is easy to see why he accepted the British proposal without asking for more. The British were astonished how quickly the Soviet representative in the EAC complied. This was an unusual experience. On 15 February ambassador Gousev submitted the Soviet draft proposals for the terms of surrender, which included a detailed description of the zonal boundaries corresponding exactly with the lines drawn on the British map. The Foreign Office welcomed this decision as a breakthrough in their relations with the Russians who now seemed to have come on board. There were no serious objections to the Soviet proposal for joint occupation of Austria, which had figured as part of the American zone. What was regarded as more important was Soviet acceptance of the principle of indirect rule and the special status accorded to Berlin as the seat of the Allied Control Commission. The only bone of contention was the island of Fehmarn, which had not been clearly marked on the British map. The principle at stake was the sanctity of existing administrative boundaries. After months of haggling and after being authorised to waive his claim, the British representative Sir William Strang eventually secured the island for the West.[13] It was not until May 1945, when British and American troops had conquered large tracts of the Soviet zone, that it occurred to one of the clerks at the Foreign Office: "The unusual alacrity with which the Russians accepted our zone proposals in the E.A.C. suggests that we gave them more than they ever expected to get".[14]

Once the Russians had accepted the British proposals for the zoning of Germany, in particular the size of the Soviet zone, the Americans had virtually no alternative but to follow suit. They were, in any case, more preoccupied with the allocation of the North-Western zone than with the size of the Soviet area. In other words, by mid-February the border between the two German states was already in place and never to change until 1990. The border between East Germany and Poland, however, was still an open question. As we know, the Allies were unable to settle this issue either during or after the war. At Yalta Churchill and Roosevelt refused to consent to the cession of the whole of Lower Silesia and the subsequent population transfer.[15] Nor did the West accept Stalin's unilateral decision to hand over all lands east of the Oder-Neisse, except for the area around Königsberg, to Polish administration. The British were particularly upset about this move since it compromised the principle of joint Allied responsibility for Germany as a whole and deprived Germany of vitally important agricultural areas, thereby endangering food supplies. Not surprisingly, the question of Poland's Western border was to turn up again in 1990 as a major obstacle on the road to unification.

Why was the German capital, by 1945 an urban wasteland, of such political significance? Here we have to return to the assumptions made during the planning stage. When the first plans for the occupation of Germany were hatched out Berlin was still the all-powerful administrative centre of the Reich. Moreover, there was a distinct probability that at the time of surrender the Allies might be faced with a non-Nazi German government. Whether or not such a government should be kept in power was a highly controversial issue both in London and in Washington. Whitehall clearly favoured indirect rule, either via a non-Nazi central government or through central administrative authorities under the control of some Allied supervisory body that would see to the strict implementation of all surrender terms. Naturally, a central German government in place before the end of hostilities would have tried to maintain the unity of the Reich. The collapse of the Hohenzollern Empire in 1918 furnished the scenario for the end of the Second World War. British belief in the Prussian ethos of *Staatsraison* was unshaken: those army generals who had helped Hitler to power, and whose dissatisfaction with their war-leader was well known in Whitehall, would know when the time had come to get rid of him and present an acceptable government to the Allies for the business of surrender. At this stage the machinery of government would still be intact and allow the Allies to rule Germany through a civilian control commission. To the British this seemed to be a rational hypothesis. Moreover, this scenario also coincided with their interests: the avoidance of military government and direct administration. In Germany the colonial principle of indirect rule was to be applied for the last time.

For the purpose of establishing an inter-Allied control machinery Berlin was to be occupied by a mixed Allied force. Nor was the German capital, as the symbol of joint United Nations occupation, to be divided into separate sectors like the rest of the country. One of the first British drafts laid down: "The United Nations Supreme Commander-in-Chief would have his G.H.Q. at Berlin, which would form a small special zone occupied by picked troops of the United Nations in order to stress further the combined occupation of Germany".[16] The Commander-in-Chief was to play a subsidiary role to that of the civilian Control Commission. He would be responsible for maintaining law and order in the combined zone and the position should rotate among the Allies. This was the theoretical model which was then exposed to constant erosion. The British Chiefs of Staff let it be known that they would never agree to serve under a Russian Commander-in-Chief in Germany. On 12 January 1944 Ministers approved the plan for a "machinery in Germany during the period of occupation", while stressing that supreme authority should be handed over to a High Commission as soon as possible. A few days later this document was submitted to the EAC as the British draft proposal. It soon emerged that the Americans favoured full-blown military government. Throughout most of 1944 the British and Americans argued over the nature of the Control Commission. As the British conceived it, a

Military Commission or Control Council would direct the German authorities, and thus be "the Military Governor of Germany as a Trinity in unity".

For much of 1944, the Soviet government were not inclined to discuss
matters such as how Germany or its capital were to be run by an Allied con-
sortium. However, after Eisenhower had entered Paris at the end of August
1944 Stalin changed his mind. With the help of French forces the Allies
might be the first to reach Berlin. Moreover, the 20 July plot increased his
suspicions about a possible collusion while its failure seemed to suggest that
at the end of the war there would be no acceptable German government to
deal with. Thus on 26 August 1944 ambassador Gousev revealed Moscow's
plans for an Allied control machinery to be set up in Berlin. He insisted that
the joint Allied zone around Berlin should also be carved up into separate
sectors. Stalin was now able to cherry-pick from the British and American
plans selecting those elements that suited him best. Like the British he
favoured some sort of indirect rule as long as the Military Governors ruled
supreme in their zone of occupation. However, contrary to British ideas, he
wanted the Control Council to be a purely co-ordinating committee devoid
of any administrative structure. Only the inter-Allied "Kommandatura" for
Berlin should have any of the trappings of a proper authority. To make
sure the Soviet Governor would not be overruled Gousev insisted that all
decisions taken by the Control Council must be unanimous. EAC negotiations now focused on the nature of the supervisory body. From the Soviet
point of view real power would have to lie with the forces in each of the
three occupation zones, rather than distributing the portfolios between
the three Allies. The most controversial aspect was the notion of "supreme
authority" in Germany. Would it rest with the Control Council or with the
individual commanders? In the autumn of 1944, a judicious compromise
was worked out which was to encapsulate the German Question for the next
half-century. The Commanders-in-Chief were to exercise supreme authority
"each in his own zone of occupation, and also jointly, in matters affecting
Germany as a whole". If the Allies could not agree on a common policy the
division of Germany would follow as night follows day. At the same time
this formula also enshrined Allied responsibility for Germany as a whole,
and this was to come to the fore in each of the subsequent Berlin crises, as
well as in the unification process in 1989/90.

Unfortunately, free access to Berlin had not been covered by the final
protocol: it was taken for granted. But that Berlin, the German capital and
seat of the Control Council, was the common responsibility of the three
(later four) Allies, was never really in dispute, much as the Soviet government later tried to question it. The fate of the city could not be legitimately

determined by any one of the Allies. In a curious way Berlin was *pars pro toto* in that it represented Germany as a whole. The capital, jointly administered, was the only counterweight to the centrifugal tendency prevailing in the zones of occupation. It was only through German authorities in Berlin that the whole country could be held together. Yet no such administration was still functioning by the time the Red Army had conquered the city in April 1945.

So far, it has been argued that the early zoning of Germany for the purpose of occupation lay at the root of an incremental process towards division. However, it is worth pointing out that this was by no means just the fault of the Western powers who were desperately trying to appease Stalin and to forestall the Cold War. If the Wehrmacht had surrendered at the right moment, as did its predecessor in 1918, Allied plans for indirect rule on the basis of a functioning administrative machine in Berlin might well have preserved German unity. Yet the German generals had long since lost their independence to their Führer who led Germany straight into the abyss of total war, total defeat and total occupation. In other words, the failure of the 20 July plot and Germany's fight to the bitter end also contributed to the eventual division of Germany.

It was more than a month after the end of hostilities before the Western Allies took over their share of the city. In the meantime the Soviet Military Administration (SMAD) had created *faits accomplis* both in Berlin and in its zone before the Control Council had had a chance to deliberate on policies affecting Germany as a whole. While the Allied Reparations Commission met in Moscow to consider how to share the spoils of war, the Russians forged ahead with dismantling entire plants and whatever could be taken away in their zone of occupation.[17] The British were most frustrated by all unilateral actions taken by the Russians. All their careful preparations for the post-war Allied régime were meant to guarantee a common approach. In the course of the last one-and-a-half years the EAC had received British and American draft directives on all aspects of German public life to be jointly implemented by the Control Commission. Stalin could not have cared less: the Soviet delegate kept saying that he had no instructions to discuss these matters since experts had not yet arrived from Moscow. They never did: it was like waiting for Godot. Gousev would only conduct negotiations about the organisational framework for occupation, never about policies to be adopted.

In May 1945, Churchill had been ready for a showdown with Stalin after Eisenhower's and Montgomery's armies had conquered large tracts of Germany allotted to the Soviet zone of occupation. When President Truman turned down his request to stay put in the Soviet zone until certain demands were met, the Prime Minister concentrated his efforts on bringing about another summit conference. Stalin agreed with Harry Hopkins, Truman's emissary, that the three should meet in Potsdam on 15 July. The main purpose of the Potsdam Conference was to implement the terms of surrender, i.e. to bring about the denazification, disarmament and demilitarisation of Germany.[18] However, the three leaders also agreed: "So far as is practical there shall be uniformity of treatment of the German population throughout Germany". In particular, Germany was to be treated as a "single economic unit". For this purpose "certain essential central administrative departments, headed by State Secretaries, shall be established, particularly in the fields of finance, transport, communications, foreign trade and industry". These departments were to act "under the direction of the Control Council".

In Potsdam it looked as though German unity had become a tripartite goal. The Russians needed an undivided country in order to exact the maximum amount of reparations. Nor did they wish to make life difficult for the German Communists who wanted to pose as the champions of German unity. What none of the Western participants in Potsdam could know at the time was that only three days earlier Molotov had pressed for central departments to be established. SMAD had already issued instructions for 11 such agencies to be set up for the Soviet zone.[19] During the following months, which were to see more unilateral action on the part of the German Communists, such as expropriation of landed estates, the British began to wonder whether Berlin would not, over time, mutate into a central administrative machinery for transforming the whole of Germany into a Communist state like other Soviet dependencies in Eastern Europe. It has previously been assumed that the central departments failed to materialise because of sustained opposition from France. However, Elisabeth Kraus has discovered that except for the Americans none of the other three Allies was making much effort to maintain German unity, despite all their rhetoric to the contrary.[20] The Russians were keen to consolidate their hold on East Germany, not least in order to bleed their zone white by the wholesale removal of stocks. It must be said, however, that when they withdrew from the Soviet zone American and British troops also carried away blueprints, machinery and part of the workforce, though generally with the consent of the owner and not necessarily as reparations.

After Potsdam the British began to have their doubts as to whether the idea of Germany being treated as a single economic unit would still work in their favour. Before their very eyes the agricultural heartland east of the River

Elbe was to turn inexorably into an economic desert. By the end of 1945 living conditions in Berlin were clearly worse than in the Western zones. What if the situation in the East were to lead to the mass migration of starving people to the Western zones? It was not until ten years later that precisely this development was to benefit the West German economy. In 1945 it would have been a horror scenario. The most controversial issue debated in Potsdam was the amount of reparations due to Russia. For the Americans and British self-sufficiency of their zones had priority over any reparations to be expected for themselves or for the Russians. The agreement reached after much haggling was clearly incompatible with the principle of treating Germany as an economic unit: each power was entitled to meet her reparations claims from her own zone of occupation. In addition, the Soviet Union was to receive 10 per cent of all the Western zones' industrial equipment that was not needed for the peace economy and 15 per cent in exchange for food and raw materials from the Soviet zone. What was the German peace economy supposed to be? This was a recipe for later discord when the level of German industry came to be assessed.[21]

In the context of this book it makes sense to analyse the unsuccessful attempts at overcoming the division of Germany that was being sealed with the establishment of two different states in 1949. The failure to implement central departments agreed upon at Potsdam was certainly the most important of all the missed opportunities, but there were others which in the course of time proved less and less effective. Between 1945 and 1955 initiatives of this kind had to come from outside. During that period the Germans were not masters in their own house, which was turned, as it were, into two semi-detached halves. Under Allied supervision they were allowed to provide their own furniture, but were unable to get their act together because matters concerning Germany as a whole were the responsibility of the Four Powers.

The Americans who wished to finish the business of occupation as soon as feasible were most frustrated by the slow progress towards a common policy. Apart from pressing ahead with the establishment of democratic institutions in their zone of occupation they were the first to submit a radical plan to overcome the growing division between the Soviet and the Western zones. The United States was forced to spend $200 million per annum on food which ordinarily would have come from the Russian zone. In many ways the American attitude to the German problem was the most detached and far-sighted, and only briefly interrupted by the Morgenthau Plan: the best way of pacifying Germany would be its integration into the free trade world economy and its total dependence on imports and exports.[22] After the war, before a Cold War mentality had penetrated all corners of government, this goal was regarded as fully compatible with Germany's political neutrality. A basic objective of American policy was that Germany should be politically independent of other powers and militarily available to none. In September 1945 Secretary of State James F. Byrnes began to test the water by consulting his colleagues about the idea of enforced neutrality for Germany.[23] When he first told Molotov of his proposal for a 25-year treaty to block the resurgence of German militarism he was encouraged by Russia's interest. On Christmas Eve 1945 he discussed the matter with Stalin in Moscow. The Soviet dictator, too, sounded positive and Byrnes began to lobby Senators in Washington, who endorsed his plans in principle. However, at the Paris Conference of April 1946 Molotov could not be persuaded by his three Western colleagues to accept the American proposal: it would postpone German disarmament, he argued. The period was not long enough and it was altogether completely "inadequate". Later he complained that the treaty evaded such problems as democratising Germany. Byrnes came to the conclusion that Moscow did not want the United States involved in the maintenance of European security for the next 25 or 40 years. In Soviet eyes security depended on their Communist agents holding on to power, which in turn required the full backing of the Red Army. Moreover, a nationalised economy seemed most conducive to exacting reparations. All this could not be guaranteed with only a small Allied inspection force on the ground.

Even though the first initiative to break the deadlock over Germany by imposing neutral status failed, similar plans were to be submitted over the next ten years and hotly debated inside Germany.[24] It seemed obvious that neutrality, or a disengagement of sorts, offered the only chance of overcoming the division of Germany, and possibly that of Europe too. In 1989/90 the idea was to surface for one last time with Gorbachev's desperate attempt to decouple Germany from NATO.

The next move in the same direction was made by the British Military Governor, General Sir Brian Robertson, in 1948 as a way of solving the first Berlin Crisis. The latter had been brought about by the Soviet's ever-intensifying blockade of the city.[25] This was their response to the currency reform in the Western zones and West-Berlin which was seen as a decisive step in a state-building process. Like most of the military experts, Robertson did not believe that Berlin could be supplied by air for long. Only an inter-Allied agreement on Germany, he felt, would release Berlin from the tightening grip of the Soviet blockade. On 4 July he submitted a plan to the Foreign Office which proposed a radical change in the Allied approach to the creation of a West German state: all four Allies should withdraw not only from Berlin but from most of the German territory, and settle in garrison quarters at the periphery.[26] An all-German government should then be formed on the basis of free elections. General Robertson and his advisors in Berlin knew that the Germans would never make a deal with the Communists, not even in order to regain their lost territories in the East. However, the old hands at the Foreign Office were still obsessively afraid of a repeat performance of Rapallo. Germany on its own might no longer pose a serious threat, but a German government either in cahoots with Moscow or under its intimidating influence was a different proposition. "In such a bloc Germany, with her capacity for war, her restless ambitions, her manpower and her industrial potential, could be a mortal peril." What also militated against Robertson's plan was that it provided for a Soviet say in control of the Ruhr industry. For the past two years the Foreign Office had been doing its utmost to keep the French and the Russians out of this sensitive area. There was no inclination in London to redirect the train that was now destined for a separate West German state.

George Kennan experienced the same frustrations as Robertson when he submitted a similar plan in Washington a couple of months later. After alerting the American decision-makers, in his famous long telegram, to the dangers of Soviet ambitions, he had become, since May 1947, head of the State Department's newly established Policy Planning Staff. As such he felt called upon to question all previous premises in order to end the siege of Berlin. He could not understand why all Western efforts were devoted to the airlift without considering the wider political context. More clearly than others he foresaw that with the implementation of the so-called "London Programme", which set forth the terms for a separate West German state, the Russians would feel obliged to follow suit and turn their zone into a Soviet satellite state. The division of Germany and Europe would be the inevitable outcome. Basically, Kennan wanted to keep things flexible, which he thought would further weaken Moscow's grip on Western Europe now that Tito had fallen out with Stalin. His superiors' first reaction was "a troubled and thoughtful silence".[27] On 12 November with no end to the airlift yet in sight, Kennan submitted his more detailed Plan A as a discussion paper for a new conference of Foreign Ministers. Like Robertson, he realised that the strategic situation in Berlin was untenable in the long run, but that the prestige of the Western powers in Germany had been greatly enhanced. He wrote: "If the continuation of the present deadlock threatens us with the loss of Berlin, it threatens them [i.e. the Russians] with the loss of Germany itself". Like Robertson, Kennan advocated a simultaneous withdrawal, so that neither the West nor the Russians would lose face. "The withdrawal of forces to garrison areas therefore appears to be the best compromise." Ninety days after the Foreign Ministers had given their approval, free elections to a Constitutional Assembly should take place under the supervision of the United Nations. A second chamber, a kind of Senate representing the *Länder* should likewise result from a free vote. Military Government would come to an end and the Control Council be replaced by an Allied High Commission, which would remain in charge of demilitarisation and reparations. What Kennan had in mind was a kind of demilitarised neutrality: no more than 160,000 troops in all – 40,000 for each of the four powers – should keep a watchful eye from the four corners of Germany. The Americans would withdraw to the Bremen enclave, the Red Army set up quarters around Stettin. Kennan deeply regretted that his initiative was simply ignored in Washington. After all, Lucius D. Clay, the US Military Governor, saw the creation of a West German state as his crowning achievement.[28] Indeed, he more than Adenauer was the true founding father of the Federal Republic. Kennan had doubts, too, as to whether Moscow would accept his plan. But he persuaded himself that the Russians must have realised that in the long run the Communist régime in East Germany could not successfully compete with the non-Communist, prosperous state in the West.

It looked as though Stalin wanted to have his cake and eat it: hold on to his "Socialist achievements" in the Soviet zone and yet prevent the consolidation of the Western zones by way of a separate state. Like the Western powers he was not prepared to take any risks at this stage. The Soviets fostered their plans for Germany through the so-called Socialist Unity Party (SED), which was the product of the forced fusion of Communists and Social Democrats in the Eastern zone in February 1946. Right from the start it was conceived as the nucleus from which a Socialist Germany might one day be generated. However, outside the Soviet zone the SED was only licensed in the Western sectors of Berlin, where the party did not appeal to the electorate at all.

When, in 1947, the Western powers had given up hope of running Germany as a single economic unit, as agreed in Potsdam, the SED was used by SMAD to put a brake on the emergence of a separate West German state. The SED now posed as the vanguard of national unity, which was allegedly being jeopardised by the Anglo-Saxon powers. The London Conference of Foreign Ministers in November 1947 appeared to be the last chance of maintaining four-power control and preventing the complete eclipse of Soviet influence from all Western affairs.[29] According to a report by the US Secret Service, SMAD approached the SED leadership one week before the conference began to convey Moscow's wish that a German national representation should be sent to London to back up the Soviet position regarding the re-establishment of German unity. If this could not stop the Western powers from proceeding with their plans, at least they should be exposed as the perpetrators of the division of Germany in the eyes of the people.

In the meantime the SED had come up with the idea of a People's Congress, which should embrace the cause of German unity.[30] In many ways it was another attempt at fostering Communist aims in the disguise of National Front tactics – an old Soviet ploy. The whole venture, which was meant to be above parties, was flawed from the start. At short notice invitations to a "German People's Congress for National Unity and a Just Peace" were issued to all and sundry: all parties, trade unions, mass organisations and the workforce of larger companies. A positive response could only be elicited from the Soviet zone, and even here the Christian Democrats refused to become involved. In the Western zones the People's Congress was a non-starter, due to the opposition of the main parties. Kurt Schumacher, the charismatic leader of the SPD in the Western zones, had already rejected beforehand a policy of empty gestures and declarations. All major parties in the West knew that Germany's fate was in the hands of the occupying powers, not in their own. The Congress met at Berlin's State Opera (6–7 December, 1947). It was mainly an East German propaganda affair. All the motions were inspired by Soviet interests. Why should German delegates be concerned about meeting reparations demanded by the victorious powers? For ordinary Germans in the West it made no sense for the SED to advocate economic reconstruction and refuse Marshall Aid at the same time.

When Molotov requested that the above mentioned delegation, as the voice of the German people, should be heard, he was told by his three Western colleagues that the People's Congress in no way represented the political climate in Germany. Indeed, only 21.73 per cent of the 1,229 delegates had made their way from the Western zones and the great majority of these (77.2 per cent) were appointees of the KPD, the Communist Party in the Western zones. The overall proportion of SED/KPD fellow-travellers was nearly 66 per cent. The whole selection procedure had been in the hands of Communist stalwarts, an indication of how elections in this part of Germany would be handled in the future.

Although the first Congress proved to be a failure, the SED believed that it had now found a way of demonstrating its all-German credentials. On 11 February 1948 Marshall Sokolovsky had asked his Western colleagues in the Control Council to lift the ban on the Congress movement, given its alleged popularity and importance for the preservation of national unity.

Robertson and Clay disputed this claim and argued in forceful terms that this was a trick by one party that was otherwise in no way representative of the German people's interests. Soon afterwards the Russians turned their backs on the Control Council for good. The Congress movement, which had begun with a specific aim, now developed a momentum of its own as a non-stop mobilisation of the population, and a substitute for real progress towards national unity. A second Congress was convened for 17/18 March 1948, the centenary of the March Revolution of 1848. Again delegates had to be elected in all *Länder*, districts and cities of the Soviet zone. At the second Congress workers and peasants were in a minority (21.3 per cent), even though the GDR was later to refer to itself as the "Workers' and Peasants' State". Again only 25.7 per cent of the nearly 2,000 delegates came from the Western zones. Nevertheless the Military Government authorities in the Western zones were worried about the unashamed appeal of the Congress to nationalistic sentiments. Indeed, public opinion polls conducted by the Americans suggested that a majority in the Western zones favoured a movement propagating national unity and accepted the Congress as the nucleus of a German government. However, 90 per cent refused to sign up when they realised that it was a Communist Front organisation.

In the course of 1948 the movement that claimed to represent the German people as a whole mutated into a Constitutional Assembly for a separate East German state. The Second Congress was asked to choose from its ranks a kind a People's Soviet (*Volksrat*) as a more permanent body, consisting of 400 delegates (100 West Germans). A special committee was to work out a constitution for a "German Democratic Republic", based on a SED draft of 1946. In response to the Parliamentary Council in the Western zones, the Third People's Congress was elected on 15 May 1949. The block vote, which left voters with no choice, contained the insidious sentence: "I am in favour of German unity and a just peace". However, only 66.1 per cent approved the list of candidates. In view of this unsatisfactory result, even semi-free elections would not be tolerated in future. As a reaction to the first meeting of the West German parliament on 7 September, the SED set up the "National Front of the Democratic Germany", which was to have no following in the West. On 7 October 1949 the 330-strong German *Volksrat*, emanating from the Third Congress, constituted itself as the provisional People's Chamber (*Volkskammer*), based on the constitution that had been passed by the previous *Volksrat* on 18 March 1949.

Thus in the early autumn of 1949 two German states came into being, two states as opposed to one another as their patrons, the new super powers. It would, however, be a mistake to see them merely as creations of these super powers: in the East the Communists had realised at a very early stage that they would exercise no power or influence in a united Germany. That is why their state-building had to be camouflaged as an appeal to national unity. This went hand in hand with the transformation of the SED into a truly Stalinist party of the "new type", accompanied by the purge of all crypto-Social Democrats and rigorous centralisation.[31] There can be no doubt that the German Communists and the Soviet leadership over-estimated national feeling in post-war Germany. Otherwise their futile attempts to manipulate German nationalism cannot be explained satisfactorily. In spite of all anti-Fascist propaganda they hoped to repeat the success of plebiscitarian dictatorship as demonstrated by the previous régime.

Although Stalin hoped that the Soviet zone would serve as a model for the whole of Germany, it actually had the opposite effect. In the West the population supported *nolens volens* the economic fusion of their zones into a separate state. It would be easy to say that in this case freedom was more important than national unity if both were unattainable, but we should guard against such easy answers. Post-war Germans did not become reformed Democrats or adherents of a free market economy over night. A mixture of fears and hopes was at work: fears of Bolshevism due to Nazi propaganda and the post-war experiences of refugees from the East, hopes of a better life and military protection under the umbrella of the United States, which had offered Marshall Aid and, by its steadfastness, had broken the Berlin Blockade. The author can remember that American school-meals formed a substantial part of his post-war diet and that ordinary pubs were converted into clubs for youngsters run by American social workers, which provided snacks, entertainment, and subtle re-education.

The road to a divided Germany was a controlled process due to the mechanics of the Cold War or, as one author put it:

German division did not emerge full-blown from any master plan conceived
in Moscow, London, Paris or Washington. It emerged from the process of
incremental decision-making, where the logic of one action followed the logic
of another with a mutual ratchet effect leading to a result that most had
not expected.[32]

As such it is a good example of the cunning of history. In other words, it was the result not of daring but of caution on all sides. Each of the occupying powers wanted to hold on to its own slice without running the risk of letting its rival have the whole. To be certain, they imposed their own political and social system on their half: socialisation in one part of the country, liberal democracy in the other West Germany's market economy, however, was the result of the first free elections in the summer of 1949. A divided Germany threatened no one, a united country might join either the Western alliance or the Soviet camp thereby unhinging the balance of power among the two opposing camps. So it is hardly surprising that political neutrality of some sort was proposed from time to time in order to overcome this dilemma. But it was never accepted as a safe option, given Germany's past record.

If both sides approached the German question with the same interest in mind – to keep their own halves for themselves – it does not mean that they followed the same policy. Recent research suggests that Stalin's aims were much more contradictory than the policies pursued by the West. Even though he was the first to impose unilaterally a new social order on his zone, thereby effectively separating it from the West, he still hoped to keep the German Question open. The GDR was, as one author has put it, "his unloved child", which he eventually had to adopt because he failed to pro-duce a legitimate Germany in his own image.[33] Even after the two German states had been founded he urged his East German protégés to press on with the idea of a "National Front" as a lobby for a peace treaty in both parts of Germany. The GDR was more the brainchild of Walther Ulbricht, the Machiavellian party secretary of the SED, than that of Stalin, though helped along by influential SMAD officials like Sergey Tulpanov who was ahead of the game in anticipating a separate East German state, and tried to secure Soviet interests by re-organising society according to the Bolshevik model. It is still an open question as to how sincere Ulbricht and the SED leadership were in their propaganda campaign for national unity. They had fed Stalin's illusions about Germany's disposition towards national socialism of an anti-Fascist brand, and then had to appease him by appearing to act upon this illusion.

The Western powers, notably President Truman and the British Foreign Secretary Ernest Bevin, followed a much more consistent line, better under-stood at the time and later: first cooperation with the Soviet Union in trying to implement the Potsdam agreements, then, when this policy ended in deadlock, a resolute U-turn.[34] The Western zones where joint decision-making was still possible were fused together, and from 1947 onwards the project of a separate West German state as part of the Western alliance was being launched. The British and Americans did a much better job of persuading the German population to go along with this idea and accept the inevitable though unwelcome consequence – the division of their country. At the end of the war, most Germans were still in favour of some kind of Socialism, a planned economy of sorts.[35] However, after three years of shortage tempered by a flourishing black market, the currency reform of 1948 was perhaps the most persuasive argument for a free market: shops full of consumer goods. While the Basic Law introduced in May 1949 allowed (and still does!) for a nationalised economy as demanded by the Social Democrats the first free elections in August brought Konrad Adenauer, the septuagenarian leader of the Christian Democrats, into power which he shared with the Liberals. These elections, not the occupation forces, were to decide the social order of the Federal Republic for good. By that time most West Germans, notably the political élite, had realised that division was the price to be paid for a life in freedom and relative prosperity. Ten years later the Social Democrats came to the same conclusion and abandoned their Marxist programme in favour of a free market economy as part of the Free World (*Godesberg Conference, 1959*).

Notes and references

1 Control Council, *Official Gazette*, No. 14, 31 March 1947, p. 262.

2 Beginning with T.H. Marshall "What to do with Germany". See Lothar Kettenacker, *Krieg zur Friedenssicherung. Die Deutschlandplanung der britischen Regierung während des Zweiten Weltkrieges* (Göttingen, 1989), pp. 150–61.

3 John Maynard Keynes, *The Collected Writings*, Donald Moggeridge (ed.), vol. 26 (London 1980) p. 334 ("The chief thing that matters is that Ministers should not suppose that the chief thing that matters is to avoid the mistakes made last time").

4 Sumner Welles, *Time for Decision* (London, 1944), p. 284.

5 Apparently this was seriously considered as part of the 20 July plot, notwithstanding the demand for unconditional surrender. See Peter Hoffmann, *The History of the German Resistance 1933–1945* (London, 1977), pp. 352–53.

6 See Winston Churchill, *The Second World War* (London, 1954), vol. 6, pp. 386–98. This concerns the negotiations of SS-General Karl Wolff in Switzerland about the capitulation of the German army in Italy.

7 See Hermann Fromm, *Deutschland in der öffentlichen Kriegszieldiskussion Großbritanniens 1939–1945* (Frankfurt a.M., 1982).

8 Eden to Churchill, 16 March 1943, Public Record Office: FO 371/34457/C3165. All further quotes and references, unless otherwise indicated, in: *Krieg zur Friedenssicherung*, pp. 270–302. See also Tony Sharp, *The Wartime Alliance and the Zoning of Germany* (Oxford, 1975).

9 *The Memoirs of Lord Gladwyn* (London, 1972), p. 127.

10 For the controversy between the COS and the FO see Kettenacker, pp. 479–86.

11 See Anthony Glees, *The Secrets of the Service: British Intelligence and Communist Subversion 1939–1951* (London, 1986).

12 For this and the following quotes see above, n. 8.

13 William (Lord) Strang, *Home and Abroad* (London, 1956), p. 215.

14 Quoted in: Kettenacker, p. 531.

15 See Alfred M. de Zayas, *Nemesis at Potsdam. The Anglo-Americans and the Expulsion of the Germans* (London, 1977). See also Hans Georg Lehmann, *Der Oder-Neisse-Konflikt* (Munich, 1979).

16 Quoted in: Kettenacker, p. 331. All further quotes and references, ibid., pp. 309–34.

17 See Alec Cairncross, *The Price of War. British Policy on German Reparations 1941–1949* (Oxford, 1986), pp. 194–218 ("Even electric wiring was removed from private houses to meet a shortage in Russia", p. 199).

18 See Charles L. Mee, *Meeting at Potsdam* (London, 1975). Protocols in the Annexe.

19 See Heinrich Maetzke, *Der Union Jack in Berlin: Das britische Foreign Office, die SBZ und die Formulierung britischer Deutschlandpolitik 1945/47* (Constance, 1996), pp. 40–44.

20 Elisabeth Kraus, *Ministerien für ganz Deutschland? Der Kontrollrat und die Frage gesamtdeutscher Zentralverwaltungen* (Munich, 1990).

21 This is discussed at length by Cairncross (see above, no. 17).

22 See John H. Backer, *Priming the German Economy. American Occupation Policies 1945–1948* (Durham, NC 1971); also: Bruce Kuklick, *American Policy and the Division of Germany. The Clash with Russia over Reparations* (London, 1972).

23 For more details see Axel Frohn, *Neutralisierung als Alternative zur Westintegration. Die Deutschlandpolitik der Vereinigten Staaten von Amerika 1945–1949* (Frankfurt a.M., 1989).

24 See now: Dominik Geppert and Udo Wengst (eds), *Neutralität – Chance oder Chimäre. Konzepte des Dritten Weges für Deutschland und die Welt 1945–1990* (München, 2005).

25 W. Phillips Davison, *The Berlin Blockade* (Princeton, NJ 1958); also William R. Smyser, *From Yalta to Berlin. The Cold War Struggle over Germany* (London, 1999), pp. 73–87 (covering post-Soviet research).

26 Most comprehensive analysis of this plan and following quotes in: Rolf Steininger, "Wie die Teilung Deutschlands verhindert werden sollte. Der Robertson-Plan aus dem Jahre 1948", in: *Militärgeschichtliche Mitteilungen* 1983 (33), pp. 49–89.

27 George F. Kennan, *Memoirs* (New York, 1967). See also Frohn, pp. 124–134.

28 See Lucius D. Clay, *Decision in Germany* (New York, 1950) as well as Jean Edward Smith, *Lucius D. Clay* (New York, 1990).

29 See Hermann Graml, *Die Alliierten und die Teilung Deutschlands. Konflikte und Entscheidungen 1941–1948* (Frankfurt a.M., 1985), pp. 178–95.

30 See Christoph Kleßmann, *Die doppelte Staatsgründung. Deutsche Geschichte 1945–1955* (Göttingen, 1982), pp. 202–208; also with documents: Rolf Steininger, *Deutsche Geschichte seit 1945* (Frankfurt a.M., 1996), vol. 2, pp. 87–115.

31 For the most recent and comprehensive history of the SED see Klaus Schröder, *Der SED-Staat. Partei, Staat und Gesellschaft 1949–1990* (Munich, 2000).

32 Smyser, p. 71.

33 Wilfried Loth, *Stalins ungeliebtes Kind: Warum Moskau die DDR nicht wollte* (Berlin, 1994).

34 See Steininger, vol. 2, pp. 13–49.

35 Gerhard Ambrosius, *Die Durchsetzung der sozialen Marktwirtschaft in Westdeutschland 1945–1949* (Stuttgart 1977).

CHAPTER 2

Cold War confrontation

On 12 September 1949 Theodor Heuss was elected as President of the new Federal Republic of Germany (FRG), followed one month later, on 11 October, by Wilhelm Pieck, appointed to the same office in the German Democratic Republic (GDR). This sequence was to be significant: the West was always one step ahead, not looking over its shoulder. The foundation of the two German republics bears all the hallmarks of the Cold War in that they both disputed each other's democratic legitimacy. The Federal Republic went one step further in not recognising the GDR as a sovereign state. Both states claimed the moral high ground, pretending to represent the nucleus of a country that longed to be reunited. The founding fathers of both states sincerely believed that this could be achieved only on their own terms, or never. Yet, on both sides the existing social and political order was judged to be more important than unity as such. When the SED régime eventually crumbled in 1989 it was pointed out, and rightly so, that socialism was the only *raison d'être* for the GDR as a separate German state. Therefore the struggle for Germany for the next forty years was fought over the political and economic order, rather than, as was claimed, over national identity and integrity. The unspoken agenda was: Which system was to yield higher benefits and was thus more likely to pull the population of the other half into its orbit? Reunification on the other hand became an article of faith rather than of practical politics, almost like belief in the Second Coming of Christ. In the East this was true of the people, who had no voice anyway until 1989; in the West it was more a tenet of official policy, but with decreasing support from the less nationally minded younger generation.

Right from the beginning the odds were clearly in favour of the West. The East Germans were the real victims of the Cold War while the West Germans were its beneficiaries – though it should be noted that most

West Germans never perceived themselves as such. West Germany was in a much more privileged position than its poor Eastern neighbour. It encompassed more than twice Germany's post-war territory, more than three times its population as well as the industrial heartland, the coal and steel plants of the Ruhr. Moreover, the Western powers took an active interest in economic reconstruction which soon became more important than exacting reparations.[1] The list of plants to be dismantled for this purpose dwindled over the years. Above all, the Federal Republic had a democratic and liberal constitution, which allowed for free elections and legitimate government with no need of constant recourse to force and falsehood.

For its own survival the GDR depended on the permanent support of the Soviet government and the Red Army garrisoned on its territory. As so often happens, defensiveness expressed itself in offensive propaganda that served only to further undermine its credibility. While the Red Army, as we shall witness in the uprising of 16–17 June 1953, sought to protect the régime from its own people, the Anglo-Saxon powers were perceived by the West Germans as their protectors (*Schutzmächte*). The showdown over Berlin in 1948, with Soviet superiority in conventional forces and US monopoly in nuclear power, had been the West's greatest propaganda success in the early stages of the Cold War. The blockade-running airlift marked a decisive turning point in relations between the West Germans and their occupying powers.[2]

Early on the two most important political leaders realised that the West had more to offer in the long run: Kurt Schumacher, the undisputed leader of the Social Democrats, propounded the so-called "magnet theory" in 1947,[3] and Konrad Adenauer, the German Chancellor, who securely anchored the Federal Republic in the Western Alliance, advocated a "policy of strength",[4] often misunderstood by contemporaries as nothing but power politics. Both states based their struggle for supremacy on premises that were not borne out by the reality of the day and had to be discarded in a long learning process. The GDR abandoned its campaign for national unity in favour of desperately fighting for recognition of it own statehood. The Federal Republic, on the other hand, reluctantly came to the painful conclusion that the "bastard" state had to be recognised for the sake of détente, as the only means of improving the existing *modus vivendi* of the two Germanys. This story will be told in the following chapter.

In the context of this study it makes sense to deal with the SED leadership and their German policy first, because of its unremitting demands for German unity notwithstanding the foundation of two German states. West German leaders were more concerned about full sovereignty of the new FRG and were more on the defensive regarding the German Question, the solution of which was enshrined in the preamble of the Basic Law as an article of faith. Experts are agreed that during his last years Stalin took a keen interest in German affairs. With the constitution of a West German state the Kremlin felt deprived of its right, as laid down by the Potsdam Agreement, to be involved in all-German affairs, be it in order to convert Germany to Socialism, to extract reparations or just with a view to depriving the West of Germany's military potential. The true aims of Soviet policy *vis-à-vis* Germany are still shrouded in mystery. Recent research, however, suggests that recouping former rights of intervention rather than a genuine interest in an agreement with the Western powers was at the root of Stalin's strategy. He could only pressurise the Anglo-Saxon powers by mobilising the German population with the help of his trusted agents, the SED in the GDR and the Communist Party (DKP) in the Federal Republic. They were called upon by their Soviet master to pose as the champions of national unity and solidarity against the "separatist" Adenauer, who had allegedly sold his soul to American imperialism. When he was appointed as East German Prime Minister on 7 October 1949, Otto Grotewohl demanded that Germany should form a "unitary democratic republic". It was at Moscow's instigation that the new East German government forced the so-called block parties, *bourgeois* satellites of the leading SED, into the *National Front*, which was to campaign for national unity in both parts of Germany.[5] The Soviet Control Commission (SKK), successor to SMAD, complained at regular intervals that not enough was being done to spread the national gospel in the West. The *National Front*, which was to appeal to *bourgeois* elements in the West, including former Nazis, was a reinvention of Soviet popular front tactics of the 1930s, enriched by a nationalist input for German consumption. Apparently Stalin and his entourage believed that this was a winning card in the German game. In the meantime, however, the SED, their chief player, had done everything to compromise this very policy in the eyes of West Germans, thereby further separating the two societies: first, it had rejected the German path to socialism in favour of the Stalinist model; second, it had purged itself of all Social Democratic sympathisers and split the block parties from their nationally-minded leaders like the CDU chairman of Saxony, Hugo Hickmann, who favoured a neutral Germany as a way of overcoming the division.[6] It is therefore doubtful whether the SED leadership really believed that they were on the right track towards reunification, and it seems more likely that the national campaign was just a means of deluding Moscow and their own population in the sense of saying: Look, we are doing everything to foster German unity and this is what happens.

On 30 November 1950 Otto Grotewohl had sent a letter to Konrad Adenauer, his opposite number, suggesting negotiations on the formation of an "all-German Constituent Council" with a view to encouraging the West Germans to support the *National Front*'s first "mass action".[7] A public opinion poll revealed that 49 per cent as against 27 per cent of West Germans were in favour of a positive answer. In his reply, delivered to the *Bundestag* on 15 January 1951, Adenauer demanded, without mentioning Grotewohl's initiative, free elections in the Soviet zone and the dissolution of the People's Police (*Volkspolizei*). Secretly he had instructed his confidant, Herbert Blankenhorn, to arrange a meeting between Heinrich Vockel, Bonn's plenipotentiary for Berlin, and Georg Dertinger, Foreign Minister and Deputy Chairman of the East German CDU. The result of these soundings was embarrassing: no sensible specifics like free elections could be elicited. Adenauer's position was strengthened by the strict refusal of Jacob Kaiser, his most nationally-minded Minister of All-German Affairs, and of the Social Democratic opposition to honour the East German régime with any kind of recognition. Bonn's official position was, and remained for a long time, that the German Question was a matter for the Four Powers as laid down in Potsdam and that the government had a license to speak up only for the interests of the East German population.

The SED was to make no headway when they launched their next campaign in 1951 under the banner "Germans around one Table" (*Deutsche an einen Tisch*). Again the initiative for what amounted to a kind of would-be plebiscite originated in Moscow. A so-called Peace Congress convened in Essen, the centre of Germany's industrial heartland, called upon the Federal Government and Parliament to organise a referendum on "Remilitarisation or Peace Treaty". Adenauer's pledge at the beginning of the Korean War to contribute to the defence of the West was very controversial. A clear majority in both parts of Germany rejected the re-introduction of national service six years after the war. More than 6 million West German voters who had been approached opted for a peace treaty followed by the withdrawal of all occupation forces. In the East the result was predictably 95.3 per cent of the 12 million voters in favour of the treaty. Communist stalwarts had daubed the walls in West Germany with slogans like "Ami go home". The demagogic character of this campaign prompted the Federal government to prohibit it altogether, since it was financed and orchestrated, as the SED stated, to incite the population to rise against the government. No doubt, the Soviet Union was increasingly concerned about the turn events had taken. It was not Germany on its own that constituted a real danger but the bulk of Germany's manpower and industrial resources reinforcing the anti-Soviet bloc.

The whole purpose of the *National Front* propaganda had been to prevent the integration of the Federal Republic into the Western Alliance. But by the autumn of 1951 the Kremlin leadership had realised that their East German agents were not up to the task and that they themselves had to enter the fray. The stark question facing Stalin was whether preventing the Federal Republic's drift into the anti-Soviet alliance outweighed the further integration of the GDR into the Soviet Empire. It was typical of the confused state of Soviet decision-making under Stalin that this alternative, though put out as bait, was never seriously seen through. Peter Ruggenthaler, who has been able to consult Soviet archives, has shed new light on Stalin's diplomatic spring offensive of 1952.[8] Apparently it was SED chief Walter Ulbricht who first suggested that the Soviet government should encourage West German opposition to integrating the FRG into NATO by offering the prospect of neutrality. The various and more explicit drafts of Stalin's notorious overtures of 10 March 1952 indicate that security was never conceived of in purely military terms, and that the abandonment of the "socialist achievements" in the East was never contemplated in earnest. This suggests that the whole venture should be seen as a last-minute attempt to put a spoke in the wheels of West German political alignment. In fact, Stalin did not offer much more than had been tentatively put out by *National Front* activists in the West: Germany would be re-established as a united state, and a single German government should be invited to negotiate a peace treaty. Germany, freed from all occupation forces, was "not to enter into any kind of coalition or military alliance directed against any power which took part with its armed forces in the war against Germany". For the country's defence Germany would have its own national forces. The so-called "Stalin Note", which created a sensation in Bonn and the capitals of the West, has aroused historical controversy ever since. Some historians saw it as the last chance to bring about German unification which would have saved the East Germans from nearly forty years of further misery. Attention is generally focused on the negative response by the Western powers and the clear backing they received from Adenauer. In the past the Soviet factor in the equation has been under-exposed because it was less well known. The vocabulary employed both in the drafts and the final note is very revealing, and suggests, for instance, that "democratic conditions" had a very different meaning in East and West. Stalin knew that a national force strong enough to defend Germany would be unacceptable to her neighbours, which were, however, quite prepared for a small German army to be fully integrated into the proposed European Defence Community. The whole process of integrating West Germany into the West European framework would have to be revised. No wonder Adenauer rejected this apple of discord. Moreover, he correctly sensed the feeling of the silent majority, who deeply mistrusted Soviet intentions and were in no mood to jeopardise economic security and military protection under the Western umbrella. Published opinion, however, was a different matter altogether: many well-meaning politicians, journalists and church leaders, mostly but not exclusively of a left-liberal persuasion like Gustav Heinemann, Thomas Dehler or Rudolf Augstein, editor of *Der Spiegel*, were advocating what they called "sounding out the Soviets". Adenauer who could not be sure Stalin was bluffing would have none of it. And his Western partners, like US Secretary of State Dean Acheson and his British colleague Anthony Eden, fully shared the Chancellor's reservations. Adenauer's attitude has often been misrepresented, as though he were only concerned with holding on to power. One former US diplomat probably comes nearest to the truth:

He favored German unification in the long run, but during the 1950s he did not want another united Germany playing an independent and potentially mischievous role in Europe and in the world. He believed that Germany in the post-war years needed democracy and stability more than it needed unity.[9]

It was the "cauchemar" of Weimar politics that haunted the old man. Adenauer's assessment of the German Question exactly reflected the views of the Western powers. Consequently, they torpedoed Stalin's initiative by demanding free elections, in the full knowledge that this was a deadly weapon, unacceptable to Moscow and its satellite régime in East Berlin. The exchange of notes went on for another six months, but with the receipt of the first reply Stalin lost interest in pursuing the matter in a serious manner. After all, he could not prevent the Federal Republic from signing the General Treaty (*Deutschlandvertrag*) on 25 May 1952, a kind of peace treaty which would end Allied control and recognise the Federal Republic's political sovereignty as soon as matters of security had been settled.

There is compelling evidence for the assumption that Stalin's diplomatic offensive and its anticipated rebuttal was but a pretext for creating an East German army, the National People's Army (NVA).[10] Only now did defence become a major topic in East Germany's propaganda repertoire, which had previously been designed to support a peace ballot movement in the West. The official youth movement (FDJ) was instructed to change the prevailing negative attitude towards military service. The *Organisation für Sport und Technik* was to engage young people in pre-military training. Further measures served to tighten Moscow's grip on its share of Germany: the transformation of the GDR's Western demarcation line into a fortified border, and further measures to impose socialism, especially the collectivisation of agriculture, on an unwilling population as a result of the second SED Party Congress in July 1952.

It is inconceivable that all these measures, which clearly contravened Moscow's apparent overtures to the West, could have been implemented without Stalin's explicit approval. Nothing disconcerted stalwarts more than the steady exodus of GDR citizens from the promised land, the so-called "escapees from the republic" (*Republikflüchtlinge*), a problem that betrayed the hollowness of all propaganda efforts and which in the end would hasten the demise of the régime in 1989. Between 1945 and 1961, the year when the Wall was built, more than 2.75 million East Germans sought a better life in the West.[11] The only answer the Party could ever come up with was a tightening of border controls. The day before the official announcement was made, on 27 May 1952, the border police were instructed to execute Action "Anvil", the clearing of a 10-metre control strip and off-limits zones of 10 km, from which all "negative elements" were to be evacuated.[12] Families were ordered out of their homesteads without notice, packed on to lorries with a few belongings and dumped somewhere in the East. Apart from foreigners and those not registered with the police, there was the category of "persons who because of their position in and attitude towards society pose a danger to the anti-fascist democratic order". The press was instructed to report on the misery inflicted on the escapees in West German camps and indeed on the friendly reception of West German scientists, doctors and engineers at their new work places in the GDR. What happened in many cases was that former entrepreneurs who had set up a business in the West had recruited workers from their old plants. This was now to be exposed as corruption of the worst kind. All this was a blatant distortion of reality, which undermined rather than strengthened the credibility of the SED régime. The resolution concerning the "planned construction of socialism" taken at the second Party Congress in July 1952 was meant to strengthen the separate identity of the GDR as a socialist state which would make German unification all the more difficult. However, the implementation of this decision had the cumulative effect of depressing living standards and alienating the population: concentration on heavy industry at the expense of consumer goods, higher taxes and a credit squeeze directed against more than 16,000 private enterprises (comprising a quarter of the industrial workforce), and forced collectivisation of agriculture. The SED even managed to alienate their own clientele: farmers who had benefited from the redistribution of large estates after the war were now asked once again to part with their plots. By the time of Stalin's death in March 1953 the frantic efforts to speed up the introduction of socialism resembled, as one author put it, "an overheated steam engine close to explosion, racing ahead without control".[13]

With Stalin's death the time for stocktaking had come. The Eisenhower administration expected a new offer on Germany, a "really big one", as Charles Bohlen, US Ambassador in Moscow surmised, "involving Soviet withdrawal from Eastern Germany".[14] However, all plans for a new initiative towards German unification under consideration in Moscow presumed the "interim" existence and, in fact, the key role of a stable East German state. Yet the SED régime was anything but stable in the late spring of 1953. The clearest indication that the one-party state was careering towards a catastrophe was the unstoppable and swelling exodus of GDR citizens. This did not escape the Soviet authorities in East Germany, least of all Beria, the former NKWD chief, who now advocated a complete U-turn. Since January 1951 nearly half a million (447,000) East Germans had turned their back on what was still referred to in the West as the Soviet zone. In the first four months of 1953 no fewer than 120,000 GDR citizens, mostly skilled workers and, since the collectivisation of agriculture, an increasing number of farmers (*Kulaks* in Soviet terminology) had left East Germany. By 1 April 1953, 7.3 per cent of all arable land, nearly 450,000 ha., had been abandoned and neglected. What enraged Moscow's leadership above all were the 2,700 Party members and 8,000 from the barracked police corps who had escaped to the West.[15] On 2 June the Soviet Council of Ministers issued an order "On Measures to Improve the Health of the Political Situation in the GDR". It referred to the refugee crisis as well as other deficiencies and stated explicitly that it was necessary to recognise the course of forcibly imposing socialism "as mistaken under current conditions".[16] This document was handed to a delegation of SED leaders summoned to Moscow on the same day. According to Grotewohl's sketchy record they were given a real dressing down by their Soviet "friends". "Don't worry about prestige; if we don't correct now", Georgii Malenkov told them, "a catastrophe will happen". Back home, the Politburo deliberated for days on how to communicate the admission of failure to their people: self-criticism was the order of the day. But the Soviet High Commissioner, Vladimir Semyonov, gave them no time to prepare the ground, fearing delaying tactics, and insisted on swift implementation of the new course. Published on 11 June, the waves of this news bombshell rippled through the whole country.[17] Party members were in shock; others believed that the admission of bankruptcy would hasten Ulbricht's resignation and the demise of his hated régime. To make matters worse, the SED leadership, in an effort to preserve its authority, insisted that the raised production norms imposed in May should remain in force. This meant a reduction in wages for building workers, who were to be in the forefront of the ensuing unrest, of between 10 per cent and 25 per cent. "Negative discussions" on the shop floor followed, demanding the dissolution of the SED. Rumours spread, according to which the leading lights of the Party had fled or been arrested. In some villages liberation parties were staged. By 16 June the workforce of most East Berlin industrial plants was on strike, quickly followed by strikes and demonstrations all over the country. The hasty decision to readjust wages to the pre-May norms could no longer ease the situation. As in the autumn of 1989 State Security officials in the provinces were left without guidelines. The following day, the memorable 17 June 1953, the whole country was in turmoil: a veritable national uprising spread to 350 places and half-a-million people demonstrated against the Communist régime. The demand for free elections and political change had replaced specific grievances, first expressed by the building workers in East Berlin. At 1 p.m. the Soviet Commandant, Andrei Grechkov, declared a state of emergency and called in Russian tank brigades. The East German barracked police were called into action and the Ministry of State Security began to round up strike leaders. Two days later no fewer than 1,400 people had been arrested. On the evening of 17 June about 50 people had lost their lives, at least 20 if not more were summarily executed, including Soviet soldiers who refused to obey orders. Ulbricht and the other leaders had taken refuge in the Red Army Headquarters in Karlshorst: they did not dare to show themselves in public. The whole régime had been utterly humiliated and discredited by the events of the day. The uprising had been brutally but successfully quelled by the occupation forces, but sporadic strikes continued to flare up throughout the country for at least another week, until security forces regained control.

Officially the uprising was dubbed a "counter-revolutionary coup", provoked by "fascist agents and spies" from the West. In actual fact, the three Western Commandants had cautioned political leaders in the Western sectors of Berlin against inflammatory speeches and editorials. The British managed to tune down a joint communiqué protesting against the allegation that the Western powers had approved of the uprising. Churchill had no qualms in recognising that the Russians, faced with uproar, had declared martial law in order to prevent "anarchy". His man on the spot had reported that the Russians had reacted "with marked restraint and moderation".[18] Much to his chagrin the events of 17 June had quashed his hopes of another four-power conference, which he believed could have settled the German Question once and for all.

Following Stalin's death the British Prime Minister believed the time had come for the West to take the initiative. In his speech to the Commons on 11 May, his last programmatic foreign policy venture, he addressed Soviet security interests.[19] The "master thought" was to be found in the Treaty of Locarno of 1925. Churchill was the first and only Western statesman to admit publicly that the proposed integration of the Federal Republic into the Western Alliance was actually incompatible with Russian security concerns. This was interpreted as favouring German neutrality as a way out of the Cold War deadlock, even though Churchill did not actually say so as such. Moscow welcomed the speech and so did public opinion in the West. However, the decision-making élite was aghast. Churchill had not consulted his own Foreign Office – Foreign Secretary Anthony Eden was in hospital. Washington feared another bout of British appeasement. No one was more worried than Adenauer, who saw his life's work cast into doubt: German security under Western protection. When he arrived in London soon afterwards he was unable to persuade the Prime Minister to change his ideas on how best to deal with the new Soviet leadership. He now relied on British diplomats, who shared his concerns, to bring Churchill back on track. That the Prime Minister was indeed toying with the notion of German neutrality has been revealed in a Foreign Office memorandum warning him against "a reversal of alliances". A neutral Germany would be tempted to side with Russia. "We should thus have created by our own action the most deadly danger to our security and to that of the world."[20] Similar plans put forward by Sir Brian Robertson and George Kennan five years earlier had met with the disapproval of their governments. Now these were even less inclined to reverse their achievement in pulling the greater part of Germany into the Western orbit. Thus the great war leader failed to make his mark in the history books as a peace-maker.

Eventually, Churchill relented and the stroke he suffered on 23 June 1953 spared the Western world further embarrassment. A day earlier Selwyn Lloyd, in charge of the Foreign Office, had told the Prime Minister what he thought about the German Question. His words have since become a much-quoted expression of how the Western Alliance really felt on this issue:

Germany is the key to the peace of Europe. A divided Europe has meant a divided Germany. To unite Germany while Europe is divided, even if practical, is fraught with danger for all. Therefore everyone – Dr. Adenauer, the Russians, the Americans, the French and ourselves – feel in our hearts that a divided Germany is safer for the time being. But none of us dare say so openly because of the effect upon German public opinion. Therefore we all publicly support a united Germany, each on his own terms.[21]

In 1953 this view was no doubt shared by the new Soviet leadership, with the possible exception of Khrushchev, who was soon to end the farce of supporting unification in public.

The Western governments, and Bonn in particular, had no wish to risk a major showdown with the Russians. Nor did Adenauer, the arch bogey-man of Communist propaganda, take a different line. He expressed sympathy with the East German demonstrators, but warned against further escalation and violence. It was because the East Germans felt they had been let down in their hour of peril that Bonn declared 17 June as a public holiday, to commemorate the victims and publicly reaffirm its commitment to reunification. Over the years, especially after official recognition of the GDR in 1972, commemorations on this day became unfashionable reminders of the Cold War, offending the spirit of détente. In the late 1970s and 1980s West German historians felt the need to play down the events surrounding 17 June as just a workers' revolt against an uncalled-for raising of their workload. This interpretation has been called into question now that the SED Party archives are accessible, and the widespread character of the unrest has been fully revealed. It extended over a longer period than was previously thought and was not confined to Berlin and a few other cities. The original perception of the events as a national uprising in the Communist bloc has been fully confirmed.[22] The playing-down of the painful and disturbing character of Communist rule in the past was inspired by political motives, the out-of-hand dismissal of anti-communism, rather than by the ethos of historical scholarship. There can be no doubt today that without the intervention of Soviet tanks the SED régime would have collapsed then, even faster than in 1989. For the SED and the Stasi the uprising remained their defining trauma for the next 36 years.

It looks as though the greater flexibility of Soviet decision-making in the spring of 1953, leading up to the new course, had offered a slightly better chance of reunification than Stalin's diplomatic initiative a year earlier. One can only speculate what would have happened if the uprising had succeeded in overturning the régime. Free elections and a peace treaty might have followed, coupled with a kind of neutrality status similar to that of Austria. The Western powers would have tried to buy off Soviet goodwill with massive reparations. While the West Germans might have had to forgo the economic miracle, the East Germans would have been spared 40 years of hardship and "nanny rule". The West Germans, less spoilt than 40 years later, would have been psychologically better prepared to accept the sacrifices inherent in the process of reunification. But this is counter-factual history to show how the West Germans benefited from the ongoing Cold War.

The aftermath of the East German uprising is quickly told.[23] Ulbricht managed to survive the power struggle, as the only man the Soviets could trust to re-establish their authority. In Wilhelm Zaisser, the Minister of State Security, and Rudolf Herrnstadt, editor-in-chief of *Neues Deutschland*, both potential rivals, he found high-calibre scapegoats who were blamed for the troubles and their alleged intention to sell out the GDR. In Moscow it was Beria who was forced to take on this mantle when the collective Soviet leadership made a concerted effort to get rid of their most dangerous rival in the bid for power. Beria had been most outspoken in his criticism of the GDR's mismanagement of the economy and was now charged with treason for abandoning socialism altogether in the GDR in favour of a *bourgeois* and neutral Germany. Since all these accusations were levelled at him by his rivals it is difficult to ascertain whether he was really prepared to opt for a solution to the German Question acceptable to the West. Ulbricht was given a free hand both in disposing of his personal enemies and all "unreliable" elements in society, and in relaxing his strict rule for the benefit of better living conditions. The unexpected uprising in June meant that the GDR had utterly failed as a launch pad for all-German policies. Not accepted by its own people, the government could hardly claim to serve as a model for a reunited Germany. There was general agreement both in Pankow, seat of the East German government, and Moscow that for the time being reinforcing the weakened structure of the GDR and enhancing the prestige of the SED should have priority over any new approaches to the West. The new course was revised in the sense that socialism should be pursued with greater regard to the needs of the people. At the same time more attention was paid to internal security and ideological propaganda. The Kremlin prepared the ground for the GDR to be recognised as a second German state.

The new determination to hold on to the GDR, come what may, was also reflected in Moscow's response to the Western powers' pressure for another Conference of Foreign Ministers.[24] Now at the Berlin Conference in January/February 1954 the Russians proposed that the two German states should co-exist with a provisional all-German government. The peace treaty should not be dependent any longer upon a unitary German state. The Western powers, however, insisted on a different procedure:

1   free elections;
2   national constituent assembly;
3   constitution and negotiations about a peace treaty;
4   and only then formation of an all-German government which would conclude a peace treaty.

Adenauer's victory in the autumn elections – an increase in the CDU/ CSU vote from 31 per cent to 35.2 per cent and the disappearance of the communists as a parliamentary party (only 2.2 per cent) – showed all too clearly that the GDR as a champion of national unity had no appeal what-soever.[25] Yet the régime had to be seen to be pursing the goal of German unification to satisfy its own people. In October 1954 Ulbricht came up with the idea of a confederation of the two German states, which would leave the GDR intact. It is interesting to note that for a short time Chancellor Helmut Kohl and Hans Modrow, the last Communist Prime Minister of the GDR, toyed with similar plans in 1989/90. In the autumn of 1954 Moscow was surprised at how quickly the Western powers, given the defeat of the European Defence Community in the French Chamber, had developed alternative plans to incorporate the Federal Republic into a European secur-ity system. Anthony Eden, the British Foreign Secretary, was the man of the hour by committing British troops to the defence of Europe. By pledging a strong British presence to balance the Germans he reassured both the French and the Americans. On 23 October 1954 the Paris Peace Treaties were signed, guaranteeing the Federal Republic's independence and its military integration into NATO: these two issues, political sovereignty and security, had been linked ever since May 1952. Moreover, security from Germany and security for Germany were closely intertwined as will be seen again in 1989/90. It was now up to the French Chamber and the *Bundestag* to ratify these agreements. There was strong opposition to West German rearmament in both parliaments. In this precarious situation the Soviet government launched its last diplomatic offensive on 14 January 1955, seeking to pre-vent the inevitable from happening. It offered free elections in the whole of Germany and made it clear that if the *Bundestag* accepted the Paris Treaties German unification would no longer remain on the agenda of inter-national conferences. A week later Adenauer rejected the Soviet proposal out of hand, to the dismay of large sections of the Social Democrats and Trade Unions, which then set out to prevent ratification of the treaties by extra-parliamentary activities. To no avail: on 5 May 1955 the *Bundestag* ratified the Paris Treaties, thereby terminating West Germany's occupation status. Only a few days later the Federal Republic was received into NATO as a new and valuable member of the Western alliance.

As so often in the past, Soviet tactics had been all too transparent: inter-vening with proposals for unification at precisely the moment when Bonn was about to make another move towards the West. Now that the Federal Republic had acquired both international recognition and security, it was definitely too late to derail the westbound train. Moreover, the Soviet offer, riddled with the same old vocabulary of "democratic and peace loving conditions", etc., did not contain any substantially new guarantees. It would be up to the German states to work out the terms of unification. The strings attached to the Soviet package were unacceptable to Adenauer. It would have meant recognising the GDR as a second German state and as the legitimate voice of its people, and at the same time alienating Bonn's Western allies who had nurtured and protected the Federal Republic from its infancy. Adenauer was such a hate figure of Communist propaganda because he had, as it were, marched his country single-handed into the Western camp without once looking over his shoulder. But then, of course, Moscow followed suit by integrating the GDR into its own empire, always one step behind the West. By mid-May the Soviet government had set up a counter alliance to NATO, the Warsaw Pact. On 20 September the GDR was endowed with the same kind of sovereignty as the Federal Republic: the Soviet High Commissioner took on the mantle of Moscow's ambassador to Pankow. However, the Red Army remained on East German territory, and since 17 June 1953 there could be no doubt that its main task was to protect the régime from its own people.

While the GDR was charged with control of its borders Moscow explicitly reserved its rights in Berlin according to the Potsdam Agreement. By sticking to Four-Power control of the capital the Soviet government made it clear that it intended to keep hold of the key to the German Question. This was incidentally the standard phrase of West German politicians during the Adenauer period: *Der Schlüssel zur deutschen Frage liegt in Moskau!* (The key to the German Question lies in Moscow). Security in Berlin was, and remained, the concern of the Four Powers. This explains the cautious approach of the three Western powers *vis-à-vis* the disturbances in East Berlin on 17 June 1953. Neither the West Germany army (*Bundeswehr*) nor the National People's Army (NVA) were allowed to have a foothold in the old capital. Thus, for the next 16 years Berlin became the focal point of East–West confrontation: here the Superpowers were staring each other in the face. In July 1955 Nikita Khrushchev, who had emerged as the strong man in Moscow, had paid East Berlin an official visit and espoused on this occasion the new theory of the two German states which had to come to terms over unification.[26] Henceforth recognition of this fact by the West became a prime target of Soviet policy. The issue of unification changed sides, as it were: it was now embraced by the Federal Republic which, with the signing of the Paris Treaties, had committed its new allies to support the goal of "German self-determination and uniformity of treatment of the German population throughout Germany".

The Germany of the 1950s was, with a few exceptions, an intensely private society, concerned above all with getting ahead individually rather than national redemption. Expressing sympathy for the "brothers and sisters" in the East was left to Sunday preachers. The venture into world politics since the 1890s had proved to be an unmitigated disaster. Thus any risk-taking in politics was frowned upon. Konrad Adenauer's most successful election slogan was: *Keine Experimente!* (No risk-taking! Safety first!) The objective of national unification enshrined in the preamble to the Basic Law was a pious wish that required no immediate action. The policy of non-recognition – the SED régime was a German scandal best ignored – fitted this picture very well.

By the summer of 1955, ten years after the war, the die was cast: two German states in the opposite camps of a divided world, with an increasingly fortified border between them. There were two peculiarities in this otherwise straightforward set-up: first, the Federal Republic refused to recognise the GDR, still referred to as the "Soviet occupied zone" or, for short *die Zone*, and persuaded the rest of the Western world to follow suit. For almost 20 years Bonn succeeded, against mounting opposition, in isolating the GDR internationally. Second, Berlin, the former capital of the Reich, equally divided, was a separate political unit inasmuch as it was still, at least officially, the responsibility of the Four Powers which maintained garrisons in the city.[27] The problem was that Berlin was situated in East Germany cut off from the West. Both German states and their respective patrons, the USA and the Soviet Union, were worried about this precarious situation: The West was concerned about free access to the city, its lifeline for survival. From the Communist point of view West Berlin was perceived as a kind of thorn in the flesh, i.e. a showcase of Western prosperity and the only loophole for refugees from the GDR opting for a better life in the West.

For the next 15 years these two problems, recognition of the GDR, which meant recognition of the *de facto* and *de jure* division of Germany, and the international status of Berlin, were to become key issues in Cold War diplomacy. The question of German unification, though still looming in the background, was no longer on the international agenda until it suddenly resurfaced in November 1989. It is always right to ask who wanted to change the *status quo*. The answer reveals the whole complexity of the German Question. In the long run it was only the FRG that adhered to the ultimate goal of reunification, as enshrined in its constitution, thereby calling into question the balance of power in Europe. The Soviet Union and its East German garrison state were determined to defend the existing set-up of states and borders, what they called "the outcome of the Second World

War". In the short term, however, the reverse was the case: the West wished to hold on to the Federal Republic as the only legitimate spokesman for Germany, and to the Four Power agreement on Berlin. The Soviet government was resolved to change the status of Berlin in order to consolidate its beleaguered East German outpost. Both issues were clearly inter-connected. The constant exodus of East Germans via Berlin discredited the SED régime in the eyes of the world, and confirmed Bonn's policy of non-recognition. By pressurising West Berlin, the weak link in the Western chain of defence, the Kremlin hoped to persuade the West to face facts and recognise the GDR.

When the Federal Republic had indisputably become a member of the other club, Khrushchev tried to make the best of the new situation by inviting Adenauer to Moscow and establishing normal relations. "Normalisation" became the new catchword of Soviet diplomacy. There was, of course, nothing normal about the German Question. A deal was struck which suited both governments: appointment of ambassadors in exchange for the return of the remaining German prisoners-of-war in Russian captivity – about 10,000 in total. The actual homecoming of these emaciated German men proved to be Adenauer's most spectacular political success and helped him to win the next elections.[28] However, Bonn was now faced with the question of how to explain to the world the existence of two German ambassadors in Moscow. German lawyers now constructed the so-called Hallstein Doctrine – Hallstein being the permanent Under-Secretary of State in the German Foreign Office, and only one of several law professors dominating German diplomacy in the 1950s and 1960s. The establishment of the embassy in Moscow was a "singular act because the Soviet Union was one of the four privileged powers responsible for Germany as a whole". The Federal Republic was alleged to be the true successor to the German Reich, which had not vanished as a legal entity in 1945. Therefore only the Federal Government was entitled to represent Germany abroad. Recognition of the GDR constituted an "unfriendly act", which would result in the rupture of diplomatic relations with Bonn.[29] A conference of German ambassadors, convened in December 1955, was to rule that recognition would imply acceptance of the division of Germany. The policy of non-recognition, they were led to believe, provided moral support for the East German population in their opposition to the SED régime. Negotiations between two German states of equal status would never lead to unification because the GDR could not be expected to agree to its own demise. The policy of non-recognition was strictly and scrupulously adhered to by all West German diplomats throughout the next 17 years. Wherever an East German delegation or the GDR flag, the so-called *Spalterflagge* ("splitting flag"), was sighted, Bonn's ambassadors lodged their protestations and raised their warning fingers. The implementation of the Hallstein Doctrine in Third World countries such as those in Africa reads like a collection of satirical short stories because naturally many local politicians saw a chance to blackmail the other state for their own benefit. Was a Ghanaian football team playing in Leipzig, or an honorary degree bestowed on its head of state by the Humboldt University an act of recognition or not? More importantly, Bonn not only managed to isolate the GDR, it also contrived to restrict its own room for manoeuvre in foreign policy. As a consequence of the Hallstein Doctrine there were no West German embassies in Eastern bloc capitals which, on instructions from Moscow, had to open their door to GDR embassies. Looking back, it is doubtful whether this policy helped to further the cause of German unification. But it must be said that this deliberate humiliation of the hated East German régime did indeed reflect the official mind in the Federal Republic during the 1950s, much as it was called into question after the erection of the Berlin Wall in 1961.

After the bloody suppression of the Hungarian uprising, Khrushchev felt that he had to give more political leeway to his Warsaw Pact allies. It was in this context that he intended to strengthen the GDR by means of a peace treaty which would end Berlin's status as an occupied city and a showcase of Western affluence. After all, East Berlin had become the official capital of the GDR – the district of *Pankow* being synonymous with the SED régime in the West German media. With his speech on 10 November 1958, in which he called into question the presence of the Western powers in Berlin, the Soviet leader triggered off the second Berlin Crisis. In his subsequent note of 27 November he specified his demands. He proposed that the three Allies should join Moscow in concluding a peace treaty with Germany. It was time to get rid of the "remnants of the war". West Berlin, situated "on the territory of the GDR", was to be given the status of a free city, without the presence of occupation forces and with no further ties to West Germany. All activities directed against the GDR were to be prohibited. The question of unification was not addressed, since this was to be sorted out by "the Germans themselves", i.e. by representatives of the two German states joined in an "all-German commission". Khrushchev, who liked intimidating gestures, backed up his demands by an ultimatum: if the Western powers refused to co-operate he would conclude a peace treaty with the GDR, which would then be responsible for granting access to West Berlin. The new Soviet leader tried throughout to force the West into compliance by the threat of nuclear war, which he readily employed in his rhetoric. By 1958 it was not yet known that these were idle threats from a man who was in fact a cautious broker. The status of a "free city" meant, of course, the very opposite: West Berlin was to be deprived of the protection provided by the three Western powers, which guaranteed its freedom and prosperity. Washington would not yield, but indicated that it was willing to attend a conference.

The Geneva Conference of Foreign Ministers led nowhere, and forced Khrushchev to climb down. Afterwards the Western powers came to the conclusion that they had to be on their guard against attempts at curtailing their rights piecemeal. Khrushchev now decided to wait for the American elections, in the hope that the new President would be more susceptible to his threats. Kennedy realised that the Soviet leader had a legitimate interest in maintaining the Communist régime in East Germany. The latter was not threatened from outside, as its propagandists would have it, but from within, from a constant stream of refugees who were using Berlin's international status as the only remaining escape route to the West. This haemorrhage of manpower, skilled workers and professionals, posed a real threat to the very existence of the "workers' and peasants' state": 100,000 East Germans had sought refuge in West Berlin since January 1961 with the staggering figure of 20,000 in June. On 21 August 1959 Ulbricht had boasted that by 1961 the GDR would overtake the GNP of the Federal. By that time, however, the gap had actually widened considerably due to the West German "economic miracle". The increasing number of refugees in the first months of 1961 was a painful reminder of Ulbricht's empty promises. In the early summer the East German Party chief began to urge his Soviet patrons to close the Berlin loophole and consolidate the border between East and West Berlin. Khrushchev gradually came round to accepting this second-best solution. He had renewed his 1958 ultimatum when he met the new American President in Vienna in June 1961: either a peace treaty with both German states by the end of the year, or a Soviet one with the GDR, which would then be in charge of access to Berlin. The threat of a nuclear holocaust over the Berlin issue was in the air. Macmillan was rattled;[30] the Pentagon engaged in contingency planning, and President Kennedy desperately sought a convincing answer to the crisis. Nuclear deterrence was no longer as effective as in 1948. Nevertheless, the credibility of the United States as a world power was at stake.[31] Dean Acheson, who had directed US foreign policy during the first Berlin Crisis, now helped to strengthen the new President's resolve, and made him realise that a trial of strength was looming. Having completed an MA thesis on appeasement,[32] Kennedy was well aware of the Munich crisis and its fallout. In early July Khrushchev tried his poker game on Frank Roberts, the British ambassador to Moscow. He invited Roberts to dinner after a performance of the Royal Ballet in Moscow, and discussed the German Question with him. He openly threatened an atomic conflagration if the West were to force its way into Berlin and added that it would be ridiculous for two million people to die because of the future of two million Berliners. Roberts reported that he was asked to convey "a very serious, solemn personal warning to Her Majesty's Government, and personally to the Prime Minister".[33] But Macmillan could not dissuade the American President from holding a tough line. On the evening of 27 July Kennedy addressed the nation on television and delivered a speech that showed that he, too, knew the political poker game: both the defence budget and the overall number of troops were to be increased. Half the strategic bomber command was to be airborne within fifteen minutes. He then referred to the "three essentials" for *West Berlin*, which must be maintained at all costs: the Western powers' right to be present in the city, free access, and the guaranteed freedom of its citizens. Kennedy was open to negotiation, but not under threat. The emphasis on West Berlin and the reference to the threatened border dividing the city were signals showing Khrushchev a way out of his dilemma. Five days later William Fulbright, chairman of the Senate Foreign Policy Committee, gave an even stronger hint when he said in a television interview that he could not understand why the East Germans did not close their border, which he thought they had every right to do. Kennedy is quoted as having said that he could hold the alliance together for the defence of West Berlin, but not in order to guarantee free access to East Berlin. Apparently there is no documentary evidence that the Americans were secretly in cahoots with the Kremlin over the closure of the Berlin border.[34] To many Western observers such a measure seemed fraught with danger since it might well ignite another uprising in East Germany with unforeseeable consequences. It seems that Kennedy's credible stance on West Berlin – and West Berlin only – eventually persuaded Khrushchev to yield to Ulbricht's more immediate demand that the Berlin escape route be blocked. According to his own memoirs he came up with the idea of a proper wall. Ulbricht, who had only thought of sealing off his part of the city with barbed wire, needed no persuasion. This was the solution to his immediate problem, that of containing his own population. As late as 15 June Ulbricht had given the public assurance that "nobody has the intention of building a wall" – with the result that the number of refugees immediately swelled even further. In order to avoid a stampede of refugees as in 1989, strict secrecy was to be observed. When Khrushchev addressed the Warsaw Pact delegates in early August (3–5 August 1961) he did not mention the Wall at all. Ulbricht referred to the enemy that was using the open border between the GDR and West Berlin to inflict severe damage on the economy by the organised traffic in human beings (*Menschenhandel*). Active measures were needed to stop this harmful development. His listeners could still think that what he had in mind was the implementation of well known intentions: a peace treaty with the GDR and the end of West Berlin's occupied status. From Ulbricht's point of view the closure of the border was meant to be the first step in that very direction. However, for Khrushchev it was the alternative to a showdown with the West which might have unleashed all-out war. In the West no one could be sure that this was in fact both the climax and the end of the second Berlin Crisis.

On 12 August, at 4 p.m. Ulbricht signed the order for the closure of the border, to be set in motion at 1 a.m. the following morning. The East German Press Agency (ADN) announced that measures were about to be implemented "for a reliable protection and effective control of the border with the Western sectors of Greater Berlin". It began with a barrier of barbed wire, soon to be replaced by slabs of concrete once it had become clear that the West would not intervene. On the same day further official statements followed, which justified the Wall as an act of securing peace in view of alleged West German preparations for a civil war. It was, of course, the erection of the Wall itself, the virtual imprisonment of the East German population, which could have ignited another uprising. However, the haunting memories of Soviet tanks crushing demonstrators on 17 June 1953 and the fate of Hungary in 1956 were still too fresh to invite repetition. Nor were the secrecy and efficiency of the operation conducive to any organised response. Ten days later border guards were given orders to make use of their weapons against those who dared to "violate the borders of the GDR". By September 3,000 people, mostly youngsters, had been arrested for the offence of "anti-state slander". The reaction of the Berlin population in the Western half of the city was one of anger and frustration at the apparent helplessness of the Western powers. The leaders of the Western world, who were enjoying a relaxing weekend, remained calm, almost mute, since the measures taken were directed against the GDR's own citizens, not against the freedom of West Berlin. After consultation with the three Western commandants, Willy Brandt, the Governing Mayor of West Berlin, advised his citizens to remain calm. *Der Westen tut nichts* (The West does nothing) was the headline of *Bild*, Germany's top-selling tabloid.[35] Adenauer continued his election campaign as if nothing had happened, not sparing with his abuse for Berlin's Social Democratic mayor. One witness describes the feeling in the chancellery on that day with the famous Wilhelmine watchword "remaining calm is the citizen's first duty".[36] Adenauer's reserve on this fateful day was deliberate and born out of a sense of responsibility. He was only too aware that the crisis could easily escalate. Nevertheless, his conduct over Berlin hastened the decline of his waning power and popularity. According to his well-disposed biographer Hans-Peter Schwarz, his Chancellorship now reached its first major "cataract".[37]

Four days later Kennedy was propelled into action by Edward R. Murrow, Director of the US Information Agency, who had happened to be in Berlin on 13 August and had sent a personal cable directly to Kennedy warning of a crisis of confidence: "What is in danger of being destroyed here is that perishable quality called hope".[38] This telegram forced Kennedy to react. He decided to increase the Berlin garrison by 1,500 troops and to dispatch Vice President Johnson and Lucius D. Clay, the saviour of the besieged capital in 1948, as his personal representatives. It was not until 1963, after the Cuban missile crisis, that Kennedy himself would set foot in Berlin and pronounce the famous words *Ich bin ein Berliner*. The arrival of Johnson and Clay in 1961 were symbolic gestures to demonstrate America's determination, rather than concrete counter-measures. Not only was the scope for possible action very limited, there was also uncertainty as to the political significance of the Wall. Would Khrushchev now be satisfied with the solution to the refugee problem and the ensuing economic consolidation of the GDR, or would he feel emboldened to make the next move by concluding a peace treaty with East Berlin and abandoning Berlin's Four-Power status? For the SED Politburo, the Wall, though greatly diffusing the Berlin problem, could only constitute the second-best solution. It could be assumed that Ulbricht would want to keep up the pressure over the status of West Berlin, which was, as it were, out of place in the GDR, and a constant reminder of the unsolved German Question. Indeed, we now know that he had begged Khrushchev for the authorisation gradually to undermine Berlin's Four-Power status by getting his hands on air-traffic control and on Allied access to East Berlin, now officially dubbed the capital of the GDR. From his point of view "Westberlin", according to politically correct GDR spelling, was still a Western stronghold bent on subverting the GDR, by means of intelligence activities as well as radio and television stations, which were making a good job of wrecking Communist propaganda efforts.

This is the background to the famous confrontation at Checkpoint Charlie, which perhaps along with the Cuban Missile Crisis was potentially the most dangerous incident in the Cold War era in Europe. For the Western powers, notably the Americans as the leading power, maintaining their rights of free access to Berlin as a whole was a matter of standing fast. Officials of the three Western powers, when entering East Berlin, refused to recognise the authority of the *Volkspolizei* and would only negotiate with Soviet representatives, in line with the city's Four-Power status. On 15 October, while crossing the border on the way to a theatre performance in East Berlin, Edwin A. Leithner, deputy US commandant in Berlin, was asked by the *Volkspolizei* to prove his identity. He refused, and contacted Lucius D. Clay, President Kennedy's personal representative in West Berlin. Later he was to cross the border twice, escorted by armed US military police without further disturbance. As an additional demonstration four American tanks positioned themselves opposite Checkpoint Charlie, the main crossing point. At first the Russians admitted that a mistake had been made. But then the Press Agency announced that the GDR Minister of the Interior had given instructions for Allied personnel in civilian clothes to be checked by the *Volkspolizei* as a matter of principle. The Americans responded by continuing with their test-drives into East Berlin, always accompanied by armed GIs. The new Soviet political adviser explained that the GDR was now in control of border crossings, whereupon Clay ordered ten American M48 tanks to be moved to Checkpoint Charlie, and the US garrison to be put on alert. Indeed, Clay was spoiling for a showdown and an opportunity to demolish the Wall by force. He had a mock wall built to see how best it could be torn down. The Soviet Secret Service, which noticed this manoeuvre, came to the conclusion that plans for aggressive action had been given the go-ahead by Washington. In fact, Kennedy and his Secretary of State Dean Rusk disagreed with Clay and tried to diffuse the situation. Meanwhile, on 27 October ten Russian tanks with live ammunition positioned themselves opposite the US front line. On the same day the President decided, much to the annoyance of Clay, that no further test-drives by US civilian personnel were to be undertaken. For 16 hours ten Soviet and ten US tanks, ready to fire in earnest, directly confronted each other. Rolf Steininger, one of the most investigative of historians, thinks he has found the answer to the climb down: secret channels of communication with the Kremlin.[39] Kennedy's brother Robert knew a KGB agent named Georj Bolshakov, attached to the Soviet Embassy in Washington. Kennedy let Khrushchev know that if he were to withdraw his tanks first, the Americans would follow suit. And this is what happened: the diffusion of a potentially explosive confrontation against the advice of hardliners on both sides, Clay and the military in the West, Ulbricht and his SED stalwarts in the East. Neither the Americans nor the Russians wished to launch nuclear war for the sake of their former enemy's capital.

A year later the KGB lines of communication were activated once more to diffuse the Cuban Missile Crisis. For a while Washington was seriously concerned that the Soviet leader, faced with quarantine around Cuba, would be tempted to retaliate with another blockade of Berlin. A NATO sub-committee busied itself with possible Soviet action and adequate counter-measures. However, Khrushchev saw that nothing further was to be gained by continuing the war of nerves over Berlin. Soon his mind was absorbed by negotiations regarding non-proliferation and the more worthwhile prospect that neither German state would ever be in possession of the atom bomb.

With the building of the Wall, all aspirations for German unification seemed to have reached a dead end. In retrospect the 1950s, notably the first half, appeared to have offered certain opportunities that were never explored. The political controversies of this period were later resumed by historians. In the 1950s the Social Democrats, certain National Conservat-ives, as well as a number of influential journalists like Paul Sethe (*Frankfurter Allgemeine Zeitung*), Hans Zehrer (*Die Welt*) and Rudolf Augstein (*Der Spiegel*) maintained that Adenauer did not really pursue every opportunity for achieving German unity. The historiographical debate centres on the Stalin Notes of 1952 and whether a chance had been missed. The Chancellor's later critics, in particular Rolf Steininger and Josef Foschepoth, point to his unwillingness to explore Stalin's offer. They seem to have been shocked to discover documentary evidence that Adenauer was deeply distrustful of his own people and their common sense in matters of foreign policy.[40] He had every reason to be – born in 1875, and having experienced both World Wars as an adult. It is not that he objected in any way to the eventual goal of German unity. During the second Berlin crisis he had secretly tried in vain to come to an understanding with the Soviet government, which for the time being would lead to a *modus vivendi* between the two German states with the prospect of unification at a later stage.[41] But before that happened, before the German nation state could throw its weight around, he wished to see the Germans securely anchored in the Western Alliance for their own sake as much as for that of Europe. A fully independent or neutral Germany would be a sort of loose cannon. The Germans, especially those in the North and East who had never been under the civilising influence of Roman cul-ture, were prone to make mischief. Most West Germans saw him as a stern, autocratic but also a caring father figure who told them what would be in their best interests given the turbulent first half of the century. By 1958 he had left Bismarck behind in public opinion polls as the German statesman who had achieved most for his country; this was an important watershed in German mentality.[42] Now even the educated middle class which had longed for the reconstitution of the *Bismarck-Staat* had accepted the West German *Adenauer-Staat*. Right from the beginning Adenauer was prejudiced against what he saw as the last Soviet spanner thrown into the smooth process of Western integration. He was "an old man in a hurry" who knew perfectly well that a united Germany such as he had in mind, free and embedded in the Western Alliance, would be totally unacceptable to the Soviet government. Even if Stalin could have been persuaded to grant free elections, he would have insisted on German neutrality in the same way as he forced neutrality on Austria. Adenauer was adamant in rejecting this idea because it would have got Germany into deep water. Weak, unable to defend herself adequately, and tempted to go for a seesaw policy, she could easily have succumbed to Soviet influence.

Notes and references

1 See Ian D. Turner (ed.), *Reconstruction in Post-War Germany* (Oxford, 1989). The Volkswagen plant on which Turner had written his PhD thesis is the most spectacular example.

2 See William R. Smyser, *From Yalta to Berlin. The Cold War Struggle over Germany* (London, 1999), p. 87.

3 Speech on 31 May 1947, quoted in Rolf Steininger, *Deutsche Geschichte seit 1945* (Frankfurt a.M., 1996), vol. 1, p. 319. See also the interpretation in Peter Siebenmorgen, *Gezeitenwechsel. Aufbruch zur Entspannungspolitik* (Bonn, 1990), pp. 83–88.

4 See the definitive biography: Hans-Peter Schwarz, *Konrad Adenauer*, 2 vols, translated from German (Oxford, 1995), esp. the chapter "That Bully Adenauer", vol. 1, pp. 516–54; also Charles Williams, *Adenauer: The Father of the New Germany* (London, 2000). As to the "politics of strength" in particular: Siebenmorgen, pp. 55–83.

5 For more details about the SED's national campaign on which the following account is based: Heike Amos, *Die Westpolitik der SED 1948/49–1961* (Berlin, 1999). See also the survey by Johannes Kuppe, *Deutschlandpolitik der DDR,* in Werner Weidenfeld and Karl-Rudolf Korte (eds), *Handbuch zur deutschen Einheit 1949–1989–1999* (Frankfurt a.M., 1999), pp. 252–67.

6 Hugo Hickmann was close to the West German Nauheimer Kreis founded by the historian Ulrich Noack, which gathered national-minded intellectuals in favour of unification. See now Alexander Gallus, *Die Neutralisten. Verfechter eines vereinten Deutschland zwischen Ost und West 1945–1990* (Düsseldorf, 2001).

7 See Michael Lemke, "Eine deutsche Chance? Die innerdeutsche Diskussion um den Grotewohlbrief vom November 1950 auf der Entscheidungsebene", in: *Zeitschrift für Geschichtswissenschaft* 43 (1996), pp. 25–40. See also Amos, pp. 67–76.

8 Peter Ruggenthaler (ed.), *Stalins großer Bluff. Die Geschichte der Stalin-Note in Dokumenten der sowjetischen Führung* (Munich, 2007). See also Jürgen Zarusky (ed.), *Die Stalin-Note vom 10. März 1952. Neue Quellen und Analysen* (Munich, 2002), especially the contribution by Gerhard Wettig.

9 Smyser, p. 118.

10 See now the documentary evidence in Christian F. Ostermann (ed.), *Uprising in East Germany 1953* (New York, 2001), Doc. No. 1: Conversation between Josef Stalin and SED Leaders, 1. and 7.4.1952, pp. 22–42.

11 Helge Heidemeyer, *Flucht und Zuwanderung aus der SBZ/DDR 1945–49–1961* (Düsseldorf, 1993). This figure excludes the refugees from the East and approx. 500,000 who returned to the GDR. The estimate for the period 1950 until 1961 is 2,020,750, pp. 43–45.

12 See the report of the border police of Halberstadt, 25.5.1952, in Dirk Hoffmann, Karl-Heinz Schmitt and Peter Syba (eds), *Die DDR vor dem Mauerbau. Dokumente zur Geschichte des anderen deutschen Staates 1949–1961* (Munich, 1993), pp. 106–09; see also the reaction of the Politburo on 6.1.1953 to westward migration (Abwanderung), ibid., pp. 128–33.

13 Armin Mitter and Stefan Wolle, *Untergang auf Raten: Unbekannte Kapitel der DDR-Geschichte* (Munich, 1993), p. 44.

14 Quoted in Ostermann (ed.), p. 7.

15 For these statistics see ibid., Doc. No. 13, pp. 100–109.

16 Ibid., Doc. No. 18, pp. 133–36. For the following see Doc. No. 19, p. 137f.

17 For the crisis of 16/17 June 1953 see, apart from the documents edited by Ostermann and by Hoffmann *et al.* (pp. 149–231), Mitter and Wolle, pp. 27–162 as well as Ilko Sascha Kowalczuk, Armin Mitter and Stefan Wolle (eds), *Der Tag X. 17. Juni 1953. Die "innere Staatsgründung" der DDR als Ergebnis der Krise 1952/54* (Berlin, 1995).

18 See the various telegrams between Berlin, the FO and Churchill in Gerhard Beier, *Wir wollen freie Menschen sein. Der 17. Juni 1953: Bauleute gingen voran* (Frankfurt a.M., 1993), pp. 129–62. On 19 June General Colemann told the FO that the uprising was spontaneous and that without the Russians' decisive intervention no doubt the government would have been toppled (p. 130).

19 For Churchill's last but unsuccessful diplomatic initiative to overcome the Cold War see Klaus Larres, *Politik der Illusionen: Churchill, Eisenhower und die deutsche Frage 1945–1955* (Göttingen, 1995), pp. 133–54 – as well as Churchill's Cold War. *The Politics of Personal Diplomacy* (New Haven/Conn., 2002).

20 Frank Roberts to William Strang ("A united, neutralised Germany"), 19.5.1953, PRO: FO 371/103660/C1016.

21 Selwyn Lloyd to Winston Churchill, 22.6.1953, reproduced in Ostermann (ed.), p. 252.

22 See Mitter and Wolle, pp. 27–162; see also Hans-Hermann Hertle and Stefan Wolle, *Damals in der DDR. Der Alltag im Arbeiter- und Bauernstaat* (Munich, 2006), pp. 62–88. For the vast volume of West German literature on this topic see Beier, pp. 380–82.

23 See summary of documents in Ostermann, pp. 178–80.

24 For the development of the German Question in 1954/55 see the two divergent narratives (*pro* and *contra* Adenauer) by Adolf M. Birke, *Nation ohne Haus. Deutschland 1945–1961* (Berlin, 1989), pp. 319–43 and Rolf Steininger, *Deutsche Geschichte seit 1945* (Frankfurt a.M., 1996), vol. 2, pp. 285–318.

25 See Hans-Peter Schwarz, *Die Ära Adenauer. Gründerjahre der Republik 1959–1957* (Stuttgart, 1981), pp. 187–96.

26 For this and the subsequent development see Smyser, pp. 129–36.

27 See Udo Wetzlaugk, *Die Alliierten in Berlin* (Berlin, 1988); also Lothar Kettenacker, *Britain as One of the Four Powers in Berlin*, in Jeremy Noakes, Peter Wende and Jonathan Wright (eds), *Britain and Germany in Europe* (Oxford, 2002), pp. 141–83. There is now an "Allied Museum" in West Berlin. See catalogue of recent exhibition on Reagan's visit in 1987: Helmut Trotnow and Florian Weiß (eds), *Tear down this Wall* (Berlin, 2007).

28 Schwarz, *Adenauer*, vol. 2, pp. 164–76 ("Moscow – a Journey into the Unknown").

29 See in defence of the controversial doctrine: Rüdiger M. Booz, *"Hallsteinzeit". Deutsche Außenpolitik 1955–1972* (Bonn, 1995). The other influential law professor apart from Walter Hallstein was Wilhelm Grewe (*Rückblenden*, Frankfurt a.M., 1979).

30 John P.S. Gearson, *Harold Macmillan and the Berlin Wall Crisis: The Limits of Interests and Force* (London, 1998).

31 For the American part in the drama see Smyser, pp. 137–92.

32 John F. Kennedy, *Why England Slept. With an introduction by Henry R. Luce, July 1940* (London, 1962). At the time Kenendy was 23 and lived with his father who was US ambassador in London and judged to be himself an appeaser by the British FO.

33 Frank Roberts, *Dealing with Dictators. The Destruction and Renewal of Europe 1930–1970* (London, 1991), p. 216.

34 See the most recent and most thoroughly researched German study on the subject: Rolf Steininger, *Der Mauerbau. Die Westmächte und Adenauer in der Berlin-Krise 1958–1963* (Munich, 2001), p. 234.

35 Quoted by Schwarz, *Adenauer*, vol. 2, p. 541 ("The West does nothing. President Kennedy remains silent. Macmillan goes hunting . . . and Adenauer sneers at Brandt").

36 Horst Osterheld, *"Ich gehe nicht leichten Herzens". Adenauers letzte Kanzlerjahre. Ein dokumentarischer Bericht* (Mainz, 1986), p. 57.

37 Title of his chapter on the Berlin Wall, Schwarz, *Adenauer*, vol. 2, pp. 522–47.

38 See Smyser, p. 162.

39 Steininger, *Mauerbau*, pp. 305–14.

40 Steininger, *Deutsche Geschichte*, vol. 2, pp. 326–33. For Steininger, Adenauer was the chancellor of the Western allies, a verdict which had first been levelled against him by his SPD opponent Kurt Schumacher. As proof and Q.E.D. of his criticism Steininger reproduces at the end a memo by Ivone Kirkpatrick about a conversation with the German ambassador (16 December 1955). "Dr Adenauer had no confidence in the German people . . . Consequently he felt that the integration of Western Germany with the West was more important than the unification of Germany." See also Joesf Foschepoth (ed.), *Adenauer und die deutsche Frage* (Göttingen, 1988). In his bibliography he lists all relevant works by Steininger on this question.

41 As to the so-called Globke plan and the plan for a temporary truce see Volker Erhard, *Adenauers deutschlandpolitische Geheimkonzepte während der zweiten Berlin-Krise 1958–1962* (Hamburg, 2003); also Hans Buchheim, *Deutschlandpolitik 1949–1972* (Stuttgart, 1984), pp. 87–104.

42 See the article in *Frankfurter Allgemeine Zeitung* "Das Jahr 1958" (2.1.2008) by Elisabeth Noelle, the grand old lady of German public opinion polls (Institut für Demoskopie Allensbach).

CHAPTER 3

Ostpolitik: Putting the East at ease

The Wall was the most telling and the most hideous symbol of the Cold War: by 1970 165 km of concrete slabs or metal fence, 3.5–4.2 m in height combined with ditches, anti-tank obstacles, watchtowers, floodlights, dog kennels. Border patrols were guarding the "state border of the GDR" day and night. It is important to be aware of the different perspectives. For the citizens of the now hermetically sealed state it was a prison wall. West Berliners were cut off from their relations and friends in the East, the West Germans realised that the division of their country could no longer be denied and for the rest of the world the Wall signified the evident failure of socialism. The Superpowers were relieved without saying so that a temporary solution had been found in a dangerous trouble spot. However, what the rest of the world regarded as a shameful monument, the SED celebrated as a great achievement, because its own population remained numbed and the West, equally surprised, did not intervene. According to the propaganda version of events, the "anti-fascist protective wall" would keep Western imperialism at bay and had prevented a counter-revolution just in time. The Wall gave the SED régime another lease of life or, as one historian has put it, it marked its rebirth,[1] because now for the first time it had full control of its workforce and could hope to consolidate its economy. With a view to increasing productivity a new economic reform was launched in 1963, aimed at decentralisation and more managerial responsibility.[2] However, prices were still fixed and a real market economy was not allowed to take root. Just two years later the whole venture was abandoned and the centralised structures of a command economy re-established.

Constructing a separate GDR identity became the chief objective of all propaganda efforts in the 1960s. This meant, above all, cutting all existing ties with West Germany, not least in the sphere of cultural life. Young FDJ activists climbed on to roofs to demolish aerials that could receive West German radio broadcasts and television. Constant pressure was put on the Protestant bishops to sever their links with the all-German church in Hanover, until in 1969 they eventually gave in and set up the *Bund der Evangelischen Kirchen in der DDR* (BEK).[3]

In the course of this demarcation policy the same SED which in the early 1950s had appealed to German nationalism now even disputed the unity of the German nation. In 1967 a new GDR citizenship was introduced that referred to two separate *Staatsvölker* and defined the GDR as a "socialist state of German nationhood".[4] A year later a new constitution followed, which now enshrined in Article 1 "the leading role of the Party", charged with the task of realising socialism. Since the SED now ruled supreme, all other human rights guaranteed in the constitution were of no real consequence. The People's Chamber, though "the only constitutional and legislative organ of the GDR", was to rubber-stamp the Politburo's decisions.

One could argue that the ten years following the erection of the Wall were one long and desperate struggle for internal and external recognition. Legitimacy at home was less important in so far as people had no choice but to stay and to adapt to what was later despairingly referred to as "really existing socialism" (*real existierender Sozialismus*). An elaborate system of surveillance by the Stasi seemed to suggest that the leadership had no reason to worry about its own people. International recognition was a different matter. As far as the non-Communist world was concerned it was mainly in the hands of successive West German governments. Therefore this chapter will deal primarily with the incremental shift in policy in West Germany culminating in *Ostpolitik*, the sea-change in the Federal Republic's relations with the GDR and Communist Europe, which ultimately proved to be a necessary, though unforeseeable, precondition for reunification in 1990.

Ostpolitik, which resulted in a series of treaties in the early 1970s that recognised the post-war order in Europe, is generally attributed to Willy Brandt, Governing Mayor of Berlin, and his close adviser Egon Bahr. It is said to have started where the previous policy had demonstrably failed: in Berlin. In an abbreviated sense this is true, but caesuras in history are never that clear-cut, new departures never quite that new. Adenauer was not just a stumbling block on the way to détente, as he was perceived by his opponents at home and by some of the FRG's allies. He did try to reach an understanding with Moscow on his own terms, but failed. To appreciate the new development one has to be aware of what went on before. During the second Berlin crisis Adenauer suspected that the Superpowers would compromise over the city's future at the expense of Bonn's vital interests. He felt under pressure to come up with his own ideas for solving the crisis, even though he really wanted to leave things as they were for the time being. Moreover, he felt strongly that the problem of Berlin could not be decoupled from the German Question as such. This is the background to the so-called "Globke Plan", Hans Globke, its author, being Adenauer's controversial head of Chancellery.[5] It was, to all intents and purposes, a kind of peace treaty with the long-term prospect of unification, which met certain Soviet demands – chiefly recognition of the GDR, and Berlin, both West and East, to become a Free City just as Khrushchev had demanded. Within five years of the treaty a ballot on unification was to take place. If no majority could be gained in either of the two German states they would become truly sovereign. In other words, the East would have to concede free elections and the West would not out-vote the smaller or less populous GDR. The voting system was specified to the last detail in order to prevent Communist manipulation by block vote. The unified Germany would be free to join NATO or the Warsaw Pact, but would not be able to opt for neutrality. The territories east of the Oder-Neisse line were not mentioned, and were virtually written off. Adenauer insisted on one condition though: more freedom, above all more freedom of movement, for his fellow countrymen in the East. The plight of the Germans "in der Zone", as he would say, preoccupied him above all. He was more concerned about the people than about borders. After the Wall had been built he told the *Bundestag*: "The Federal government is willing to discuss many a matter, as long as our brethren in the Zone can organise their lives as they wish. For us, humanitarian concerns carry more import-ance than national considerations."[6]

The Globke Plan, the final version of which was put into treaty form, was never tabled or submitted as the official West German proposal for solving the Berlin crisis. Nor was it ever made known to the public at the time. Adenauer had no intention of releasing the Four Powers from their respons-ibility for the German Question. Indeed, nothing worried him more than the idea that they would carry on with détente without prior agreement with West Germany. But he peddled various elements of the plan, notably in his talks with American and British diplomats. Although he was always paranoid about conferences and contacts between the Superpowers, behind the scenes he tried to keep open channels of communication with the Kremlin, mainly through the Soviet ambassador Andrej Smirnov and his own ambassador Hans Kroll, who had established a personal relationship with Khrushchev and had unrealistically high hopes of a rapprochement. The Chancellor held on to Kroll after the latter had lost the trust of his superiors at the German Foreign Office (*Auswärtiges Amt/AA*) as a result of his uncalled-for initiatives.[7] In June 1962 Adenauer proposed to Smirnov a formal truce, i.e. a *modus vivendi* without constant threats, for a period of ten years, on the condition that Moscow would see to it that living conditions in the East improved. Adenauer was convinced that time was on the West's side, both because Soviet Russia would not be able to sustain an armaments race with the United States for long, and also because the threat posed by China would make it more compliant in Eastern Europe. To what extent Adenauer introduced other elements of the Globke Plan, such as free elections at the end of this period, or whether he insisted on the removal of the Wall as a necessary precondition, is not quite clear since the Soviet version only refers to an unconditional truce, which it nevertheless rejected out of hand. As mentioned before, the Cuban Missile Crisis relieved the situation in Berlin: nuclear deterrence had passed its first real test and there was no need for a repetition over Berlin. In effect, a kind of undeclared truce between the Superpowers as regards the German hotspot had been arrived at. Bonn constantly defended, come what may, its policy of non-recognition and its sole right to represent Germany abroad. Every small deviation from this rigid position caused an uproar in Bonn. When the GDR signed the Test-Ban Treaty, Bonn would only accede to the international agreement after US Secretary of State Dean Rusk told the Senate that this did not imply international recognition of the East German government.

One can well imagine that Bonn's legalistic stance in matters of international relations was not well received in Washington and London. Brandt's more pragmatic and flexible approach in Berlin was more in tune with the policy of détente as it unfolded after the Cuban Crisis. It is important to stress both the continuity and innovation of *Ostpolitik*. Adenauer's overtures to Moscow were always carried out in secrecy and close consultation with Washington and Paris. The basic principle was: no détente without simultaneous progress on the German front, as though a relaxation of tension was mainly in the interests of the Soviet government. *Ostpolitik* proper, as conceived by Brandt and Bahr, meant a reversal of priorities. In the age of a potential nuclear holocaust, détente was important for its own sake, and was, at the same time, a necessary precondition – not a result – of progress over the issue of Berlin and German unification.

For Brandt, the security and prosperity of the city, which depended on a *modus vivendi* with the East German authorities, was more pressing than German unification. Under Adenauer the two issues were regarded as inseparable. The Berlin Wall made no difference to the way in which the German Question should be tackled. For Brandt and Bahr it made all the difference in the world: prior to the Wall 60,000 East Berliners had been working and shopping in the West of the city, 10,000 West Berliners in the East. Extended families lived in both parts of the city and were, from one day to the next, cut off from each other. The division of the city, though merely reflecting the partition of the whole country, was more immediately absurd and painful. Something had to be done. In retrospect, all efforts to overcome the Wall also contributed to German unification. However, few people realised this at the time. Nor would this policy have been successful if propagated in these terms: first Berlin, then Germany as a whole. At the time it was not at all obvious that under the prevailing circumstances the best way of overcoming the division was to accept it as a temporary reality.

The intellectual origin of *Ostpolitik* has been traced to a speech by Egon Bahr at the *Evangelische Akademie* in Tutzing (Bavaria) in July 1963.[8] Bahr, previously RIAS Berlin's chief commentator, had been Brandt's press spokesman, and as such an important adviser to the Governing Mayor. He was then the sharpest mind in Brandt's brains trust. It is in Tutzing that the famous concept *Wandel durch Annäherung* (change via rapprochement) had first been muted. Both Brandt and Bahr referred on this occasion to Kennedy's "strategy for peace". A month earlier the US President had received an enthusiastic welcome in West Berlin when he uttered the famous words *Ich bin ein Berliner*. Bahr was the first to explain convincingly that the Kremlin could not be forced to turn the key and that the door was not to be opened by just one turn. He rightly suggested – and this was a new insight – that reunification would not be achieved by one single act, but as a result of a patient process, what he termed a "process of many small steps and many stages". *Wandel durch Annäherung* and *Politik der kleinen Schritte* were to become the key concept of *Ostpolitik*. At the time they were the first signals of a new departure. Bahr dared to suggest that changes and improvements were only possible in cooperation with the hateful East German régime. He explained in some detail that even without formal recognition the GDR had been acknowledged by the Western Allies and the Federal Republic in many ways. Trade was the vehicle best suited to improving the lot of the East Germans. Some might worry, he argued, that in this way the unhappiness of "our fellow countrymen" would be reduced. However, this was to be welcomed because it would also reduce the danger of uncontrolled developments, which were bound to be set-backs to achieving reunification. The fear of another uprising in the East was one of the most important elements in *Ostpolitik*, as it also was later, in the 1980s, when it was skilfully exploited by Honecker to extract more financial support from Bonn. As mentioned before, Adenauer, too, was concerned about living conditions in East Germany, but the emphasis was on more freedom, which would put pressure on the régime. Now, for the first time, the opposite effect was advocated: more stability for the shaky party state in the hope that this would encourage the SED to overcome its inferiority complex. What Bahr was recommending was a kind of therapeutic treatment for men who were still regarded by most West Germans as despicable Communist stooges. Not surprisingly, then, his ideas were widely criticised, not only in West Germany but also in the East. Otto Winzer, the East German Foreign Minister, called Bahr's suggestions "aggression in slippers". Anti-Communist journalists in the West, notably the Springer Press which ruled the roost, were most upset and preached a no-surrender attitude, as though there was no alternative other than victory or defeat. Even within the SPD Bahr's views fell on stony ground. After all, it was only a few years since the party had decided on its historical U-turn by subscribing to Adenauer's foreign policy. However, Brandt, though more restrained in his own utterances, protected Bahr and urged him to put out feelers. Yet he too felt it necessary to qualify Bahr's view as a "private contribution to the discussion which required further thought". At first only one liberal paper, *Frankfurter Rundschau*, supported the reassessment of old assumptions. More importantly, Brandt and Bahr's new thinking had the tacit support of the US administration which was now engaged in the policy of détente. The concept of *Wandel durch Annäherung* was sufficiently vague and ambivalent to allow for a variety of interpretations. For Vogtmeier, who has studied Bahr's political philosophy, the phrase expressed the dialectic nature of later *Ostpolitik*.

In spite of early reservations *Wandel durch Annäherung* soon gained acceptance within the SPD. In many ways this was less a theoretical concept than a practical approach to justify attempts at creating a *modus vivendi* in the divided city: how to facilitate visits to East Berlin, arrange for travellers' cheques, improve rail connections, etc. All this could only be negotiated with the GDR government and implied a degree of recognition.

The first visa arrangement between the Senate of West Berlin and the GDR was signed in December 1963, just in time for Christmas, allowing one-day visits, after due checks. During the two weeks it was valid, 1.3 million West Berliners seized the opportunity to visit relations in the East of the city. Further such arrangements were to follow, in spite of serious objections on the part of the new Chancellor Ludwig Erhardt and the CDU, but with the support of the Liberal Party and its chairman, Erich Mende, the Minister for All-German Affairs. Reluctantly the same Ministry also approved one of the most controversial actions of the Cold War: the exchange of prisoners-of-war, those sentenced for attempting to turn their back on the republic, for valuable foreign currency. Between 1963 and 1989, 40,000 people were released in this way, for ransom money raised over the years from DM 40,000 to DM 95,000 per person.[9] These shady deals, disguised as human relief measures, reflected badly on the character of the East German régime, which in its propaganda sought to occupy the moral high ground over the Federal Republic. It suited both sides that these negotiations, as distinct from the visa arrangements, were conducted in great secrecy with the help of East German lawyers as unofficial brokers. In their efforts to break the Cold War ice Brandt and Bahr had to tread carefully because of the restraining influence of their coalition partner, the Berlin CDU, and because of the city's total dependence on Bonn's financial lifeline. When, in early 1963, Brandt was tempted to meet Khrushchev in East Berlin, he was stopped at the last minute by his CDU deputy Franz Amrehn, who threatened him with the collapse of the government. He argued that West Berlin should not conduct its own foreign policy. Soon afterwards the Berlin SPD won an overwhelming victory (61.9 per cent) and terminated the coalition.

West Berlin was not, after all, an integral part of the Federal Republic.[10] It was by no means clear that Bonn, in its international trade agreements, had the right to represent the interests of the city. Formally, West Berliners were still subject to occupation status, its young citizens could not be recruited by the Federal Forces (*Bundeswehr*), Lufthansa had no landing rights at West Berlin airports, its deputies elected by the Berlin Chamber had no voting rights in the Federal Parliament. West Berlin's internal relations with Bonn were those of a German *Land* (like Hamburg), its external relationship, however, that of a member of a confederation. For its economic prosperity Berlin had to rely on the Federal Republic, for its security on the three Allies. In other words, the implementation of *Wandel durch Annäherung* required careful co-ordination with both the Allies and the Bonn government.

After a while it became obvious that the political terrain of Berlin did indeed only permit "small steps". No wonder, then, that Brandt sought the larger playing field of the Federal Republic. However, when he first walked on to the pitch as Foreign Secretary in 1966 he was, much to the dismay of his party's younger generation, again under the restraining influence of a conservative coalition partner, now in the driving seat. Bahr had not been in favour of a Grand Coalition with the CDU/CSU either. It was not until a year later that his appointment as head of the *AA*'s planning staff could be secured.

This was the time when Berlin became the hotbed of student unrest, especially after Benno Ohnesorg, who was harmlessly demonstrating against the Shah's visit, had been shot by a panicky policeman. The Grand Coalition in Bonn gave left-wing students the impression that without a functioning opposition democracy was being eroded. Thus they formed the Extra-Parliamentary Opposition (APO), which took to the streets of Berlin.[11] They directed their frustrations against Axel Springer, the right-wing press tycoon, who had erected his headquarters right next to the Berlin Wall. Their chief target was West Germany's foremost tabloid, *Bildzeitung*, the mouthpiece of the silent majority. Ordinary Berliners had little sympathy for anti-Vietnam demonstrations while the Americans were guaranteeing the freedom of a city surrounded by Russian tank divisions and a Communist régime eager to take over. When Rudi Dutschke, the charismatic leader of the student rebellion, was shot by a right-wing sympathiser on Maundy Thursday 1968, students stormed *Bild*'s headquarters and set cars on fire. Berlin saw the worst civil unrest since Weimar days. All of a sudden Berlin, the besieged fortress of the West, seemed to be threatened from within. However, with the Soviet reaction to Prague's struggle for freedom and with the end of the Grand Coalition a sober mood returned to the city.

On election night at 28 September 1969 Willy Brandt, though hesitant and reflective by nature, grasped his chance to abandon the Grand Coalition and to enter into a coalition with the Free Democrats under Walter Scheel.[12] The SPD had gained in strength, but the Conservatives remained the strongest party. Under majority voting, as in Britain, Brandt would have had no chance. His foreign policy venture would have been doomed from the start. The change of guard, the first since the founding of the Federal Republic, was possible because the Free Democrats in opposition had been campaigning for a new and more pragmatic foreign policy that would recognise the GDR as a political reality, though not as a foreign country. They also urged reform in the fields of higher education and law, and fully subscribed to Brandt's slogan "We want to dare to be more democratic". No wonder that Brandt, the émigré and anti-Nazi German, became the darling of the Western world, expected to introduce a healthier, more liberal climate in West Germany. His departure in foreign policy looks more radical in retrospect than at the time. In his first government statement he pledged to continue the policy *vis-à-vis* the GDR inaugurated by his predecessor: a contractual agreement on a *modus vivendi*, but no binding international recognition. He insisted on Germany sharing the right of all nations to self-determination. However, the emphasis was different: the government's task was to preserve the unity of the nation by overcoming the tension between the two parts, and living up to their common responsibility for maintaining peace in Europe. His reference to the "two German states" that were not foreign to each other marked the crucial shift, to which his predecessor took exception. Kurt Georg Kiesinger complained that the government had abandoned the legal principle of sole representation. Walter Scheel, in his new capacity as Foreign Secretary, did not yet invite Third World countries to recognise the GDR. But he wondered how the policy of sticking rigidly to one's principles had helped the East Germans. More than before the emphasis was now on trying to improve the lot of the other half, even if this meant negotiating with their unelected masters. The Conservatives, on the other hand, were not even prepared to grant the GDR the status of a proper state, given its unrepresentative leadership. It has been a feature of German political culture to confuse the rule of law with an uncritical reliance on legality. The Hallstein Doctrine was an outgrowth of this mentality. It needed a new critical reappraisal of Germany's past to overcome this stalemate.

Brandt and Bahr were not in the least tempted to side-step Four-Power responsibility in favour of closer relations with East Berlin. Here continuity prevailed: the Kremlin gates had to be unlocked first, and this required the firm backing of the Western Allies who should not be given any reason to be suspicious. After all, President Nixon's rapprochement with China forced the Soviet government to reassess its political priorities and to come to terms with the *status quo* in Western Europe.

In his first policy statement Brandt also announced that his government would sign the Non-Proliferation Treaty, which was bound to please Moscow. Moreover, he was prepared to enter into negotiations with the Soviet Union concerning a treaty on the non-use of force, a German offer that had been on the table for some time but which was only now being taken up. Why was the Soviet Union more amenable now? Apart from the impression that a German government under Brandt was more favourably disposed towards détente, there are three possible reasons for Moscow's more mellow stance: first, the growing conflict with China, second, the desire to mend fences after crushing Prague's fight for freedom, and third, awareness of the widening technological gap between East and West and the hope of improving trade relations with the Federal Republic. William E. Griffith, one of the foremost experts on *Ostpolitik*, stresses the interdependence on what happened on both fronts of the Soviet Empire. On 2 March 1969 the Soviets had interfered with flights to West Berlin carrying members of the *Bundestag* on their way to elect the new Federal President because this act was alleged to violate Berlin's international status. On the same day news about a serious clash of troops along the Sino–Soviet Ussuri border had reached Moscow. "On the following day the flights occurred without incident, as did the Presidential elections, a fact hardly unrelated to the Ussuri incident."[13]

Negotiations in Moscow began in earnest on 8 December 1969, at first conducted by the German ambassador Helmut Allard. In the past the Soviet government had refused to enter into talks unless the GDR was first recognised. Such conditions had now been waived, much to the annoyance of the SED chief Walther Ulbricht. That Brandt had attributed to the GDR the hallmarks of a proper state did not fully appease the SED leadership, which felt uneasy about the emphasis on the continued existence of the German nation and the special relations between its constituent parts. Not to be outdone by Moscow, Ulbricht offered negotiations on 17 December, enclosing in his letter to President Heinemann a draft treaty "on equal relations". The letter was answered by Brandt, addressed to his East German opposite number, Minister-President Willi Stoph, saying that he was ready for talks between "our two states" on the non-use of force and practical steps "to ease the lives of persons living in divided Germany". Brezhnev, the Soviet leader, now opened a secret channel with Bonn through KGB contacts attached to Bahr who would brief him on Ulbricht's manoeuvres and also help him to handle his own stubborn Foreign Secretary Andrei Gromyko. It was a clear signal that the Soviet government would remain in control of inner German relations.

It might have been due to Soviet pressure that Ulbricht agreed to an exchange of visits between the two heads of government, as suggested by Brandt. The two meetings between Brandt and Stoph, first in Erfurt on 19 March 1970, and then in Cassel on 21 May, were media events of great symbolic significance, but did not lead to much progress in relations between the two governments. Bonn was not yet prepared to grant full diplomatic recognition. What had happened on the streets proved to be more telling than what was going on in the conference chamber: to the annoyance of the authorities national feelings erupted in Erfurt when thousands crowded the streets and shouted "Willy, Willy". Only a massive show of force could contain public excitement. In Cassel, West German police failed to stop right-wing fanatics from tearing down the East German flag (*Spalterflagge*), which had been hoisted for the first time in the Federal Republic. Abroad the impression prevailed that neither government could vouch for their people and that the German Question was far from being settled.

For the Lib–Lab government Erfurt and Cassel were sideshows, given what was at stake in Moscow. Nothing had changed the general feeling amongst the West German political class that, as the saying went, the key to the German Question lay in Moscow. Since negotiations about normalisation had stalled Brandt decided to entrust Egon Bahr, his confidant and special adviser, with these difficult negotiations.[14] These lasted for 50 hours altogether, dragging on between 13 January and 22 May 1970, interrupted by two intervals during which Bahr consulted his government at home. The

German goal was to achieve normalisation of relations on the basis of a non-use of force agreement regarding any change of the post-war order. For the Soviet Union this meant a binding recognition of existing borders, for Bonn a *modus vivendi* in peace without forfeiting the German right to national self-determination. Bahr was convinced – and eventually proved to be right – that in history the *status quo* had never been maintained by trying to tie it down. Territorial changes achieved by mutual agreement should always be possible. The question was how to incorporate a reference to German reunification in the treaty adamantly rejected by Andrei Gromyko, the Soviet negotiator. Bahr therefore came up with the idea of a "letter regarding German unity" (*Brief zur deutschen Einheit*) which should be accepted along with the formal treaty. This was the sticking point of the negotiations. When Bahr threatened to return to Bonn empty-handed the Soviet side relented. They had also, after much haggling, agreed that the borders should be "invulnerable" rather than "unalterable". The final stage of negotiations was conducted by Walter Scheel, to make sure that the treaty would also meet the interests of Bonn's Western Allies. The Moscow Treaty, the first of a whole ensemble of such agreements, was signed on 12 August 1970 by Willy Brandt and Soviet Prime Minister Alexei Kosygin.[15] The Soviet government had dropped the demand for formal recognition of the GDR, and accepted West Germany's presence in West Berlin. Without being too specific, Bonn had, to all intents and purposes, recognised the loss of territories in the East. Moscow was prepared to acknowledge receipt of the controversial "letter regarding German unity" without expressing consent. It was also understood, and this point was crucial to Scheel, "that the treaty would only come into force if the Four Powers reached a satisfactory agreement on the status and security of Berlin". Putting an end to the Berlin crises of the past was, after all, one of the chief objectives of *Ostpolitik*. Yet, as a matter of international law, Bonn was in no position to prejudge Allied rights in Berlin. With some justification Gromyko refused to discuss Berlin in his negotiations with Bahr, for whom the fate of his native city was of immense importance.

It was not really in the interests of the Soviet government to consent to an agreement on Western access to Berlin. For obvious reasons the GDR was even less enamoured by this prospect: West Berlin was a thorn in its flesh and a constant reminder that the German Question remained open. Bonn needed and received the full support of the US government. Henry Kissinger, the new President's chief adviser, though somewhat suspicious of Bahr's KGB contacts, was the architect of a complicated diplomatic linkage system by which progress on SALT (Strategic Arms Limitation Talks) between Washington and Moscow, Four-Power negotiations on Berlin, and ratification of Bonn's Moscow Treaty were closely connected in order to put utmost pressure on the Soviet government. To the Superpowers, to Nixon and Brezhnev in particular, it was obvious that détente had to cover Berlin, or rather West Berlin if it were to make sense at all. In no uncertain terms Kissinger had complained to Anatoly Dobrynin, the Soviet Ambassador in Washington, about Ulbricht's mischief making regarding access to Berlin. By August 1969 all three Western powers had approached the Kremlin proposing talks about the situation in Berlin. Negotiations between the four ambassadors had begun in earnest on 26 March 1970 in the former head-quarters of the Allied Control Council in Berlin. In Valentin Falin Moscow had dispatched a new ambassador to Bonn who was to become one of the chief players in the game of *Ostpolitik*.[16] The villain of the piece was Walther Ulbricht, who tried to keep West Berlin under pressure in the hope of cutting all ties with the West. The way in which East German border guards harassed travellers to the West is described by Smyser in some detail:

They increased tolls dramatically (up to tenfold) without warning. They left border traffic lights on red for hours. Vopos forced drivers to buy East German license plates for a trip to Berlin, or they conducted interminably meticulous searches of cars, persons and luggage. They randomly confiscated written material as subversive propaganda or as intelligence documents.[17]

Such harassment by the badly paid border guards would show the wealthy Westerners who was in control. It was the pay-back currency of those who were suffering from lack of personal and official recognition. For Ulbricht this was also a means of blocking an understanding between Bonn and Moscow, which to him contravened the GDR's true interests. He wished to monopolise relations with Bonn and West Berlin as an equal partner. In the end he had become such a nuisance to his "friends" in Moscow that Brezhnev saw no way out of this dilemma but to remove him from the scene and to replace him with the more cooperative Erich Honecker.[18] This transition of power in May 1971 made it abundantly clear who was calling the shots. Soon afterwards Honecker and an SED delegation made a "pilgrimage" to Moscow and pledged to support a speedy conclusion to the quadripartite talks on Berlin. They specifically abandoned their previous premise that West Berlin was on GDR territory and accepted its "special political status", a formula to which the West could not object. After the overdue departure of Ulbricht, who was seen by many as a relic of the Stalin era, agreement on the essentials for Berlin was reached in due course. The draft text was initialled on 23 August 1971.[19] It has been suggested that the final stage of negotiations was eased by Nixon's announcement in July that Kissinger had returned from Beijing, and that he himself would visit China in 1972. There is no doubt that in view of these developments Moscow wished to have it "all quiet on the Western front", and this could best be achieved by recognition of the *status quo* by Germany, the very power that had the greatest interest in changing it. As far as borders were concerned this seemed to play into Moscow's hand. In the case of Berlin it was the West that benefited from confirmation of the *status quo*. The two most important concessions concerned access rights to Berlin and the existing ties between the Federal Republic and West Berlin. The Soviet Union took responsibility for traffic routes across East Germany and promised that transit traffic would be "unimpeded". East German guards remained at the checkpoints, but under Soviet supreme authority. The agreement permitted existing ties to be "maintained and developed", but Bonn had to recognise that West Berlin was not "a constituent part of the Federal Republic". Moscow was, however, prepared to accept West German passports for West Berliners. In return for this important and hard fought-for concession Moscow could install a Consul-General in West Berlin. However, the agreement, only being initialled, would not be signed until the *Bundestag*, West Germany's parliament, had ratified the Moscow Treaty.

So far only two of the three most important cornerstones of the whole diplomatic edifice called *Ostpolitik* have been placed. Three more elements were necessary to complete the building: the Basic Treaty between the two German states, perhaps the most important component, and the two treaties with Warsaw and Prague that were to lend crucial support to the seriousness of German intentions. All these negotiations went on more or less simultaneously. Those with Poland were of particular significance because Bonn would have to sign away the loss of German lands in the East, a quarter of the territory of the former Reich (1937). In view of the substantial number of well-organised refugees from East Prussia, Pomerania and Silesia, no conservative government in Bonn had hitherto dared to tackle this issue. Most West Germans knew in their heart of hearts that the loss of the Eastern territories was the price Germany had to pay for the invasion and occupation of Poland that had triggered off the Second World War. On the other hand, more than 12 million Germans had been expelled from their homes in a process of ethnic cleansing in the wake of which nearly 2 million people had perished. Not unlike the formula of acknowledging a second German state without granting international recognition, Brandt now managed to find a solution to the Polish problem: the Federal Republic would recognise "existing boundaries", following the decision at Potsdam, as "the Western state frontier of Poland". But the final solution to the question of all German borders had to await a peace conference, and a future all-German government engaged in such negotiations would not be bound by the present treaty. Thus Brandt hoped to appease both the Poles and West Germany's refugee organisations, which could claim that no final decision had been taken. This is why the issue had to be taken up again in 1990 so as to be settled once and for all as part of the diplomatic process leading to reunification. In 1990 Helmut Kohl, the Chancellor of unification, had to overcome the same unwillingness of national conservative elements to face reality as Brandt had in the early 1970s. The CDU/CSU opposition felt that Brandt had sold the country short without gaining anything worthwhile in return. Nor did they appreciate the photograph showing the Chancellor of the Federal Republic falling to his knees in front of the monument to the victims of the Warsaw ghetto. However, it was this very image that endeared Brandt to the younger generation in West Germany and to the rest of the world. On 17 December Brandt and Josef Cyrankiewycz, the Polish Prime Minister, signed the Warsaw Treaty.[20]

Negotiations with Prague are less relevant in the context of Germany unification than those with Moscow and Warsaw. However, they were the most protracted and confined to a single issue: the validity of the Munich agreement of 29 September 1938. Bonn was prepared to concede that the agreement had become meaningless, even invalid, as a result of Hitler's invasion but not, as Prague insisted, that it had been so all along (*ab initio*). This would have meant that throughout the war all Sudeten Germans were Czechoslovak citizens, and as such traitors who had forfeited all rights as German citizens. Their expulsion in 1945/46 would then appear to be a matter of justice. The Sudeten Germans in the Federal Republic, as a whole more the political clientele of the Bavarian CSU, did not make life any easier for the Lib–Lab government by demanding that any treaty should include their *Heimatrecht* (right to their homeland), i.e. the right to return to the Sudetenland to recover their property, or at least be indemnified for it. The compromise reached after much legal haggling, and not signed until December 1973, took care of both concerns: the Munich Agreement was "void as stated in this treaty", but Article 2 specifically excluded legal consequences in that it did not affect legal status or nationality.[21] Important for Bonn in all these treaties were: renunciation of the use of force, recognition of historical boundaries, and the inclusion of West Berlin in the Federal Republic's jurisdiction.

The treaties with Moscow and Warsaw had to be ratified by the *Bundestag* before the crucial agreements on Berlin would come into force. This was the deal. The *Bundestag* debates gave Rainer Barzel, the leader of the opposition, a chance to topple the Chancellor, or so he thought. He did not attack Brandt's *Ostpolitik* as such, but argued that better terms could have been negotiated, notably Moscow's explicit acknowledgment of Germany's right to national self-determination. According to the Basic Law, the only way to topple a government mid-term was the so-called "constructive vote of no-confidence", which meant that the old government had to be replaced by a new one immediately. This procedure had been introduced to make sure that the country was not left without a functioning government, as had happened so often during the fateful Weimar years. The opposition counted on just enough defections from the SPD to win the necessary majority of votes to install Barzel as Chancellor. But they miscalculated: Barzel's motion failed by just two votes. The general assumption was, and it has not been refuted since, that votes were bought – people were paid, probably on both sides. Moreover, the Soviet government went out of its way to help Brandt. Before the decisive vote on 24 April 1972 Brezhnev confirmed Germany's right to eventual self-determination and announced the release of many ethnic Germans who wished to settle in the Federal Republic. Honecker's simultaneous offer to ease travel restrictions, however, was declined, since support for Brandt by German Communist leaders was judged to be counter-productive. Whatever the circumstances surrounding this fateful vote, a different result, in other words a change of government by dubious manoeuvres rather than fresh elections, would have been a blow not only to *Ostpolitik*, but to German democracy as well. Opinion polls showed widespread support for Brandt and his Eastern treaties. When the treaties were put before the *Bundestag* on 17 May 1972 the CDU/CSU was well advised to abstain rather than registering opposition, so that ratification was possible. By now most Germans had realised that there was no alternative to détente and that this was the only guarantee of securing the future of Berlin and the only hope of easing the burden of division. On the same day that the two Eastern treaties came into force by exchange of documents, 3 June 1972, the final Four-Power Protocol on Berlin was also signed. The linkage could not have been more obvious. Brandt seized the opportunity and called for early elections in November 1972. The electorate returned him with a comfortable majority, thus endorsing his foreign policy.

By this time, in the autumn of 1972, negotiations between the two German governments had entered a crucial phase. No doubt Brandt was aided by the fact that the Basic Treaty (*Grundlagenvertrag*), the climax of the whole complex of *Ostpolitik*, had been initialled on 8 November 1972, just before the elections. Through the instrument of linkage, the momentum of timing was one of the most characteristic features of this strategy. Negotiations on "normalisation of relations between the two states" began as soon as the two Eastern treaties and the Berlin Protocol had cleared the way. The first meetings between Egon Bahr and Michael Kohl, his East German opposite number, between 15 June and 2 August, served as an exchange of views. At that time it was not at all clear whether agreement could be reached before the election on 19 November. In the past the GDR government had been most suspicious of the motives for Brandt's *Ostpolitik*. West German attempts at rapprochement were met by stressing demarcation lines. During Ulbricht's last days Honecker had denounced *Ostpolitik* as "*Sozialdemokratismus*", one of the worst Communist heresies. "Nowhere", writes Vogtmeier, "was the Cold War as cold as between the 'hostile brothers'".[22] With all their baggage of inferiority complexes *vis-à-vis* West Germany the East German leaders were in a psychological situation that differed considerably from that of the Russians and Poles. However, when all the Eastern bloc leaders met at the end of July Honecker was brought into line. Although they were suspicious of the FRG's intentions, they much preferred to deal with Brandt rather than with Barzel or Franz-Josef Strauss, allegedly West Germany's Cold War warrior *par excellence*. Moreover, the SED would not tolerate Moscow and Warsaw being on better terms with Bonn than East Berlin. After returning from the Crimea Honecker discussed the whole catalogue of problems with Bahr. He made it clear that the question of German unity was not to be mentioned in the treaty. However, the treaty was not to be in conflict with the Federal Republic's Basic Law which obliged Bonn to strive for unification. On 10 October 1972 they should only have an exchange of views. The GDR adamantly rejected any reference to the continued existence of a united German nation. In the end the same ploy was used as in the case of the Moscow treaty. Bahr wrote a letter saying that the treaty was "not in conflict with the political aim of the Federal Republic of Germany to work for a state of peace in Europe in which the German nation will regain its unity through free self-determination". This letter was accepted as an integral part of the treaty. What had been deemed permissible by their Soviet masters could not possibly be rejected by the East German leadership. The preamble to the treaty confirmed the agreement to disagree on the national question. For Bonn it was all-important that this book remained open and that no final line was drawn. Two years later the GDR reacted to this interpretation by expunging all references to the German nation from its 1968 constitution. It was a very German, almost theological approach to politics to think that questions of national faith and feeling could be settled by promulgating a new concept such as "people of the GDR". Owing to the elections which saw the SPD emerge for the first time as the leading German party the Basic Treaty was approved by an easy majority in the *Bundestag* on 11 May 1973. Bavaria tried to wreck it by appeal to the Constitutional Court. When the Court ruled that the treaty was perfectly compatible with the Basic Law, the last hurdle had been cleared.

In the long run the *Grundlagenvertrag* did indeed achieve the desired effect: it relaxed tensions and eased relations between the two Germanys, and thus softened the ground for eventual unification. At the time the balance sheet looked somewhat different, because the GDR seemed to be the chief beneficiary of the immediate and tangible gain: the suspension of the much-maligned Hallstein Doctrine that upheld the Federal Republic's sole right of representation. East Berlin had achieved one of its most cherished goals, recognition by the United Nations and the international community of states, with which diplomatic relations could now be established. However, its enhanced international status did not do much to legitimise the régime in the eyes of its citizens who cared more about better relations with the other half of Germany than with the rest of the world. The nature of diplomatic relations between Bonn and East Berlin was quite revealing of the convoluted state of inner German relations. On the insistence of the West, no ambassadors were to be accredited, only "permanent representatives". While the West German official was attached to the East German Ministry of Foreign Affairs, his opposite number had to deal with the Federal Chancellery. This explains why Kohl, and not Genscher, was to be in charge of the unification process in 1989/90.

From now on Bonn had a vested interest in furthering rather than slowing down détente. Yet hopes of a new *modus vivendi* between the two states on the basis of normal relations were not to be fulfilled in the near future. Travel restrictions on visits to East Berlin and the GDR were eased but not *vice versa*. Apart from old-age pensioners, who were no loss to the economy if they chose not to return, the number of visits to the Federal Republic for special family reunions, etc., was still very limited (40,000 per annum). The East German government also continued to release political prisoners only in return for hard currency. In financial terms, the Basic Treaty, with its various agreements on travel, postal and other services,[23] proved to be an important source of income for the GDR. That the capitalist Federal Republic should be held to ransom for all kinds of facilities seemed to be quite in order. It was a case of being too clever by half, since the cash-flow from the West led to a dependency culture which, in turn, bred delusions as to the true state of the economy. A normalisation of relations, as with other civilised states in the Western world, was not yet on the cards. As soon as the Basic Treaty had been concluded, the GDR reinforced security measures along the borders with the West, installing mines and automatic firing devices. Methods of supervising and repressing the population were greatly enhanced and refined, mainly due to a substantial increase in official and unofficial informers employed by the Stasi. No doubt, the SED saw contacts with the West as a constant source of contamination. However, the authorities were unable to shield their charges from the Western media, notably television, which could be received everywhere in the GDR except for the area around Dresden and further east (*"Tal der Ahnungslosen"* – "valley of the unsuspecting"). Nor could they prevent more comparisons between living conditions in the two parts of Germany resulting from private visits and the exchange of journalists. In many respects the East German leaders were right to fear that the repercussions of détente might undermine the stability of their régime, except that they themselves unwittingly contributed to erosion of authority by excessive counter-measures. Over time the small but constant doses of fresh air proved to have devastating effects on a closed society.

Notes and references

1 Dietrich Staritz, *Geschichte der DDR* (new extended edition Frankfurt a.M., 1996).

2 As to the *Neues Ökonomisches System der Planung und Leitung der Volkswirtschaft* (NÖSPL) see Klaus Schroeder, *Der SED-Staat. Partei, Staat und Gesellschaft* (Munich, 2000), pp. 178–83.

3 See Robert Goeckel, *The Lutheran Church and the East German State* (Ithaca, NY, 1990). For the first twenty years see also Mary Fulbrook, *Anatomy of a Dictatorship. Inside the GDR 1949–1989* (Oxford, 1995), pp. 87–106.

4 See Johannes Kuppe, *Deutschlandpolitik der DDR,* in Werner Weidenfeld and Rudolf Korthe (eds), *Handbuch zur deutschen Einheit 1949–1989–1999* (Frankfurt a.M., 1999), pp. 252–67 (with bibliography).

5 See n. 41, ch. 2.

6 Quoted by Hans Buchheim, *Deutschlandpolitik 1949–1972* (Stuttgart, 1984), p. 104 (translation by the author).

7 More details about direct contacts between Bonn and Moscow: Peter Siebenmorgen, *Gezeitenwechsel. Aufbruch zur Entspannungspolitik* (Bonn, 1990), pp. 264–300. See also Hans Kroll, *Lebenserinnerungen eines Botschafters* (Cologne, 1967). The *AA*, generally dominated by atlanticists, was only too aware of the Rapallo trauma of the Western allies.

8 See Andreas Vogtmeier, *Egon Bahr und die deutsche Frage. Zur Entwicklung der sozialdemokratischen Ost- und Deutschlandpolitik vom Kriegsende bis zur Vereinigung* (Berlin, 1996), pp. 59–79. See also the most recent and readable study, Heinrich Potthoff, *Im Schatten der Mauer. Deutschlandpolitik 1961 bis 1990* (Berlin, 1999), pp. 31–43.

9 Ludwig Geissel, *Unterhändler der Menschlichkeit. Erinnerungen* (Stuttgart, 1991).

10 For the city's post-war status, Udo Wetzlaugk, *Die Alliierten in Berlin* (Berlin, 1988). Otherwise the most authoritative history is that edited by Wolfgang Ribbe, *Geschichte Berlins*, 2 vols. (Munich, 1987).

11 See the critical reassessment of the student revolution by Götz Aly, former activist turned historian: *Unser Kampf 1968. Ein irritierter Blick zurück* (Frankfurt a.M., 2008). After studying the Nazi period for the last 25 years it had dawned upon him that there was an uncanny affinity between both "totalitarian youth movements", an argument put forward by the older generation of academics who at the time were attacked by their own students. See also the more global perspective of the movement: Norbert Frei, *1968. Jugendrevolte und globaler Protest* (Munich, 2008).

12 The most detailed and popular account: Arnulf Baring, *Machtwechsel. Die Ära Brandt-Scheel* (Stuttgart, 1983).

13 William E. Griffith, *The Ostpolitik of the Federal Republic of Germany* (Cambridge, MA., 1978), p. 166.

14 See Vogtmeier, pp. 121–40.

15 English text in *Documentation Relating to the Federal Government's Policy of Détente*, edited by The Press and Information Office of the Federal Government (Bonn, 1978), pp. 17–27. See also Benno Zündorf, *Die Ostverträge* (Munich, 1979) and the Oxford DPhil thesis now published, Julie von Dannenberg, *The Foundations of Ostpolitik. The Making of the Moscow treaty between West Germany and the USSR* (Oxford, 2008). The author comes to the conclusion that *Ostpolitik* had been an indispensable precondition for German unification.

16 See his memoirs, Valentin Falin, *Politische Erinnerungen* (German translation Munich, 1993), pp. 165–208.

17 William R. Smyser, *From Yalta to Berlin. The Cold War Struggle over Germany* (London, 1999), p. 244. This is part of his excellent chapter on the negotiations about "Keystone Berlin".

18 See Staritz, pp. 266–75; also Monika Kaiser, *Machtwechsel von Ulbricht zu Honecker* (Berlin, 1997).

19 Text in Documentation, pp. 87–153.

20 Text in ibid., pp. 31–66.

21 Text in ibid., pp. 67–82.

22 Vogtmeier, p. 154 (translation: L.K.). Two opposing hilltop castles along the Rhine valley are called "feindliche Brüder".

23 All listed as part of the treaty in Documentation.

CHAPTER 4

A precarious relationship

Throughout the last decade of the Cold War, the two Super-powers were suspicious about the loyalty of their respective German allies. In fact, the policies of the two German states towards one another, though different in practice, were based on very similar principles: the desire to combine security in the case of the Federal Republic, and stability in the case of the GDR, with the continuation of calm, civilised inner-German relations. The determination of both Germanys to maintain that precarious balance provides the key to understanding their relationship in the run-up to the events of 1989 onwards.

During the first 20 years of its existence the Federal Republic was seen as a barrier to détente between the Superpowers, opposing or hampering progress in relations at every stage. That impression was reversed with the commencement of *Ostpolitik*. The policy of gradual engagement with the GDR led, for the next 20 years, to concerns among the Western allies that their German protégé might be tempted to concede too much ground to the enemy in the East. Before 1969, Bonn was worried that a rapprochement between West and East might sideline the German problem and confirm the division of the country. Only a fundamental change within German political culture could convince governments – very reluctantly in the case of those led by the CDU – that détente had become a crucial precondition to the development of relations between the two states. For both German governments, *Ostpolitik* allowed for a foreign policy that may have required the backing of their respective allies, but which was nonetheless marked by a new sense of independence. For Bonn, a firm foothold in the Western alliance – NATO, the European Community and the special relationship with France – was imperative.[1] Shared Allied responsibility for Germany as a whole did not prevent the two German states from engaging with one another as best they could under prevailing circumstances. Although Bonn did not recognise the GDR as a foreign country, the latter's international status was greatly enhanced when both German states joined the United Nations in 1973 and were invited to participate in the Helsinki process in 1975. The arrival of *Ostpolitik* represented a new departure in inner-German relations. Official contacts had been virtually non-existent before 1970. Now transit between the two states began to blossom at all levels, especially among civil servants negotiating trade, postal, health, cultural and other exchanges.

In late May 1973 Herbert Wehner, a former Communist now in charge of the Federal Ministry for *Innerdeutsche Beziehungen* (Inner-German Relations)[2] paid a visit to his former comrade Erich Honecker.[3] This meeting between the *eminence grise* of German Social Democracy and Honecker had been arranged by an East German lawyer (Wolfgang Vogel) who specialised in buying the freedom of East German political prisoners for hard currency. Wehner's official mission was to iron out problems that had arisen from an agreement to reunite families separated by the iron curtain. The actual, ulterior agenda was to establish secret channels of communication unknown to the "Big Brother" Soviet Union – an expression allegedly used by Honecker.[4]

However, from the start, there was a crucial difference in the two states' expectations of *Ostpolitik*. While Bonn was concerned to improve human contacts, East Berlin was primarily interested in gaining hard currency and strengthening its international position. Bonn thus felt bitterly let down when, in November that year, the East German government doubled the obligatory daily exchange for FRG citizens visiting the GDR to DM 20. The forced exchange was regarded as ransom money in the West and it now became a key aim of all Bonn governments to reduce it – in the same way that they worked for a reduction in the age of potential visitors from the East. Only those past pension age were permitted to holiday in the West.

A further blow to inner-German relations came in April 1974, when a close aide to Chancellor Willy Brandt was exposed as a Stasi spy. Günter Guillaume was, of course, only one among hundreds of East German agents who had successfully infiltrated Bonn's ministries, but Guillaume had made it to the very top.[5] Historians are agreed that this event as such only served as the trigger for Brandt's resignation, which proved a great embarrassment to Honecker. Brezhnev, the Soviet leader, had established a personal relationship with the Chancellor and did not wish to endanger the position of Brandt's government, or indeed any other Social Democrat government in Bonn. Andrei Gromyko, the Soviet Foreign Minister, had hoped Brandt would serve as a lever separating Western Europe from the United States.[6]

Throughout the 1970s and early 1980s, Moscow continued to hope that it could use the SPD with its devoutly pacifist rank and file to further its own security interests. Thus Honecker came under increasing pressure from his patron to mend relations with the new SPD government led by Helmut Schmidt. Ironically, the two soon got on so well that the Soviets began to have second thoughts.

Both regarded themselves as pragmatists as far as inner-German relations were concerned – though both continued to pursue opposite aims. Schmidt, more down to earth than Brandt, knew how to exploit the growing financial problems of the GDR to ease human contacts between the two societies. Honecker, meanwhile, had expunged reference to the "German nation" from the GDR's constitution in October 1974. In other words, while Bonn tried to foster links between what it saw as two halves of one nation, East Berlin saw the relationship as being one between states and governments. Still, there were sufficient overlapping interests for both sides to be satisfied with the outcome. It could be argued that increases in human traffic, purchased through trade and financial concessions, did more to erode the rigid fabric of GDR society than any other factor. The statistics are certainly impressive: between 1970 and 1979, the number of visitors from West Germany and West Berlin to the East more than doubled to 8 million, telephone calls rose from 1 to 17 million, cargo shipments nearly tripled in tonnage. And every year the GDR released more than a thousand political prisoners, receiving an average of DM 50,000 for each. William Smyser, a diplomat with the US embassy in Bonn in the late 1970s, who produced these figures, comments: "From the standpoint of inner-German relations, each visitor and even each telephone call helped maintain the unity of the German nation".[7] He also knew that West German money was the most important lubricant in the relationship: "swing" credits were increased to cover the GDR's balance-of-trade deficit, Bonn paid hundreds of millions of DM for transit fees, the construction of a new motorway between Hamburg and West Berlin, the maintenance of roads and so forth. Many of these concessions were agreed between Schmidt and Honecker when they met at the Helsinki conference.

Gradually, the GDR developed what could be described as a culture of dependency. To contain any unwelcome consequences, the SED reverted to tightening its grip on society, not only, as mentioned before, by increasing the number of Stasi spies and ordering border guards to shoot at those attempting to escape[8] but also by disciplining dissidents and expelling critical West German journalists, such as the television journalist Lothar Loewe and *Spiegel* correspondent Jörg Mettke. The expulsion of the popular cabaret singer Rolf Biermann in 1976 led to widespread protest among East German writers and artists. For its leaders, the GDR's growing international recognition proved ambivalent. The pledge to respect human rights contained within the Helsinki agreement (basket III), for instance, fuelled a nascent civil rights movement, which made use of its ability to appeal to an international commitment signed by its government.

The *modus vivendi* between the two German states received a severe blow in the mid-1970s, when the Soviet Union challenged the military balance of power by introducing a new nuclear missile system. Known as SS-20 in the West, the weapon was designed to cover a distance of over 3,000 miles. The security of Western Europe rested on NATO's deterrence strategy, whereby the superiority of the Warsaw Pact in terms of conventional forces – twice the number of divisions and three times that of tanks – would be checked by a nuclear missile shield. No European country felt more exposed to the new Soviet threat than West Germany, and no statesman was personally more incensed by this development than Helmut Schmidt. He feared that Moscow's nuclear superiority would be used to blackmail Germany into submission. Only the United States were capable of meeting the new threat and force the Soviet government to abstain from deploying the new system.

Relations between Washington and Bonn were not in good shape. The leaders of the two countries certainly did not think much of one another.[8a] The German chancellor looked upon Jimmy Carter as a Christian do-gooder, unsuited to hard-nosed Realpolitik. Carter, meanwhile, was puzzled as to how Schmidt expected to be able to confront the Soviet threat whilst maintaining a measure of détente. Bonn did not see itself as having a choice in the matter. The government needed to pursue the two apparently conflicting strategies if it wanted to safeguard both the security of the Federal Republic and the blossoming special relationship with East Germany – with the consequent advantages for the citizens of both countries. Schmidt therefore continued to grant the Soviet government favourable terms of trade, while going out of his way to warn the world against Moscow's military ambitions. The unease between Washington and Bonn grew worse when the Pentagon devised a new ploy to meet the Soviet threat. The so-called neutron bomb, an enhanced radiation weapon, was designed to kill enemy tank crews, for instance, while leaving their hardware intact. The coalition government in Bonn was furious at the prospect of such a nuclear weapon being deployed on German soil. The neutron bomb was, indeed, soon denounced throughout the world, including within America itself, as representing the height of militaristic perversion. However, in March 1978, after

NATO had given the weapon its stamp of approval, Schmidt finally agreed to its deployment in Germany. In doing so, he risked his political future, not least because of the overwhelming opposition within his own party. Then, suddenly, overcome with moral reservations to the bomb, Carter changed course and cancelled production. Schmidt, understandably, was infuriated by what he saw as an act of betrayal.

The two leaders were now entirely divided in their approach to the Soviet Union. Carter and his security adviser Zbigniew Brzezinski wanted to put the Soviet government under pressure by formally recognising China and launching a human rights campaign under the Helsinki umbrella. Schmidt wished to maintain relations with both Washington and Moscow, and had no interest in antagonising Brezhnev, who he hoped would eventually come to his senses and withdraw the SS-20 missiles. According to William Smyser, Brzezinski did not understand Schmidt's stance, and described Germany as having been *finlandized*, "a term of opprobrium that sounded more sophisticated than 'neutralized' but meant the same thing".[9]

By late October 1977, Schmidt was so concerned about the new Soviet threat that he expressed his anxieties in a public lecture at the London Institute for Strategic Studies. It was a wake-up call for NATO, but the episode with the neutron bomb had delayed an effective response to the Soviet challenge. Schmidt continued his policy of persuasion, some might argue a little unsuccessfully, when the Soviet leader visited West Germany in May 1978, even making a detour to the chancellor's modest home in Hamburg.[10] Although the Soviet leader could not be moved to withdraw his SS-20 missiles, Bonn was nevertheless prepared to sign a trade agreement. It seems clear that Moscow believed it could slowly decouple the FRG from the West. However, Schmidt won important allies in his fight for an alternative to the neutron bomb with Giscard d'Estaing, the French President, and Margaret Thatcher who took office in May 1979. Eventually, Carter, too, realised that he couldn't maintain his Christian attitudes towards facing the nuclear threat, while Soviet influence in Africa and Central America continued to grow. On 12 December 1979 NATO decided to deploy nearly 600 new intermediate-range nuclear missiles (INF) in Europe: the ballistic Pershing II along with so-called Cruise missiles, which were slower but capable of flying below the Soviet radar systems. What became crucial was the "dual track policy" of offering to abandon the new INF system if Moscow was prepared to dismantle the SS-20 missiles directed against Western Europe. On Schmidt's initiative and as a kind of bonus NATO agreed to withdraw 1,000 nuclear warheads from Germany. History might have taken different course if the Soviet government had accepted this offer. We now know that Brezhnev was, by this time, already a frail man and had no choice but to succumb to military hardliners. The Kremlin opted to maintain the race for military supremacy and, more damagingly, pushed Brezhnev to invade Afghanistan a few weeks later. The generals had the backing of Andrei Gromyko, the long-standing foreign minister and survivor of Stalin's purges, who was rarely prepared to yield an inch. The apparent failure of Carter's dual track policy, which had Schmidt's full backing, thus marked the end of détente between the Superpowers.

In the context of German unification, the complicated process of the two Superpowers coming to terms about disarmament is of little significance. Yet the fall-out from NATO's dual track policy set off a chain reaction of developments that came to a head in 1989/90. Ronald Reagan, the new American President, proved a better poker player than Gromyko when he pressed on with the armament race by launching his Strategic Defence Initiative (SDI) in March 1983, known as the "Star Wars programme". NATO's deployment of Pershing and Cruise missiles, coupled with Reagan's plans – no more than half-cooked ideas at the time – generated popular peace movements in both West and East Germany. In East Germany, the campaign for disarmament and peace gained a far greater historical momentum than in the FRG. This is in spite of the fact that West Germany saw much bigger demonstrations, producing a steadily growing grass-root opposition backed up by local Protestant ministers. The Soviet economy, already creaking under the costs of the Afghan adventure, could not keep up with the pace of rearmament in the United States. Therefore Moscow was forced to raise the price of oil and gas deliveries to the GDR, which led to a growing sense of alienation between patron and client.[11] East Berlin turned to Western banks for help. In order to finance these credits, the government was forced to squeeze consumption at home and to facilitate contacts between the two German societies in exchange for hard currency. All this will now be told in more detail.

In an important statement in the town of Gera (October 1980) Honecker insisted on the recognition of the GDR's citizenship as a precondition for "normal relations". He also demanded that the West German office at Salzgitter, which recorded his government's acts of violence, should be closed. Both requests were turned down. Every East German who managed to escape to the West was entitled to the FRG's passport.

Nevertheless, Helmut Schmidt and Erich Honecker were determined to prolong the inner-German dialogue against all odds. After Brezhnev had twice vetoed Honecker's visit to West Germany, the GDR sent its economic supremo, Günter Mittag, instead. Naturally the Soviets became increasingly suspicious about possible deals being worked out without their knowledge. Eventually, it was the West German Chancellor who visited his Communist opposite number in the latter's hunting lodge at Lake Werbellin in December 1981. No startling breakthrough was achieved and when Schmidt wished to mingle with ordinary people in nearby Güstrow the police kept citizens at bay. Relations between the two German states could not be shielded from the new frosty atmosphere among the Superpowers. During Schmidt's visit to East Germany, martial law had been proclaimed in Poland to suppress the Trade Union Solidarnosc and thus prevent an intervention by the Red Army. The SED saw the Polish uprising as a deadly virus and congratulated the government for its swift action, while ordering the NVA to be on standby to intervene.[12] Schmidt on the other hand went out of his way in his speech to the *Bundestag* to express his whole-hearted support for the Polish workers and hope that martial laws would be lifted.[13]

In spite of these glaring disagreements, the two German leaders tried to sustain a measure of understanding. They were only too aware that in the case of an escalation of the Cold War, Germany would become the main battleground. The catchwords were stability, dialogue, later *Verantwortungs-gemeinschaft* (union of joint responsibility) – in other words, cooperation beyond the deep gulf of ideological antagonism. The visit of Chancellor Schmidt had set a precedent; from now on many prominent West German politicians and managers were keen to shake hands with Honecker, offering financial assistance and assuring him that the West was not plotting against his government. The whole public attitude towards the GDR changed, based on a sense of wishing to be fair. The leading GDR expert, Peter C. Ludz, argued that the theory of totalitarianism would no longer explain the social reality of the GDR, which had to be judged by its own criteria.[14] The first West German *quasi*-ambassador in East Berlin, Günter Gaus, went native and praised the authentic, traditional atmosphere of a land and a people uncorrupted by Western consumerism and redevelopment. He evoked a fairytale country of old Germany by closing his eyes to its unpalatable aspects.[15] A team of journalists of *Die Zeit* who visited the GDR a few years later painted an equally rosy picture by marvelling at the landscape and closing their eyes to the activities of the Stasi, the run-down hallways of pre-war blocs and the messy old factory yards.[16] In retrospect this well-meaning reappraisal of the other Germany in the name of détente helped to lull the SED leadership into a false sense of security that was not conducive to introducing reforms and overhauling the system. In reality the GDR was to become a state on credit, indebted to its rival in the West.

As hard as they tried, the leaders of the SED never managed to match West Germany's standard of living, despite Honecker's early promise to pursue a "unity of economic and social policy". There were too many areas of unproductive expenditure, such as the army, the Stasi and an oversized bureaucracy. Yet the GDR depended on its exports within Comecon, especially to the Soviet Union, in exchange for vital raw materials such as oil, which to some extent were sold on to the West for hard currency. When Moscow began to raise prices to world market levels the GDR's balance of payment deteriorated sharply. The decision to establish an industry in micro-electronics in order to compete with Japan and the Superpowers was a costly disaster and demonstrated that the old guard did not know its limitations. What they did know, however, was that securing a reasonable living standard was crucial for the stability of the régime. The memoirs of Günter Mittag, Honecker's close confidant and minister of economics, present a fairly realistic picture of the GDR's final collapse. He tells us that increases in the price of oil, gas and other raw materials from Comecon countries between 1979 and 1988 cost the GDR 145 billion Marks.[17] The additional expenditure could only be covered by exporting more and more mechanical engineering products, which would then be missing for the modernisation of their domestic industrial infrastructure. Since oil deliveries from Russia had also been reduced the GDR was forced to intensify the mining of lignite, which was an expensive and ecologically damaging business. It was a vicious circle from which the leadership hoped to escape by relying increasingly on support from the FRG.

By 1982 the tensions between Schmidt and the SPD had reached breaking-point. The governing party was no longer prepared to accept responsibility for the Chancellor's insistence on implementing the new missile system and for the FDP's economic priorities. The Liberals under the leadership of foreign minister Hans-Dietrich Genscher swapped the sinking ship for the Conservatives' lifeboat. Schmidt lost the vote of no confidence and was succeeded by Helmut Kohl who was then confirmed in power through mid-term elections a year later. Soon Kohl established a close rapport with the new American President. Now and later the FRG's loyalty to NATO remained unshaken. The hopes of SED and Soviet hardliners to benefit from popular anti-Americanism were doomed.

Kohl's careful approach to the German problem has been scrutinized by various authors who all more or less agree that it oscillated between change and continuity or as one expert put it between *deklatorischem Wandel* and *operativer Kontinuität* (change in rhetoric based on continuity in decision making).[18] In other words, he emphasised the government's firm adherence to the Western alliance, in particular the decision to deploy medium-range missiles regardless of popular dissent, while continuing business as usual in its relations with the GDR. Peter Bender, one of the best commentators on the German Question, put it this way: "Whoever will be chancellor in Bonn he must have his support leg in the West and his free leg in the East".[19] Genscher, the FDP foreign secretary, who was born in Halle, East Germany, was asked to remain in office and ensure all existing links with East Berlin were maintained. Throughout his tenure of office Kohl favoured his own brand of dual track diplomacy, by cultivating personal relations with the US and French presidents, Ronald Reagan, later George Bush and Francois Mitterrand. In this way, he managed to shield his government's dealings with the East, which he left to his foreign secretary and to Franz Josef Strauss, the Bavarian Prime Minister, from public view. The three essentials that guided him throughout his tenure of office were the Atlantic Alliance, Europe and the German nation. In his first government statement he reintroduced the old rhetoric, which many on the left had discarded: The FRG was called upon to hold on to the right of self-determination so as to restore unity and freedom to the nation. But he avoided using the term "reunification" until autumn 1989. His aim was to keep the German *Kulturnation* alive, despite the break-up of the *Staatsnation*. This kind of terminology allowed for a working relationship with the GDR. On the occasion of Brezhnev's funeral in November 1982, the Federal President Karl Carstens told Honecker that the new Chancellor set great store on continuity and dialogue. He confirmed the government's standing invitation for the General Secretary to visit the FRG.[20]

During his first telephone conversation with Honecker on 23 January, Kohl intimated that he was aware of a substantial credit which had been secretly discussed between emissaries from both sides. Towards the end of June, the public learnt that Bonn had guaranteed a bank credit worth DM 1 billion in the hope of improving inner-German relations. It was unprecedented that no political strings were attached to the deal, something Schmidt would never have accepted. Yet it proved a worthwhile investment; a year later, the GRD government began dismantling the intolerable automatic firing devices along the border, as a first step towards gaining more trust – and securing future credit. In spite of severe reprimands from Soviet leaders, Honecker now banked on life-support from Bonn for the GDR's economic survival. In his memoirs, Mittag is full of praise for Franz Josef Strauss, hitherto the incarnation of the Cold War warrior, who had been instrumental in helping East Berlin secure the credit. By then, he argues, the entire Politburo should have realized how desperate the balance of payment situation had become. Without that money the GDR would have been unable to meet its international financial commitments. "No doubt Strauß had realized", he writes, "that in view of the critical climate between the Soviet Union and the United States, as well as NATO, and in the face of the deployment of medium-range missiles on German soil, a collapse of the GDR at that time might have resulted in a disastrous military conflict".[21] Minutes of all those secret talks held during the 1980s between the two sides are not yet available. But we can assume with some certainty that West German contacts were regularly confronted, if not blackmailed, with the following scenario: *A drastic reduction of consumption due to the shortage of foreign exchange would provoke unrest among the population which in turn would invite the Red Army to intervene. This would put a definite end to our special relationship. Look at what happened in East Berlin in 1953, in Budapest in 1956, in Prague in 1968, in Poland in the early 1980s! The stability of the GDR is in both our interests.* At a hearing in the *Bundestag* in November, 1993 Kohl admitted that the bank credit – and more were to follow – helped stabilise the régime. But he was sure that it was the right decision at the time, because it gave millions of East Germans a chance "to get to know the real conditions in the Federal Republic beyond all propaganda".[22] In its final days, he argued, the Politburo of the SED had realised the implications of three-and-a-half million citizens having had first-hand experiences of life in West Germany. He was candid about his government's policy of using the deteriorating economic situation of the GDR, revealed for the first time by many emissaries from the East, "to extend the corridor of travel permits in exchange for financial help". In retrospect, of course, this proved the right approach. However, in 1983 Mikhail Gorbachev's revolution was not yet on the horizon. Two general-secretaries of the CPSU were to die before his rise to the top in March 1985, which gave him the chance to change the course of world history by abandoning the armament race and the Cold War.

Kohl and his government were, of course, fully aware of the almost neurotic fixation ordinary East Germans had with the FRG. While most West Germans, especially the younger generation, did not much care about the fortunes of the GDR, "the West" – synonymous with West Germany – was the closest place to the "promised land" in the eyes of many East Germans. Stefan Wolle, a young East German historian, remembers that "everyone waited for the desired *Westpakete* or for *Westbesuch*, which would hopefully leave behind some *Westgeld* or at least bring *Westschokolade* and *Westseife*.[23] Western goods could be purchased with hard currency received from West German relations in so-called *Intershops*. "The West" became a more enticing concept for young East Germans in the 1980s than it had been for those living along the East coast of America in the nineteenth century. While the Americans had been able to pack up and go, East Berliners could only realise their dream by tuning in to West German Television. *Westfernsehen* was a daily ritual of virtual emigration. In 1987, about 85 per cent of the population admitted to watching "enemy channels" on a regular basis.[24] However, there was always the sneaky suspicion, fostered by Communist propaganda, that the Western world as portrayed in television, might not correspond with the realities of life across the border. Now, all those millions of visitors who were entitled to a travel visa, mostly old age pensioners or people who could put in a claim for urgent family reunions, would return with the message that everything was, indeed, more colourful, more plentiful – better. There was, they would report, more choice in supermarkets and department stores, greater leisure and travel facilities, there were better cars, and a more modern infrastructure in the form of roads, public transport, schools, stations, post offices and hospitals. The political freedom that went with those benefits was of interest only to a few intellectuals or what was left of the traditional middle classes. All this, every such experience passed on by an old uncle or a fortunate neighbour, was to contribute to that unexpected surge when, during the holiday season of 1989, there appeared the opportunity of a quick escape to "the West".

At the time, when secret deals between West and East German officials were being arranged behind closed doors, the Cold War had reached a new intensity owing to NATO's determination to meet the Soviet missile challenge. During the four years between the dual track decision in December 1979 and the *Bundestag's* 1983 vote to deploy Pershing II rockets and Cruise missiles, Germany turned into a battlefield for peace. Or rather two battlefields: one in the West, consisting of huge battalions of demonstrators – at one time a rally of at least 300,000 in Bonn – and one in East Germany, where a fast spreading network of small groups, sheltered by the Protestant Church and under constant surveillance by the authorities, demonstrated against rearmament in general and the growing militarisation of their society in particular.[25] The West German campaign, an alliance of Greens, Communists, Social Democrats and left-wing Protestant pastors, failed in its attempt to prevent the West counter-arming. East German pacifists, however, spear-headed the civil rights movement that eventually triumphed in 1989. Yet both movements had so much in common that the SED, which supported the West German campaign in every respect, was reluctant to stamp down on its own pacifists for fear of compromising its support for their sympathisers in the West. The most important link between the two movements was the Protestant Church and its concern for peace that went back to the famous Stuttgart *Schuldbekenntnis* (Admission of Guilt – in the face of the criminal war) of 1946.

Historians are agreed that East Germany's Protestant Church played a crucial role in the revolutionary process of 1989 that culminated in German unification a year later. It was mainly owing to the Church that mass protests unfolded in a peaceful, non-violent way that in turn was a precondition for their eventual success. But the *Bund der evangelischen Kirchen in der DDR*, separated from the *Evangelische Kirche Deutschlands (EKD)* since 1968 and yet heavily subsidised by the latter, had no secret agenda for reuniting the divided nation. The Church was the only autonomous organisation within the SED dictatorship. However, in order to maintain this status, the Church pursued a highly ambiguous course. This was encapsulated in a dubious terminology which was, possibly deliberately so, open to different interpretations: *Kirche im Sozialismus* (Church within Socialism).[26] It was employed from the early 1970s both to define the Church's position and to appease the government after two troublesome decades. But what did it mean? Did the Protestant Church embrace socialism as the social order ordained by God or was it simply indicating its location? Naturally, the state secretary in charge of Church affairs, Klaus Gysi (father of Gregor Gysi, chairman of PDS/*Die Linke*), a very diplomatic functionary, wished to assume the first meaning while the Church maintained, more specifically after than before the *Wende*, that it saw itself simply as "the Church in the GDR". There can be no doubt, however, that many East German theologians, ordinary ministers as well as bishops, believed that the idea of socialism, though not necessarily the kind implemented in the GDR, was more pleasing to God than capitalism. That this is a perfectly legitimate world view requires no further explanation. What matters here is that the belief in "true socialism" or "socialism with a human face" was played down after 1990 even though the events of 1989/90 cannot be fully understood without the ideological affinity between anti-Mammonism (or more accurately anti-Consumerism in today's world) and anti-Capitalism.

A high-level meeting held on 6 March 1978 between Church leaders, led by Bishop Albrecht Schönherr and Erich Honecker, was perceived by both sides as an important turning point in relations between Church and State. The conference did manage to establish a lasting *modus vivendi* between the two institutions. But if the General-Secretary had hoped to contain the Church's activities within the strict limits of its religious calling, he was soon to be disappointed. Within weeks of the meeting, the government introduced military education as a compulsory subject in schools. For many Protestants, the systematic dissemination of hatred implicit in such instruction was incompatible with Christ's teachings and therefore had to be opposed. In the early 1960s, when the State introduced compulsory military service, the Church had negotiated an exemption for conscientious objectors. Young men from Christian homes were granted permission to serve instead as *Bausoldaten* ("soldiers of construction"). Now, the growing militarisation of society led to the arrival of a new breed of East German protagonists for peace – a variety of small groups that began forming an ever expanding network of the like-minded. Since the GDR was supposedly "peace-loving" by definition, there was no reason or room within its borders to demonstrate for peace. The situation became more complicated the following year, when NATO took the decision to counter-arm lest the Soviet Union refuse to dismantle its new generation of medium-range missiles. This sparked a popular campaign for nuclear disarmament in West Germany on an unprecedented scale – a movement that soon enjoyed the full backing of the SED leadership. But how could the GDR cheer West German demonstrators while persecuting its own pacifists?

Since most pacifist groups in the GDR had close links to the Church, it made sense for the State to ask its leaders to keep an eye on their flock. This was not an unreasonable request in view of the fact that in former centuries, this had been exactly what the State expected the Church to do: to exercise social discipline on behalf of the secular authorities. However the churches in the GDR were no longer powerful institutions with vested interests to defend. So, ironically, it was the attitude as well as the expectation of the State that afforded Church leaders a measure of influence they had not enjoyed for some time. Pastors like Rainer Eppelmann[27] were happy to offer a safe haven to youngsters who embraced the peace issue but had hitherto not been on close terms with the Church. These new recruits, motivated by their opposition to a godless state that was trying to manipulate their consciences, injected a new vigour into churches at the local level. In the early 1980s peace initiatives began to sprout all over the country, supported by local pastors and anxiously watched by the bishops and their bureaucrats. These initiatives took the form of peace prayers, peace seminars and "peace weeks" (*Friedensdekaden*). The basic principles behind them were that all Christians were obliged to work for peace, and as such they were also to demonstrate against the proliferation of weapons that threatened peace. This view did not spare one side or the other in the Cold War. The first peace week in the autumn of 1980 chose as its badge the biblical image of *Schwerter zu Pflugscharen* (swords into ploughshares), originally a sculpture donated by the Soviet Union to the United Nations and as such hardly incriminating – much to the annoyance of the authorities. It was, however, ultimately banned when it became a widespread symbol of protest and unrest.

The growing peace movement in West Germany, enjoying as it did the backing of many SPD deputies, and even of such a prominent figure as Willy Brandt (always keen to be adored by the younger generation), raised hopes in East Berlin that the *Bundestag* might be persuaded to vote against the deployment of Pershing II and Cruise missiles. Indeed, the "peace-loving" Protestant Church in both German states was considered an important ally in achieving Soviet military preponderance in Europe. After all, the Church was represented throughout the country, down to the smallest, most remote community. The mistaken assumption was that parliament would not dare defy public opinion should the latter reject the principle of nuclear deterrence. In fact, the founding fathers of the Basic Law had seen to it that the *Bundestag* would remain sovereign, and able to take decisions regardless of fluctuating public opinion. After the *Wende*, Bishop Eduard Lohse, who had been President of the West German Protestant Church (EKD) in the early 1980s, told the *Bundestag* Commission how he and his East German colleague Albrecht Schönherr had been wooed by GDR officials and Soviet diplomats. All of a sudden the close community of the two German Churches was welcomed and encouraged in view of their common responsibility for the preservation of peace. Of course, to the Church, peace was indivisible in the sense that it could not be monopolised by either side in the Cold War. However, the formula *Absage an Geist und Logik der Abschreckung* (rejection of the logic and spirit of deterrence), the mantra of the German peace movement, suited Communist officials because it appeared to be directed at the Western concept of military deterrence. It did not please Chancellor Kohl, when on the occasion of the EKD's synod in Worms in October 1983, shortly before the crucial *Bundestag* vote, the Saxon bishop Johannes Hempel proclaimed that he did not believe additional missiles would further peace in Europe. "We are convinced that what our government wants is the preservation of its integrity, more or less the same kind of security and real peace."[28] Behind the scenes, he was reprimanded for his interference in West German politics. Later on, under Gorbachev, confrontation was to be replaced by a *Sicherheitspartnerschaft* (security partnership), a term favoured by SED and SPD. Kohl, meanwhile, was as convinced as Schmidt had been that peace would be better guaranteed by nuclear deterrence based on a balance of power rather than by Christian thinking.

Over the years, tensions between Christian activists and the hierarchy of the East German Church led to an organisation which called itself *Kirche von Unten* (Church from Below). One of the most important groups was *Initiative für Frieden und Menschenrechte (IFM)*, which was founded in January 1986.

The *IFM* did not rely at all on the support or patronage of the official Church. "The basic aims of the *IFM*", writes Mary Fulbrook, "were focussed on domestic social peace: on the democratization of society, on the rule of law, the right to strike, the establishment of independent courts, and guarantees of the freedom of speech, of the press, or organisation".[29] In other words, here the narrow concepts of peace in the sense of disarmament or of "socialism with a human face" were overcome in favour of demands that would come to fruition in 1989/90.

With the arrival of Gorbachev in 1985 the East German civil rights movements shifted their focus towards domestic issues such as democratic reforms and concern for the environment. While the peace movement had been a mild nuisance to the authorities, the public campaign for fundamental reforms was seen as a more dangerous virus, with the potential to infect the body politic of the régime. What was most worrying was the appeal of activists to *glasnost* and *perestroika*, the reform programme propagated by the new Soviet leader. This time, the régime could not hide behind the Church, or compel the latter to discipline the unruly elements. While the campaign against NATO's counter-armament had been in the interest of the whole Soviet bloc, the SED's fight against domestic reforms was not. From now on, Honecker and his Politburo of Communist veterans were left to their own devices. However, to start off with, this was seen as an extension of the GDR's political independence, especially in relations with the FRG. Honecker first welcomed the new and much younger man at the helm of Soviet politics. Under his predecessors Andropov and Chernenko, relations between the two governments had worsened due to growing suspicions at the Kremlin about the GDR's financial dependence on the FRG – Honecker was twice forbidden to accept an invitation to visit West Germany.

Soon, however, Gorbachev became impatient with Honecker's refusal to consider making any reforms in the face of growing unrest. Whereas in the early days the German path to Socialism might have been progressive, "Socialism in the colours of the GDR" was now a reactionary, if not outright Stalinist, brand. Rafael Biermann, who has studied Moscow's struggle with German unification in detail, making use of all available source material and personal interviews, thinks that the estrangement between the two leaders and their parties went much deeper than has hitherto been realised.[30] They first clashed during the two-party congresses of the CPSU and the SED in the spring of 1986. Honecker was shocked to witness the new climate and the open debates in Moscow, which were incompatible with his concept of "democratic centralism". He flatly refused to follow the Soviet example when Gorbachev, disappointed about the sterile atmosphere at the SED

Party Congress, had asked him specifically about his plans. For decades, East Germans had been told on numerous posters "To learn from the Soviet Union means to learn how to achieve victory". No longer. A year later, the conflict between the two "brother parties" over human rights reached the public domain. Faced in an interview with unpleasant questions about apparent differences between Moscow's and East Berlin's concept of human rights, Kurt Hager, chief of ideology of the SED, expressed the view: "If your neighbour redecorated his house, would you feel the need to do the same as well?"[31] This now famous retort was, of course, a highly offensive interpretation of what Gorbachev had in mind. From now on, Western observers closely followed the alienation between the Liberals in Moscow and the SED hardliners. Soviet magazines such as *New Times* or *Sputnik* were banned from East Germany. The media were ordered not to report on events in the Soviet Union without Honecker's explicit approval, while the GDR embassy was requested to inform on elements of opposition as well as the growing crisis in the Soviet Union. One of the most worrying aspects for Honecker was the growing rapprochement between the Soviet and West German governments. Hitherto, he had imagined himself to be the FRG's chief contact, assuming the role of exclusive mediator between Bonn and Moscow; now he feared being sidelined. There had been ominous signs in the past: when, in 1986, he had pleaded with the Soviet leader to discipline the writer Yevtushenko after the latter called for German unification, his request was turned down. Now with the retirement of Gromyko and the arrival of Eduard Shevardnadze as the new foreign secretary, Honecker grew increasingly concerned about the new band of Soviet advisers who were beginning to question Moscow's traditional approach to the German Question.

No doubt the process of rethinking in Moscow set in long before the decisive breakthrough in 1989. In many ways, it followed the same logic as in East Berlin, but was applied with greater consistency and had radically different consequences. After all, the Soviet Union, too, faced serious economic and financial difficulties resulting from a desolate infrastructure and the maintenance of an extensive and expensive empire. Naturally it also wished to benefit from closer economic relations with the prosperous FRG, and was considering ways in which to improve the atmosphere. At first, personal relations between Gorbachev and Kohl left much to be desired, especially after the latter's *faux pas* in comparing the Soviet leader with Goebbels (October 1986).[32] And when Ronald Reagan, like Franz Josef Strauss, a hate figure of the international Left, agreed to consider a zero option with regard to medium range missiles (Reykjavik, October 1986) Kohl had second thoughts and felt that the American president had gone too far.[33] But the signing of the INF treaty a year later convinced Bonn that due to Gorbachev's reform efforts, Soviet foreign policy had indeed changed for the better. It is important to remember that West German governments of whatever political composition never wavered in their firm belief that "the key to the German question lay in Moscow" (i.e. not in East Berlin). The Soviet government, as one of the Four Powers responsible for Germany as a whole, had more to offer than a moratorium on the shooting of fugitives, easing transit to West Berlin or reuniting families. The first German visitor to be received by Gorbachev in Moscow was not Kohl but Federal President Richard von Weizsäcker, whose speech on 8 May 1985, the anniversary of Germany's unconditional surrender 40 years before, had made a most favourable impression on the Russians. He had told the Germans that they had a lot to apologise for, not only *vis-à-vis* the Jews but also in view of the atrocities committed in Russia, and he urged friendship with the people of the Soviet Union. It is indeed true, that during the Cold War, the criminality of Hitler's warfare in the East, the death especially of millions of Soviet citizens in Leningrad and prisoners-of-war in German camps, had been subject to a kind of amnesia.[34] Von Weizsäcker was welcomed in Moscow, because he seemed to represent a reformed West Germany, very different from the GDR's projected image. When the President broached the German Question Gorbachev referred vaguely to the unpredictable nature of history, which was his way of avoiding giving clear answers – a tactic he would make extensive use of in coming months and years. What was to happen within three years was rhetorically left to the next century: "Nobody knows what might happen in a hundred years". Even in October 1989, German diplomats would fend off questions with the same ploy.

In 1988, Gorbachev convinced the conservative elements within the CPSU that a more cooperative foreign policy was required. However, Kohl was not easily persuaded to go to Moscow on bended knees. It was only when Shevardnadze managed to arrange an exchange of visits that the German Chancellor was prepared to make the first move in October 1988.[35] Kohl arrived with a huge delegation, including many captains of industry as well as the Bavarian symphony orchestra, in order to emphasise the importance he attached to this visit. And while no far-reaching decisions were made, the outcome of the trip was nevertheless momentous. It marked a new departure in relations between the two countries and, above all, between the two leaders, who now established a close rapport. Kohl, of course, would stress that the Germans should have the same right to political self-determination as the rest of Europe. And the Soviet leader would express his hope for closer economic cooperation.

In the meantime, in early September 1987, Honecker had got his long-awaited chance to visit the FRG – a state visit of sorts which he regarded as the climax of his aspirations. He saw it as proof that the GDR was being recognised as an equal to the Federal Republic. For Kohl it was to be the most embarrassing and awkward moment of his political career.[36] It was, above all, symbolic that a man who after all represented the brutally enforced division of Germany should be received with all pomp and circumstance. Matters of protocol therefore became an issue of some controversy in the run-up to the visit. Was it to be a proper state visit or just a working conference, who would receive Honecker at the airport, what would be his motor escort, was Bonn to be flagged or just the chancellery, should he meet the Federal President?[37] Eventually, a compromise was agreed: Honecker would get the red carpet treatment, and be granted some if not all the paraphernalia of a full state visit, if in return he accepted that the dinner speeches given by the two leaders would be broadcast live in both parts of Germany. As a gesture of goodwill, the General Secretary had revealed that during the first eight months of 1987 3.2 million East Germans had been permitted to travel to the FRG. According to Kohl's memoirs the easing of contacts between the two parts of the nation were uppermost in his mind. In his dinner speech on 7 September he made reference to this, and expressed a view of history which, at the time, was somewhat at odds with the West German Zeitgeist: "The consciousness of the unity of the nation is as alive as ever and the will to preserve it is unbroken. This unity finds expression in a common language, in a common cultural heritage, in a long-lasting and continuing common history".[38] He pointed out that the German Question remained open, but that its solution was not on the political agenda. Honecker's performance was comparatively weak. He used his allotted time to paint a rosy picture of the GDR and its standard of living, showering his audience with all kinds of data and statistics meant to demonstrate the successful record of the GDR which, according to Kohl in his memoirs, could not be verified at the time, but proved to be completely incorrect after the fall of the Wall.

Honecker must have felt more at ease in other parts of Germany such as Bavaria where he was received by Franz Josef Strauss with full honours. But what he enjoyed most was the visit to his native Saarland. There he found a kindred spirit in Oskar Lafontaine, who gave him an especially warm welcome. In 1989/90 the Prime Minister of the Saarland and the SPD's candidate for the chancellorship, turned out to be anything but an enthusiastic supporter of German unification.

There was a platform of common interests to which both governments pledged to adhere: securing peace by furthering disarmament. However, this did not mean that they both favoured the same approach. Kohl had been most upset about a joint SPD–SED paper on security and other questions published shortly before Honecker's visit at the end of August 1987. It was the result of a long lasting discussion between representatives of both parties who had come together in a *Grundwertekommission* (Commission on Fundamental Values). The two social systems, it was argued, should enter into a peaceful competition; no one should deny the other the right to exist; both systems were open to reform. Conservatives regarded the SPD as barmy to even think the social market economy could be compared to socialism as practiced in the GDR. Nor could they stomach some of the SPD's ideas on security. In 1986, a working group of both SED and SPD members had come up with "Principles for a nuclear-free corridor in middle Europe". Egon Bahr, the chief architect of *Ostpolitik*, advocated a withdrawal of both NATO and the Warsaw Pact from German territory.[39] This was exactly what Moscow hoped to achieve when it gave its first blessing to the idea of German unification in February 1990. Moreover, the GDR's opposition, an odd mixture of Marxists, Social Democrats and pacifists, pursued the same goal in their search for a third way even though it had been ignored by the SPD which did not wish to compromise their new relationship with the SED.[40]

When Honecker returned to East Berlin, he felt that his position had been strengthened in every respect, not least *vis-à-vis* the Kremlin. For many ordinary citizens in the West, but probably also for the rising stars of the SPD such as Oskar Lafontaine and Gerhard Schröder, the visit confirmed that the GDR was just a normal state, more or less accepted by its people and not really a dictatorship as they had been told by hardened anti-Communists of the past. Opinion polls favourable to the GDR reached their peak in the autumn of 1987.[41] Honecker had noticed that in his talks in Bonn he had not met with a great deal of support for the GDR's dissidents. Kohl had expressed his relief when told about a general amnesty for political prisoners; but that was all. So he believed he now had *carte blanche* to deal with these troublemakers as he saw fit, without endangering his relationship with Kohl and his government. It is indeed true that Bonn's political establishment – and that includes the SPD, except for a few independent minds like Erhard Eppler and Gert Weisskirchen – greatly underestimated the potential of the East German opposition. Timothy Garton Ash has exposed this lack of empathy for those who dared to raise their voice and wonders whether it was right to keep appeasing a régime that by then was already fairly isolated in Eastern Europe.[42] Most politicians in the West did not wish to antagonise the party in power and thus risk the benefits of détente for the sake of some odd groups of apparent idealists. Fortunately, and due to the tenacity of the civil rights activists, this regrettable miscalculation had no serious conse-quences. On the contrary, the régime's renewed determination to put its foot down proved counter-productive, because it encouraged the groups during the last two years to draw more attention to the constant viola-tion of human rights and the damage done to the environment. To give just one example: in mid-November 1987 the authorities searched the *Umweltbibliothek* (Environmental Library) attached to Berlin's Zionskirche and arrested several people. This action triggered off widespread solidarity with those peace and environmental activists who had been taken prisoners. The response of the authorities was to make further arrests in various cities. In January, participants in a traditional march in memory of Rosa Luxemburg's murder, who carried posters with their heroine's words "Freedom is always the freedom of nonconformists" (*Andersdenkende*) were the object of extensive police action followed by trials for treason. In churches throughout the country people prayed for their release. The frantic actions and reactions only revealed that the system was under siege. Yet in his state of the nation speech on 1 December 1988 Kohl would say that the government was concerned about the troubles the SED was facing: "We have no interest in the further increase of domestic difficulties of the GDR".[43] Was it business as usual or hypocrisy in the service of political pru-dence? Prudent it certainly was because it reassured Honecker and his old guard in the Politburo that they had nothing to fear from Bonn which they still saw as the hotbed of potential mischief.

Notes and references

1 Bericht der Enquete-Kommission *Aufarbeitung der Geschichte und Folgen der SED-Diktatur in Deutschland*, Deutscher *Bundestag* (ed.) (Baden-Baden, 1995; from now on: 1. EKB), vol. I, p. 427.

2 As a result of *Ostpolitik* the former *Ministerium für Gesamtdeutsche Fragen* (All-German Affairs) had been renamed; a purely cosmetic measure to appease East Berlin.

3 Heinrich Potthoff, *Im Schatten der Mauer. Deutschlandpolitik 1961 bis 1990* (Berlin, 1999), pp. 121–34.

4 According to the FDP deputy Wolfgang Mischnik in an interview with Timothy Garton Ash, *In Europe's Name: Germany and the divided Continent* (London, 1993), pp. 131–32.

5 For the Guillaume affair see Markus Wolf, *Man without a Face. The Autobiography of Communism's Greatest Spymaster* (London, 1997), pp. 168–72.

6 Michael Ploetz, *Wie die Sowjetunion den Kalten Krieg verlor* (Munich, 2000), pp. 208–14.

7 William R. Smyser, *From Yalta to Berlin. The Cold War Struggle over Germany* (London, 1999), p. 275.

8 Altogether about 938 people were killed while trying to escape (Potthoff, p. 141).

8a See Klaus Wiegrefe, Das Zerwürfnis: Helmut Schmidt, Jimmy Carter und die Krisedertich-amerikanischen (Beziehungen (Berlin, 2005).

9 Smyser, p. 284.

10 See Potthoff, p. 153.

11 The economic reorientation of the GDR from the Soviet Union to the FRG is best described by Ploetz, pp. 253–91.

12 See Panel discussion in 1. EKB, vol. IV/1, pp. 197–237.

13 Verhandlungen des Deutschen *Bundestages*, vol. 120, p. 4289. See also the documentation edited by the Bundesministerium für Innerdeutsche Beziehungen (Bonn, 1986): *Innerdeutsche Beziehungen. Die Entwicklung der Beziehungen zwischen der Bundesrepublik Deutschland und der Deutschen Demokratischen Republik, 1980–1986.*

14 See Jens Hacker, *Deutsche Irrtümer. Schönfärber und Helfershelfer der SED-Diktatur im Westen* (Berlin, 1992), pp. 423–24.

15 Günter Gaus, *Wo liegt Deutschland? Eine Ortsbestimmung* (Hamburg, 1983).

16 Theo Sommer, *Reise ins andere Deutschland* (Hamburg, 1986).

17 Günter Mittag, *Um jeden Preis. Im Spannungsfeld zweier Systeme* (Berlin, 1991), p. 273.

18 Christian Hacke, in Werner Weidenfeld und Hartmut Zimmermann (eds), *Deustchland-. Handbuch* (Munich, 1989). See in particular Karl-Rudolf Korte, *Deutschlandpolitik in Helmut Kohls Kanzlerschaft. Regierungsstil und Entscheidungen 1982–1989* (Stuttgart, 1998). Also Matthias Zimmermann, *Nationales Interesse und Staatsraison. Zur Deutschlandpolitik der Regierung Kohl 1982–1989* (Paderborn, 1992). *Summary in Christian Hacke, Die Außenpolitik der Bundesrepublik. Weltmacht wider Willen?* (Berlin, 1997), pp. 302–12.

19 *Peter Bender, Deutsche Parallelen. Anmerkungen zu einer gemeinsamen Geschichte zweier getrennter Staaten* (Berlin, 1989), p. 134.

20 Potthoff, p. 211.

21 Mittag, p. 87 (translation by L.K.).

22 1. EKB, vol. V/1, pp. 919 f.

23 Hans-Hermann Hertle and Stefan Wolle, *Damals in der DDR. Der Alltag im Arbeiter- und Bauernstaat* (Munich, 2006), p. 331.

24 Ibid., pp. 331–39.

25 See the most comprehensive history of the dissident movement before 1989, Ehrhart Neubert, *Geschichte der Opposition in der DDR 1949–1989* (Berlin, 1997). Memories of individual members, Ulrike Poppe *et al.* (eds), *Zwischen Selbstbehauptung und Anpassung* (Berlin, 1995). See also the bibliography following the article by Ilko-Sascha Kowalczuk in *Handbuch zur deutschen Einheit* (Frankfurt a.M., 1999), pp. 163–76.

26 See Mary Fulbrook, *Anatomy of a Dictatorship. Inside the GDR 1949–1989* (Oxford, 1995), pp. 106–09. The role of the Churches, especially the Protestant Church, has now been extensively discussed by the first Enquete-Kommission des *Bundestags* (1.EKB) in 2 volumes of 1646 pages. As to "Kirche im Sozialismus" see Richard Schröder, 1. EKB, vol. VI/2, pp. 1164–429.

27 Rainer Eppelmann, *Fremd im eigenen Haus. Mein Leben im anderen Deutschland* (Cologne, 1993).

28 Eduard Lohse, *Der Bund der Evangelsichen Kirchen in der DDR (BEK) und die Evangelische Kirche in Deustchland (EKD) in ihrem Verhältnis zueinander und zu den beiden Staaten in Deutschland*, in 1. EKB, vol. VI/2, pp. 997–1025 (quote p. 1017, translation L.K.).

29 Fulbrook, p. 218.

30 Raphael Biermann, *Zwischen Kreml und Kanzleramt. Wie Moskau mit der deutschen Einheit rang* (Paderborn, 1997), pp. 106–12.

31 *Stern* (magazine), 9.4.1987 (translation L.K.).

32 Kohl was much embarrassed about this incident. See Helmut Kohl, *Erinnerungen 1982–1990* (vol. 1, Munich, 2005), p. 450.

33 Smyser, p. 307.

34 The cruel fate of Soviet prisoners of war had been shunned by German historians for a long time and was first tackled by Christian Streit, *Keine Kameraden. Die Wehrmacht und die sowjetischen Kriegsgefangenen 1941–1945* (Stuttgart, 1978).

35 Smyser, p. 313. According to Kohl (p. 659) it had been Lothar Spät, Prime Minister of Baden-Wurttemberg, who had negotiated the twin visits.

36 Kohl, vol. 1, pp. 544–50.

37 See the most detailed account, in Korte, pp. 324–75; summary in Potthoff, pp. 268–72.

38 Reproduced in his memoirs, pp. 566–68 (translation L.K.).

39 See Andreas Vogtmeier, *Egon Bahr und die deutsche Frage* (Bonn, 1996), pp. 265–93.

40 See Christof Geisel, *Auf der Suche nach einem dritten Weg. Das politische Selbstverständnis der DDR-Opposition in den 80er Jahren* (Berlin, 2005).

41 Potthoff, p. 273.

42 See n. 4. Timothy Garton Ash's book is still the best account in English but now superseded by Potthoff who gives him due credit.

43 Quoted by Potthoff, p. 285. For the context of this speech in which Kohl as usual invoked the unity of the German nation, see Korte, pp. 409–14.

CHAPTER 5

The People's Revolution

History is what happened in the past. It also constitutes the never-ending attempt to make sense of it in retrospect. Historians are inclined to believe that those who are involved in the unfolding of events hardly knew what they were doing and that it is up to them to provide clarification and meaning. This is particularly true of the cascade of events leading to German unification in 1989/90. Except for the US ambassador Vernon A. Walters,[1] nobody anticipated in the spring of 1989 what the world would look like in a year's time, neither politicians who believed themselves to be in control of inner-German affairs, nor political scientists who claimed to be experts on the GDR, nor historians who had already written off the concept of a German nation state.[2] Left-wing academics of the younger generation had argued that the German Question was "closed" since the Federal Republic had learnt its historical lesson and reached the stage of a "post-national state". For Wolfgang J. Mommen, one of many such voices, "the phase of consolidated nation-statehood from 1871 to 1933 [sic] was merely an episode of German history".[3] These were questionable attempts to make sense of the *status quo* even though, as Joachim Fest has put it most succinctly: "Die Geschichte schreibt keine letzten Worte"[4] (history does not write last words), a truth which German historians, under the influence of historicism, often forget. Speakers for the government were more circumspect. Wolfgang Schäuble, head of the Chancellery and later one of the driving forces for reunification, expressed common wisdom when he said in February that hopes for German unity in the not too distant future were "illusory".[5] It may be this experience of ignorance confronted by the raw nature of history that accounts for the later explosion of historical literature on the GDR. Most of that literature has been written by West German experts who had failed to predict the instability of the East German régime at the time and who now tried to save their reputations.

There is no doubt that the great change in German affairs – *die Wende* is a German understatement – came about through ordinary East German citizens who were not told what to do when they turned their back on the GDR or demonstrated in the streets of Leipzig for thoroughgoing reforms. At the time they could not know where their accumulated actions would lead. However, one can be sure that individually they knew exactly what they were doing. After all, they had a much better grasp of what the GDR stood for than most of their West German brothers who posed as experts on East German affairs and who would later purport to tell them how they felt. No doubt, the overall political climate in Eastern Europe was propitious. But somebody had to provide the constant impetus that would, in a kind of chain reaction, bring down the whole fabric of an artificial state in the midst of Europe.

The barely seven months between May and December 1989 are almost a model for the surreptitious workings of history as it surprises contemporaries who think that they are the masters of events. For Chancellor Kohl, who was born along the banks of the Rhine, the river symbolised his idea of history, as he explained to Gorbachev in June 1989: With the same certainty as the Rhine would find its way to the sea, German unification would occur one day.[6]

Claustrophobia was probably the dominant feeling among people in East Germany. Thousands of citizens had jeopardised their social standing by applying for exit permits. By the end of June 1989 the number of applicants had risen to 125,000.[7] The authorities had no clue as to how many more would leave the country given half a chance. Western Europe remained forbidden territory. Only Eastern Europe was open to travellers. On 2 May the Hungarian authorities began to dismantle the barbed wire that had sealed the border with Austria since 1956. This decision by the government must have been sanctioned by Gorbachev who, while visiting Budapest a month previously, had quietly dropped the Brezhnev doctrine that had served to legitimise Soviet intervention in Eastern Europe. However, the Hungarian government had seen no need to consult East Berlin. Nor had they expected or planned for the mass exodus of East Germans that was to follow. Even before this, the less fortified Hungarian–Austrian border had been a favourite escape route for citizens of the GDR on their way to the promised land of the Federal Republic which did not regard them as foreigners. A seemingly inconspicuous measure soon turned out to be the first leak in a solid dam holding back a flood of potential refugees.

Within the next couple of weeks, more than 200 East Germans managed to cross the border, but twice that number were turned back by Hungarian border guards, who did not arrest them, but sent them back (not to the GDR), so they found their way to the compound of Budapest's West German embassy. With the onset of the holiday season the number of escapees rose steadily. Throughout July and August, Hungary appeared to be the main gate to freedom. On 13 August, overcrowding forced the German embassy in Budapest to close its doors, with the result that the Red Cross had to set up a camp site around the embassy for would-be refugees. Less than ten days later, a festival near the Austrian–Hungarian border provided the opportunity for 660 GDR citizens to flee with the tacit approval of border guards.[8] The Hungarian government, under pressure from both Bonn and Pankow, faced a dilemma: If they decided to return the refugees as demanded in the name of socialist solidarity by Oskar Fischer, the GDR foreign minister, they would risk Bonn's goodwill and economic support. In the end the prospect of substantial credits from the West tipped the scales. On 10 September, the government resolved to cancel the travel agreement with East Berlin and to open the border. The following day 6,500 GDR citizens left for Vienna where they collected their West German passports. By the end of September, some 30,000 East Germans had left their country via Hungary.

West German television, eagerly watched beyond the border, covered the drama of mass migration day by day, thus persuading many East German families to join the "Trabi-trek" to the Federal Republic. The old American dream of making one's fortune in the West seemed to have gained a new meaning. Indeed, the role of the media in all this cannot be overestimated: while West German television revelled in reporting this unprecedented exodus the media of the GDR kept an ominous silence. On 29 August, with Honecker in hospital, the Politburo debated this burning issue for the first time.[9] A fortnight later *Neues Deutschland* blamed the Western "media circus" for what by then had turned into a veritable stampede of migrants. The apparent lack of public concern suggested to ordinary citizens either that the authorities might be forced to put a stop to the haemorrhage as they had done in 1961 (which prompted many to pack up and go) or that they would lose control altogether, which would encourage people to demand the freedom to travel and thus to leave the country for good anyway. In fact, both scenarios were to reinforce one another and contributed to the accelerating process of disintegration. Gregor Gysi, who was to rise to prominence as the leader of the SED's successor party, recalled that when he had asked a member of the Politburo why they had kept silent about the situation in the Eastern bloc embassies, the answer came: If you have no solution to a problem hush it up.[10] In other words, the gerontocracy at the top was at its wit's end.

During the summer months West German and international attention was focused almost exclusively on what happened to East Germans who were leaving their country. According to the British press, the news was devastating for the GDR's reputation. On 28 August, *The Times*, under the headline "Voting with their feet", which soon became a cliché, wrote that "there is no greater indictment of a government than when a large number of its brightest and most ambitious young people seek their future else-where".[11] When, on the request of East Berlin, Czechoslovak authorities blocked the road to Hungary, would-be refugees, now faced with an insuper-able border to Bavaria, began to seek asylum in the West German embassies of Prague and Warsaw. The large compound of the Lobkowicz palace in Prague was soon crammed with thousands of people desperate to make it to the West. Food and sanitation facilities soon reached breaking point with no let-up of further arrivals, among them many families with young children. The pictures of this site, the signs of both hope and desperation, travelled the world and highlighted the drama of a state in agony. Throughout his career Hans-Dietrich Genscher, Bonn's foreign minister, never faced a similar emotional challenge. Frank Elbe and Richard Kissler devote a whole chapter to the diplomatic wrestling behind the scenes of the UN plenary session in New York.[12] Genscher's Polish colleague, Krystof Skubiszewski, proved to be amenable and promised to find a humanitarian solution for the refugees encamped at the Warsaw embassy. Not so Jaromir Johanes, Prague's foreign secretary, who coldly referred Genscher to his East German opposite number Oskar Fischer. By that time, 2,500 people had found refuge in the embassy compound and could not be persuaded to go home on the promise of an exit permit within six months. The US and French foreign ministers offered to exercise pressure on Prague. However, the crucial factor in finding a solution was probably Eduard Shevardnadze who showed concern for the 500 children among the refugees.[12a] Soviet pressure on East Berlin lead to a face-saving exit strategy worked out between Fischer and Genscher: the GDR citizens would be allowed to leave for West Germany by train via the GDR which would expel them officially by collecting their passports on board. Immediately upon his return from New York on 30 September, Genscher rushed to Prague to announce from the embassy balcony that people, addressed as "dear fellow countrymen", were free to leave. Within 48 hours their number had swollen to 3,500. However, after the initial outburst of joy, he needed all his rhetorical skill to convince the campers that the detour via East Germany would still safely land them in Hof, West Germany. Frank Elbe, Genscher's loyal assistant, who accompanied one of those trains describes in some detail what happened *en route*: just before departure some 50 people, arriving on the opposite platform from Bratislava, jumped on the train to freedom. In Reichenbach, Stasi officials boarded the train to collect passports without, as had been promised, delivering exit permits. As a gesture of defiance, a young locksmith then threw all his East German money out of the window. Soon the whole platform was covered with money, membership cards, keys and other items no longer required in the West. In front of Stasi officials, the station master waved good-bye, as did onlookers whenever the train slowed down in towns. On later occasions, ugly scenes occurred in Dresden when hundreds of youngsters hoped to board the trains only to be beaten back by police in the most brutal manner. It is easy to imagine how all this, portrayed live on television, contributed to the rapid loss of respect for the GDR government: the fabric of state and party authority was disintegrating day by day.

However, more dangerous for the government than the mass exodus was its impact on those who preferred to stay and vent their anger. On 22 August, Patricia Clough had written in the *Guardian* newspaper, that "there is virtually no active internal opposition". She dismissed "the handful of tiny protest groups" sheltered by the Protestant church.[13] The idea that Germans' sense of discipline would prevent all pressure for change still prevailed. If that had ever been the case, it certainly was not so six weeks later. Two strands of opposition emerged and, for a while, reinforced each other:

1   Popular demonstrations for freedom in Leipzig following the traditional Monday peace prayers in the Nicolai-Kirche, grew in force from one week to the next, in spite of massive police intervention.

2   The proliferation of political groups demanding thorough-going reforms began with an appeal of *Neues Forum* in early September for a "democratic dialogue", signed by dissidents and human rights activists.

It makes sense to deal with those developments separately because in the end they would diverge: the demonstrations in Leipzig, and later elsewhere, had as their constituents ordinary citizens who expressed their frustrations, whereas the new crop of political groups consisted of an intellectual élite, which in one way or another had benefited from state patronage and were thus reluctant to part with socialism.

The first address of *Neues Forum* on 9 September was anything but a call to arms against the GDR. The signatories wanted a better supply of consumer goods but at the same time "a rejection of uninhibited growth", more scope for economic initiatives but "no degeneration into an elbow society".[14] In retrospect it is easy to see why popular dissent proved to be more decisive than élitist malaise. However, at the time, the new groups which, by demanding a say in politics, challenged the monopoly of party power, appeared to be more dangerous to state security than amorphous masses of demonstrators. Soon people on the streets of Leipzig and elsewhere demanded official recognition of *Neues Forum*. This group attracted members in large numbers, not least because it wished to be a citizens' movement and not another party. As had happened after 1945, people were fed-up with parties and party politics. However, democracy required political parties prepared to engage in public discourse and free elections. *Basisdemokratie,* the favourite watchword of East Germany's human rights activists was no basis for a functioning parliamentary system. Therefore other groups, with a slightly more realistic programme, emerged in no time. On 12 September a number of Lutheran ministers, among them the later foreign minister Markus Meckel, published an appeal for the foundation of an ecological and social democracy that demanded the separation of powers, the rule of law and a return to parliamentary democracy.[15] Less than a month later, a foundation document was signed without waiting for official approval. The party now named itself, according to its provisional statutes, *Sozialdemokratische Partei in der DDR (SDP)* and called for the establishment of local organisations. What is most significant for the whole process of unification is that the new party received no support, secret or public, from the SPD, its big sister party in West Germany, which at that time was still in cahoots with the SED. Thus the first party with a claim to an honourable political tradition was left to its own devices – in the hands of well-meaning pastors.

By mid-September 1989, other groups of dissidents emerged and stood up for their ideals, notably *Demokratischer Aufbruch/DA* (Democratic Awakening) and *Demokratie Jetzt/DJ* (Democracy Now), all making more or less similar demands. Almost in every case church ministers were in the forefront of the movement. This is particularly true of DA, which was the foundation of distinguished churchmen such as Rainer Eppelmann, Friedrich Schorlemmer and Heino Falcke who appealed to more middle-class elements of society and who wanted a return to a market economy as far as small businesses and the service industry were concerned. DJ was more left-leaning, as was *Vereinigte Linke/VL* (United Left) an odd and, on the whole, insignificant collection of dissatisfied SED members. Judged in retrospect, most of these new political groups shared, apart from their democratic credentials, two important congenital defects:

1   They made it quite clear that they wished to reform the GDR and not become part of the Federal Republic.

2   They were united in their hope of realising "democratic socialism" or "socialism with a human face" without any understanding of how to put that idea into practice.

No wonder the groups were to be deserted by the majority of ordinary citizens once they had the chance of a free vote. However, it must be noted at this point that questioning the existence of the GDR and socialism before the Wall fell was a treasonable offence. Moreover, these groups were keen to enter into a dialogue with the government, not realising how much it would compromise them in the eyes of ordinary people. Yet the offer of cooperation with the SED was bound to undermine their will to hold on to power, indefensible as it was. In a sense, the dissidents, by their determination to initiate reforms, contributed to the collapse of a state they hoped to save.

The driving force for change, for "the only peaceful revolution in German history", occurred in the streets of Leipzig. Only two days before, the régime had celebrated its 40th birthday in East Berlin. While police kept demonstrators at bay, the old guard enjoyed, for one last time, the orchestrated salute of the people, complete with all pomp and circumstance – though this time in the presence of a sceptical Gorbachev, who was reported to have made the now famous remark that "life will punish the latecomer". Of the three crucial events that determined the development towards unification, 9 October was perhaps the most important and, since it did not attract the same media attention as the fall of the Wall or the first free elections, the least recognised turning point. It may have happened in the evening following Monday's peace prayers in the Nicolai Church, but in historical terms it was "High Noon", the menacing confrontation between around 70,000 unarmed citizens and the armed authorities of the GDR, determined to put an end to such defiance of law and order once and for all. All witnesses are agreed that it could have ended in a terrible bloodbath, a kind of Tiananmen Square massacre, but it ended without a shot having been fired. On previous occasions the police had arrested individual "trouble makers" without being able to disperse the masses. This time, they pursued a policy of systematic intimidation: public warnings to stay at home, the presence of a huge riot police force (28 battalions of 80 men) as well as army units and the so-called *Betriebskampfgruppen* (armed factory workers) ready to intervene, armoured police cars blocking side streets, news about local hospitals being supplied with stocks of blood and doctors on stand-by duty.[16] However, people were not deterred and turned out in even greater numbers than the week before – about four times as many. These 70,000 people brought down the régime, by their personal courage and their disciplined rejection of any form of violence: a huge impenetrable wall of people defying a menacing police force. Among calls for "no violence!", "Gorbi! Gorbi!" and "Admit *Neues Forum*", the devastating slogan "*Wir sind das Volk!*" (We are the people) could be heard for the first time. A month earlier people had been calling "*Wir wollen raus!*" (We want to get out). Now, the majority of demonstrators were shouting "*Wir bleiben hier!*" (We're staying here). The East German historian Hartmut Zwahr, who has written an eye-witness account of the events, is certain that the decision not to use force, i.e. not to give the order to shoot, was taken on the local level, not in Berlin. While the top leadership around Honecker and Krenz were still pondering their options, a triumvirate of Leipzig SED officials contacted Kurt Masur, the prominent conductor of the Gewandhaus orchestra, and other well-known public figures to make an appeal for calm and peaceful dialogue, which was then read out in public again and again. The utter peacefulness of the occasion, owing in large measure to the Church's influence and organisational skills, as well as the refusal of the Red Army to intervene, forced the authorities to abstain from a showdown. By the end of the night, the authority of the government had been weakened beyond repair. People had lost their fear of the régime and were now, throughout East Germany, taking to the streets in their hundreds of thousands. The initiative of two daring East German photographers (Radomski and Schefke) played a crucial role. From a church tower they filmed the whole scene of defiance only to smuggle their footage to a West German television company (ARD/Hamburg) on the same night. The "dictatorship of the proletariat" had been brought down by its own people who, after 40 years, decided to take control of their lives.

The retreat of the SED from power began the following day, when district commissioners opened dialogue with representatives of *Neues Forum*, the strongest opposition group, which had refused to become a political party. A week later, Egon Krenz toppled his master by marshalling his friends in the Politburo. Up to the last moment, he had hoped for an amicable handover of power.[17] The lack of any legal transition of power helps to characterise any dictatorship – officially Erich Honecker resigned for health reasons (which at the age of 77, and given his long-standing poor health, he should have done much earlier). Two of his close confidants, economy supremo Günter Mittag and Joachim Herrmann, in charge of propaganda, could not save their skins by changing sides and had to go as well. However, Erich Mielke, the hated head of State Security, being one of the conspirators, managed to stay on for the time being. The Soviet leader, Mikhail

Gorbachev, had been informed in advance and had given his blessing. The following day, the Central Committee of the SED elected Egon Krenz as Honecker's successor by unanimous vote.

All those involved in the coup ardently hoped that the change of guard would appease the angry masses, and that the party would regain the initiative. However, Krenz, who saw himself as another Gorbachev, was too close to the previous régime to be trusted: he had, after all, been Honecker's deputy and successor designate. No wonder the West dismissed him as a transitional figure. So did the people in the streets of Leipzig a week later by chanting "*Wir sind keine Fans von Egon Krenz*" (We are no fans of Egon Krenz) and with their many derogatory banners such as "*Demokratie unbekrenzt*" (a pun on Krenz: democracy without limits set by Krenz) or "*Die Karre steckt zu tief im Dreck, die alten Kutscher müssen weg*" (This cart is stuck in the mud, the old drivers have to go).[18] Krenz was also blamed for having approved of the Tiananmen Square massacre, and for manipulating local government elections in May. Rolf Biermann, the popular song-writer, expelled in 1976 for his loose tongue, gave his first concert in Leipzig on 1 December characterising Krenz in the following verse:

> *Hey, Krenz, du fröhlicher kalter Krieger*
> *Ich glaube Dir nichts, kein einziges Wort*
> *Du hast ja die Panzer in Peking bejubelt*
> *Ich sah Dein Gebiss beim Massenmord*
> *Dein falsches Lachen. Aus Dir macht Fritz Cremer*
> *Ein Monument für die Heuchelei*
> *Du bist unsere Stasi-Metastase*
> *Am kranken Körper der Staatspartei (. . .)*[19]

Less than a week later, public pressure forced Krenz to resign all his posts. During the previous six weeks he had tried desperately to rally the faithful and save his bankrupt party; its shortcomings, above all the corrupt lifestyle of its leaders, being now exposed in the media day by day. To no avail. Both the exodus to West Germany and the mass demonstrations, now spreading from Leipzig all over the country, grew rapidly in strength: the number of migrants almost doubled from September (33,000) to October (57,000) and that of demonstrators in Leipzig rose within three weeks (9 October to 30 October) from 70,000 to half-a-million.[20] Jens Reich, one of the founding fathers of *Neues Forum*, would later say that it was the overwhelming experience of having lost their fear which prompted people to take to the streets. By the end of October the so-called block parties, Liberal Democrats (LDPD), National Democrats (NDPD) and the Christian Democrats (CDU), which

had served as democratic fig-leaves for the SED, now tried to distance themselves from the ruling party by demanding a free and secret ballot. Local
party bosses hoped to stave off the day of reckoning by inviting people all
over the country to enter into a public dialogue, thereby meeting one of the
first demands of *Neues Forum*.

In the meantime, Egon Krenz rushed to see Gorbachev in Moscow so as
to give the impression that he was one of his followers. Back home he
announced the resignation of the old guard of the Politburo, among them
Erich Mielke, and published an "action programme" that contained all sorts
of promises for the future without addressing the main grievance: the lifting
of travel restrictions. To judge from the posters carried along during mass
rallies in Leipzig and elsewhere this was one of the most burning issues next
to the demand for free elections. During the last week of October placards
and choruses demanded the suspension of travel restrictions in no uncertain manner, from the mildly demanding *"Die Mauer muss weg!"* (The Wall
must go!), to the more ascerbic *"Mit dem Fahrrad durch Europa, aber nicht als
alter Opa!"* (On bicycle across Europe but not as Grandpa) and so forth.
Krenz and his crew tried to trim their sails to the "winds of change" by
preparing a new travel law and claiming that public demonstrations would
henceforth be part of "Berlin's political culture".[21] It was with their authorisation that, following an appeal by writers and artists, a mass rally was being
staged at Berlin Alexanderplatz on 4 November, the last stand of critical
loyalists or, as Jarausch put it, "the climax of the socialist movement for
change".[22] With at least 500,000 participants it was the biggest demonstration in East Berlin, the capital of party and government officials who had
much to lose by the downfall of the GDR. However, the times of crowd control were over: speakers of the old régime, like spymaster turned dissident
Markus Wolf and Berlin party boss Günter Schabowski, were booed by the
masses. Christa Wolf, East Germany's most prominent writer, revelled in the
experience of "people power", in a "socialist society" being turned "upside-
down, back onto its feet". "Imagine", she dreamed, "there was socialism
and no one ran away."[23] For a short while German intellectuals seemed to
experience true *"Volksdemokratie"*. Given half a chance they would have
turned it into a Jacobin "dictatorship of virtue", to make sure people would
not again run away from a reformed type of socialism.

Reisefreiheit – the freedom to travel – was a euphemism for the right to
leave the country for good: it concerned the very existence of the GDR. How
it was handled says much about mismanagement during the last weeks and
months if not during the whole lifetime of this state which had an obsession
with being in control without itself being controlled by the people. On

24 October the Politburo passed the draft of a new travel law requiring applicants to hand in their passports for a temporary visa (and expect 30 days for dealing with their case). Since the state was bankrupt, there was no mention of foreign exchange. It was not until 6 November that *Neues Deutschland* published the draft and invited the public to discuss the matter. However, the revolutionary mood would not tolerate such delaying tactics. The same day, half-a-million people turned out in Leipzig to demonstrate against the new law amidst a forest of banners mocking Krenz, the old party gang and the Stasi: *"Das Reisegesetz beweist, es herrscht der alte Geist!"* (The travel law proves the old spirit is alive) or *"Visa ohne Geld, da lacht die ganze Welt"* (visa without money makes the whole world laugh)[24] and so forth. The following day, the government of the GDR resigned jointly and parliament, the *Volkskammer*, which now listened to the people, turned down these proposals as too timid. A day later, 8 November, the Politburo resigned at a meeting of the Central Committee of the SED: instead of the previous 21 members, 11 were now being elected into the governing board of the party, among them reformers like Hans Modrow, soon to be the new Prime Minister, and *"Wendehälse"* (turncoats) like Egon Krenz and Günter Schabowski, as well as a few conservatives such as the minister of defence Heinz Kessler. The new leaders hastened to announce all sorts of reforms concerning the economy, the forthcoming elections, the media and recognition of *Neues Forum*. Amid this mad rush a new draft law prepared by the ministries of the Interior and State Security and meant to ease travel regulations was waved though by the Central Committee.[25] It was Thursday afternoon, 9 November: Krenz handed the text to Schabowski saying *en passant* that this could be a sensation.[26] Indeed, it would be, though not as intended. Schabowski, who had no time to attend the debate on the issue, was on his way to brief journalists on the day's far reaching decisions. There was no time to explain the details of a law which would come into force the next day and which provided for visas to be issued without delay by the relevant police departments. Towards the end of the press conference, an Italian journalist enquired whether the government had passed new travel regulations. Schabowski said yes and when asked for more details, rummaged through his papers until he found the text which he read out. The gist of it was that henceforth East Germans could travel out of the country at any time and via any checkpoint. At that moment it seemed to go without saying that people had to apply for exit visas. Asked by Tom Brokaw of NBC News whether this meant that the Wall was open he said "yes" and when pressed for details and timing was understood to have mumbled *"sofort"* ("immediately").[27] Apparently he did not know at the time whether the

Soviet authorities had been notified. Exhausted and tired, he went home not realising that with the media at his heels he had just opened the Wall single-handedly. Not quite: it was the people of East Berlin who, on hearing the breathtaking news, put in its nutshell version by the West German media, stormed the wall: the hated symbol of a corrupt ancien régime. Border guards were left without instructions from headquarters when faced with a fast growing and angry crowd. Nor did the caretaker government know what to think of the situation, which had been brought about by a decision of the party. Krenz later interpreted his own indecision as having given the go-ahead for letting people cross the border. In actual fact, this was a decision taken by the besieged border guards on the spot more precisely by Lieutenant-Colonel Harald Schäfer who had to cope without orders from above: first by stamping exit visas on identification cards, then an hour later, 23.20 hrs at Bornholmer Strasse, by letting everyone through without bothering. By midnight all border crossings along the entire Wall separating East and West Berlin had been opened. The sensational news now spread all over the world: it was the most forceful manifestation that a historical epoch known as the Cold War had come to an end. The genie of freedom was out of the bottle.

The fall of the Wall sparked off the second half of the revolution, "*die Wende in der Wende*" (turn within the turn). It is not uncommon in revolutions that the second wave swallows those who had been in the forefront of the first movement. When Krenz saw Gorbachev nine days earlier it was agreed that "German unification was not on the agenda". Now all of a sudden it was: not yet for the international community but for those who mattered more and more: ordinary people all over East Germany. By the end of the weekend 4.5 million East Germans had visited West Berlin and the Federal Republic on day trips, not counting those who had crossed the border without a visa during the first 12 hours: altogether probably two-thirds of the whole population. They were entitled to collect a "welcoming bonus" of DM 100 with which they often bought oranges and bananas and other consumer goods rarely available in the GDR. It is one of the more unpalatable attitudes of certain West German intellectuals and evidence of their political inadequacy that they accused these people of having sold their souls for bananas.[28] From now on, the call for free elections and for a plebiscite regarding German unification grew in intensity. One of the most popular slogans in the streets of Leipzig and elsewhere now referred to the suppressed version of the GDR national anthem: "*Deutschland, einig Vaterland*" ("Germany, united fatherland") reminding the government that they had once been the champions of German unity. "We are the people" changed into "We are one people".[29] One of the most telling banners emerged on 4 December: *"Kein neues sozialistisches Experiment, sondern Wiedervereinigung"* ("No new socialist experiment but reunification"). Another equally symptomatic slogan said: *"Wir leben nur einmal – dann Ja zur Einheit Deutschlands"* (We only live once – therefore Yes to German unity). It was not pan-German nationalism, as some West and East German intellectuals would have it, but an appeal for national solidarity, a cry for help addressed to their West German fellow countrymen who had enjoyed a better life for the last 40 years. By crossing the border people could judge for themselves that the TV image of West Germany did not distort reality, as they had been made to believe. What was now on offer was either another utopia, maybe under the leadership of pious clergymen, or the West German model which many had just been witnessing for the first time: not only a choice of consumer goods but also a public infrastructure that was much superior to their own. No wonder ordinary citizens began to distance themselves from their old and new leaders who called for a socialist alternative to the Federal Republic.[30] The social composition of those opting for unification among the Leipzig demonstrators is very revealing: the great majority, skilled workers and graduates/employees (between 70–90 per cent), were in favour of reunification, while most students (79 per cent) were against.[31] Students with little experience of real life were more opposed to a capitalist economy and knew that under the existing system they could be certain to have a good job.

Following the fall of the Wall, the recently rejuvenated SED régime began to woo the Federal government. On 11 November Krenz rang Kohl expressing his gratitude if the Chancellor would help to calm the situation.[32] He told him about the lifting of travel restrictions and their plans for a complete renewal of politics, but insisted that unification was not on the agenda. Kohl did not agree and referred to his obligation under the Basic Law. However, he assured Krenz that he and his government had no interest whatsoever in people leaving the GDR. Less than a week later, Hans Modrow, the new Prime Minister who had the reputation of an unselfish Party stalwart, presented his programme of thorough-going reforms to the *Volkskammer*. He revealed unsparingly that the economy was in dire straits, not least due to the hidden credits which had not hitherto been exposed. He then pleaded for "strengthening the community of responsibility of the two German states through a treaty-based union".[33] In fact, he came cap in hand asking Bonn for a credit of DM 15 billion. A social democratic chancellor in Bonn might well have entered into that kind of co-operation without further ado. Not so Helmut Kohl and his entourage who analysed this speech and came to the conclusion that they were meant to prop up a régime that was only offering the rhetoric of reforms and no substance, no promise of truly free elections, no abandonment of the leading role of the SED or a planned economy. In the official history we read: "In this way the Federal government was to contribute to keeping the SED in power. If the situation among the population had calmed down, so they calculated, their power-structures would again be consolidated".[34] In their common sense, the demonstrators in the streets of Leipzig knew better – as one of their slogans had it: "*Erst nach freien Wahlen wird die BRD zahlen*" (Only after free elections will Bonn pay).[35]

Insisting that an issue is "not on the agenda" often means that it is in fact uppermost on people's mind. For the SED the survival of the GDR was at stake, not just their monopoly on power. And the *raison d'être* for the GDR was its socialist foundation. Once they gave up the claim to socialism, there was no need for a separate German state. In early December they came to the conclusion that abandoning their leading role and recognising other powers in the land was the only viable chance for preserving the GDR. Therefore the government went along with the Protestant Church's initiative to set up a so-called Round Table as a response to the call for dialogue, which had been one of the demands of *Neues Forum* right from the beginning. The SED had by now realised that most of the new groups wished to hold on to the GDR and some kind of socialism (that is to say their leadership, because the first representative public opinion poll on 7 December indicated that a majority of *Neues Forum* (62 per cent) were in favour of unification).[36] The Round Table saw itself as "an institution of public monitoring in our country" with the purpose of continuing "its activities until free, democratic and secret elections have been held".[37] However, the reference to "our country which is in a serious crisis" and the option "for its independence and permanent development" suggested that most members on the panel did not visualise German unification as the final goal. It was the only basis of understanding with a government which otherwise was not trusted to carry out the necessary reforms. The question was whether the country could be saved once "the ecological, economic and financial situation", as demanded, had been "made public". If unwittingly, the Round Table was thus helping to dig the grave of a country that it hoped to save from its agony – another example of the dialectics of history at work throughout the process of unification. At the Round Table, government and opposition were facing each other just as in a democratic parliament: the SED and the old bloc parties such as CDU, LDPD, NDPD, etc. *vis-à-vis* a larger contingent of delegates from the new groups such as *Demokratie Jetzt, Neues Forum, SDP, Demokratischer Aufbruch*, etc. The government was not only numerically in a weaker position: to be more attractive to voters in the forthcoming free elections, the former bloc parties elected new leaders with a more progressive image. The SED tried to do the same by convening an extraordinary party congress on 8 December which changed the party name to *Party of Democratic Socialism* and elected the young and rhetorically gifted lawyer Gregor Gysi as chairman after Krenz had resigned from all his offices two days earlier.

Apart from the Wall, which gave people a feeling of imprisonment, the Stasi and its comprehensive surveillance system figured as the most hated aspect of the GDR. As Klaus Kaden, Protestant pastor and a central figure of the opposition in Leipzig, put it: "The Stasi was very good in conveying to the GDR citizen that they were quite capable of obtaining any information they wanted to, so people were scared. I think people were considerably more scared in East Germany than in Poland".[38] Not surprisingly, the abolition of State security was one of the first vocal demands in the streets of Leipzig. According to many banners, their countless and useless agents should be productively employed: "*Dem Volk zum Wohle die Stasi in die Kohle!*" (For the benefit of the people send Stasi agents into coal mines). However, Krenz had no intention of putting down what was termed "the sword and shield of the party". In the meantime Erich Mielke, the octogenarian head of the Stasi (born 1907), was busy destroying compromising material.[39] Hans Modrow, the new Prime Minister, in his first statement on 13 November, mentioned the secret police only in passing by announcing a change of name (now Office for State Security) and "new thinking in matters of public order and state security", whatever that meant in practice. Mielke was replaced by Wolfgang Schwanitz, just another top official of the same ministry. One of the most memorable if grotesque scenes took place when Mielke exclaimed in his resignation speech: "But I love you, all of you!".[40] His words, though received with laughter by members of the *Volkskammer*, should be taken seriously, i.e. as the expression of a paternalistic mindset, the suffocating love of a well-meaning *Vater Staat* who disciplines those he cares for. This attitude was, by the way, shared by many high-ranking Protestant clergymen who feared for their flock because they were worried about the temptations of the consumer society once the gates of the "authoritarian kindergarten"[41] were flung open. The Round Table would not tolerate the survival of the Stasi under a new name and at the first meeting demanded its definite abolition. Further attempts by the government to create two allegedly new services for the protection of the constitution and for gathering intelligence were equally foiled. While delegates at the Round Table discussed the process of winding down the activities of that monstrous ministry officials used the time to shred compromising files, to "privatise" financial resources and to transfer personnel to less obnoxious positions in the civil service such as police, customs, transport and the like. To gain control, citizen committees sprang up in many cities with a view to stop the systematic removal of evidence. On 15 January people in East Berlin were so frustrated about the government's delaying tactics that 100,000 stormed the central headquarters of the Stasi in Normannenstrasse in order to save as many documents as possible. Eventually Modrow promised not to set up a successor organisation to the Stasi until the elections. On the insistence of the Round Table these were now scheduled for 6 May.

Since the press was no longer subject to censorship it could now report freely about the sheltered and privileged life of the old leadership in the suburb of Wandlitz (nicknamed Volvograd) with its Western style supermarket where everything was on offer. Except for their hunting lodges, the life of the GDR nomenclatura was not exceptionally luxurious compared to that in the West. But ordinary citizens had the feeling that Honecker and his cronies were guilty of hypocrisy. More important though for the general awakening was the constant flow of information about the desperate state of the economy: the national debt, the rotten infrastructure, the uncompetitive output of industry and so forth. Now, for the first time, the glaring contrast between West and East Germany after a divergent development of 40 years became the focus of public concern. Due to the open border, two economic worlds collided that could not be more different. As the West German magazine *Der Spiegel* saw it, in the West there was one of the most highly developed countries in the industrial world and "in the East an economy where everything is in short supply, cars with engines which had been designed before the war, a telecommunication system with a ten year waiting list for private lines, products which in order to find buyers abroad had to be sold at a loss".[42]

Soon the East German currency was in free fall *vis-à-vis* the Deutschmark so that West Berliners could buy everyday commodities like bread in the other half of the city for virtually nothing. The daily migration of thousands of professionals and skilled workers from East to West made an already deteriorating situation worse. By the end of the year, 343,854 East Germans, the equivalent of a large city, had left the country overnight, and deserted their workplaces in factories, schools, and hospitals. From every corner of the country party bosses reported a breakdown of public morale, not least among party members who cancelled their memberships in their thousands.

Modrow's government tried desperately to stabilise the country by seeking help from different quarters, financial aid from Bonn and moral support from those elements of the opposition that held on to a "reformed socialist church" as it were. He had the backing from an appeal "For our Country" signed by 200,000 East Germans, among them many prominent artists and clergymen who warned against "a sell-out of our material and moral values, due to the harsh economic realities and unreasonable conditions that influential economic and political circles in West Germany attach to their offers of aid to the GDR, leading sooner or later to a West German takeover of East Germany".[43] Often without realising it many intellectuals and dissidents had been influenced by Communist propaganda to which they had been exposed for 40 years. The same phenomenon could be observed in West Germany in 1945 after 12 years of Nazi dictatorship. Again, ordinary citizens in the streets had retained more common sense and knew that their country's "material and moral values" were more imagined than real.

To West German captains of industry the economic and financial liabilities of a merger became more apparent by the day. It was the good fortune of East Germans that Chancellor Kohl was more driven by historical and emotional impulses than by economic considerations. His government was well advised to pursue a policy of procrastination as far as Modrow's offer of a "community of responsibility" was concerned. Kohl's chief negotiator in East Berlin was his head of office Rudolf Seiters, who made it quite plain that certain demands had to be met before Bonn was prepared to sort out the mess into which the GDR had manoeuvred itself: the most important being free elections, recognition of opposition parties, abandonment of the SED's monopoly of power and the introduction of certain mechanisms conducive to a market economy. As Kohl's Ten Point Programme of 27 November[44] shows, the Chancellery was aware that German unification could now be envisaged but he had no clue how long it would take for the train of events to reach that final destination: ten years or maybe only five years?

With the worsening of the situation in East Germany, above all the unrelenting flow of migrants (2,000 a day on average) and the unmistakable popular calls for unification, the timescale began to shrink. However, it was Kohl's enthusiastic reception by the crowds in Dresden and the emotional impact it had on him and his entourage that convinced the Chancellor that a fast-track solution to the German problem was now called for. The visit on 19 December was his "crucial experience in the process of German unification". When he stepped down from his plane and saw the "sea of flags in the national colours" he turned to Seiters and said: *"Die Sache ist gelaufen"* ("It's done").[45] One of Modrow's chief concerns was the monetary impact on the GDR economy since the Deutschmark had virtually become a second currency. Kohl gave the assurance, as he always did on such occasions, that he had no wish to witness more and more East Germans moving to the Federal Republic: people should see light at the end of the tunnel, he said with Modrow's approval.[46] Soon it would appear that the prospect of a currency union was the only way to bring the exodus to a halt. The joint communiqué with Modrow, at the end of the visit, once again listed all the good reforms the GDR would carry out for the sake of an agreement, "that cooperation between the GDR and FRG be increased comprehensively and that relations be elevated to a new level and made closer and more long-term".[47] While Kohl gave his blessing to such commitments for the future, he knew perfectly well that in the short term free elections would sweep the government out of office and make all these undertakings meaningless. The most visible result of that meeting was the opening of the Brandenburg Gate, Berlin's iconic symbol, to pedestrians on 22 December.

Kohl left Dresden with a much clearer notion of how to assess the domestic situation in East Germany. What mattered now was the precise schedule for free elections and how to prepare for them. Yet it would be wrong to assume that he and his advisers already anticipated the likely time span for unification. Papers produced at the Chancellery at the end of January still referred to a period of "years" in order to establish a monetary and economic union between the two states.[48] Bonn's main focus was the international scene, which required a careful and possibly time-consuming approach. Yet it was the pace at which the implosion of the GDR proceeded that dictated the development. With an influx of nearly 50,000 migrants in January, who had to be looked after, the social facilities in the Federal Republic reached crisis point. The two governments came to the realisation that only the prospect of unification could persuade people to stay. What mattered now were the conditions in which this aim should be achieved. On his return from Moscow, Modrow presented a long-term plan for German unification on 1 February: the "creation of a confederation between the GDR and the FRG with joint organs and institutions" that would lead to a federation based on a "unified constitution" and "military neutrality"; in other words the merger of two states on an equal footing.[49] No doubt under normal circumstances this proposal would have made perfect sense. However, it did not address the impending collapse of the GDR, which required a kind of crisis management. Therefore Modrow agreed to form a "government of national responsibility" by appointing eight members of the Round Table as ministers without portfolio and by bringing forward the elections scheduled for 6 May to 18 March. He may have banked on a left-wing majority in the *Volkskammer* consisting of a revamped SED – now PDS – and the SDP, which now called itself SPD after having been adopted at long last by its West German sister party. A forecast in early February among 1,500 citizens suggested a majority for the SPD of 53 per cent (PDS 12 per cent). In that case, and provided the GDR did not collapse in the meantime, German unification would be realised over a period of five to ten years and on the basis of a new constitution according to the GG (Basic Law) § 146.

Kohl and the Chancellery's "Committee on German Unity", set up around the same time, were surprised by the announcement of early elections but not unprepared. After the visit to Dresden, and in view of the ongoing exodus, they had come to the conclusion that a change of strategy was required. To achieve a fast-track solution the GDR should be invited to join the Federal Republic according to GG § 23, which provided for simple accession, as happened in 1956 with the Saarland. This approach commended itself for various reasons: the Basic Law and thus the constitutional and legal foundations of the Federal Republic would remain intact as most West Germans wanted; by adopting the administrative, economic and social structure of the Federal Republic as the German "Kernstaat" (core-state) unification could be facilitated and consequently expedited. It was important, however, that people in the streets of East Germany, and not Kohl, would appear to be the driving force.[50] Therefore the idea had to be sold to those leaders in the GDR who were seen to be in sympathy with the West German CDU, to favour a kind of fast fusion and to express the *volonté générale* of the people.

It was only at the end of January that Kohl first met the leaders of the conservative parties who by now were in favour of German unification without ifs and buts: Lothar de Maiziere of the CDU, Wolfgang Schnur of *Demokratischer Aufbruch* and pastor Hans-Wilhelm Ebeling of *Deutsche Soziale Union*, which had been fathered by the Bavarian CSU. The East German Christian Democrats (CDU), in the past one of the bloc parties dominated by the SED, shared only its name with the West German sister party. But – and this was now a crucial consideration – it was the only partner that disposed of a network of offices and loyal party workers throughout the country. Moreover, to Protestant politicians within the West German CDU like Wolfgang Schäuble, it was important that the East German CDU maintained its links with the Church and could thus contribute to a more balanced relationship between the Catholic and Protestant membership within a future all-German CDU. Schäuble tells us, too, that the inner circle at the Chancellery was fully aware of the uphill struggle against the SPD in the forthcoming elections. Allusions were made to Churchill who had won the war only to loose the elections.[51] With Kohl's prompting the three parties formed the "Alliance for Germany" in West Berlin less than a week later. Lothar de Maiziere was no easy man to deal with. When he was put in charge of the party in November, he had given the West German tabloid *Bild am Sonntag* an interview defending "democratic socialism" and declaring, ten days after the fall of the Wall, that unification was "not the order of the day" but "a matter for our children or grand-children". Teltschik had entered in his diary: "This interview fuelled our suspicion about de Maiziere".[52] And now, even though associated with the Chancellor and his party, he could not resist Modrow's invitation to join the "government of national responsibility": it was less opportunism than a sense of wishing to please everyone for the sake of the country. Kohl made no bones in his memoirs that he disapproved of de Maiziere's decision to enter the government in view of a hopeless economic situation and forthcoming elections.[53]

Many of the human rights activists at the Round Table, most of them intellectuals with a penchant for wishful thinking, still believed the political system could be reformed once the SED had been deposed. Kohl and his advisers had a more realistic notion of what was required. Their intention was not to stabilise the existing order but to prevent further chaos. The growing disarray due to mass migration could not be overcome, at least not in the short run, by a "treaty of cooperation" between the two states coupled with the distant prospect of unification. In anticipation of a forthcoming cap-in-hand visit by Modrow and his new coalition partners, they considered the possibility of a monetary and economic union in the near future:[54] that would provide East Germans with the cherished Deutschmark and should persuade them to stay instead of trying to make their fortune in the West and thus strain the latter's resources. This was a proposal of unification in all but name. Since it entailed many risks it was not uncontroversial among Kohl's advisers. Conventional wisdom suggested that a currency union only made sense once the GDR economy had caught up with the West. That was the view of the government's panel of economic advisers who predicted many of the problems that would indeed emerge in the aftermath of unification.[55] However, people in the East had no patience to put up with such a long-term process: they wanted quick results. A linkage of both currencies as proposed by the SPD would, so Kohl was told by his advisers, endanger the stability of the Deutschmark. Monetary union seemed to be the only, if risky, solution that would satisfy ordinary citizens even though it meant a substantial loss of sovereignty for the GDR government. The latter would have to open its books, as it were, to the West German receiver. When Modrow arrived in Bonn on 13 February he hoped for a favourable reception in view of his more representative delegation from the Round Table. To no avail: Kohl was not prepared to subsidise the old government shortly before the elections by granting the DM 10–15 billion he was asked to fork out as a "solidarity contribution". His position had been greatly strengthened by Gorbachev's green light for unification, in principle, during his recent visit to Moscow. He told his guest that Bonn's projection of migrants for February amounted to 100,000: only a monetary and economic union – a plan to be discussed by a committee of experts – could now stop this haemorrhage which both countries could not sustain for any length of time. Modrow had no choice but to agree while Kohl tried to demonstrate his goodwill with a financial packet of DM 6 billion for immediate measures, to be raised through a supplementary budget. Apart from money for medium-sized private enterprises, the largest sums were to be allotted to fund travel expenses and medical provisions for GDR visitors.[56] In other words, the idea was to support the needs and entrepreneurial spirit of ordinary citizens not the government as such. No doubt, this was also Kohl's entrance ticket for a successful election campaign: he only had four weeks left in which to turn the tide of opinion polls, which suggested a clear victory for the SPD.

In retrospect, members of the Round Table blamed the "unwanted" intervention of Kohl and his party for their stunning defeat in the first free elections. However, it could as well be argued that the reactions of the various political parties to the proposal of monetary and economic union were a more decisive factor. Only the "Alliance for Germany", notably the East-German CDU, welcomed the idea with no further ado. Angela Merkel, spokeswoman of *Demokratischer Aufbruch*, said: "We see this as a step in the right direction".[57] Not so other parties and groups at the Round Table, which expressed reservations of one kind or another. Markus Meckel of the SPD complained that there had been no actual results accruing from the talks in Bonn, above all "no immediate aid could be expected in the coming days". In the eyes of *Demokratie Jetzt*, Kohl's proposal posed "a threat to the process of democratization and the right to self-determination of the people of the GDR". For the Green Party it was "clear that there will be no gradual growing-together of the two German states, but only unconditional annexation of the GDR by the FRG". Then and later this became a standard quotation by the opponents of unification who would not admit to themselves that the take-over of a bankrupt state was a costly business, costlier than any capitalist venture of that kind. All their spokesmen complained that the issue of European security had not been addressed. Since many civil rights activists had experienced their formative years in the peace movement they could not imagine a united Germany as a part of NATO: Germany had to be a neutral and, if possible, a demilitarised state, in short a lighthouse of peace for the rest of the world. Ordinary people realised that this question, which would best be left to the Four Powers, could be an impediment to speedy unification. With the approach of the elections, the Round Table lost touch with the electorate and thus proved that it lacked the know-how of professional politics. As late as 20 February it resolved that "a future Germany's membership in NATO is in conflict with the aim of German unity within the framework of a peaceful European order and is therefore rejected on principle". And so was "annexation of the GDR or individual states to the Federal Republic under article 23 through an extension of the territory".[58] It was the clearest indication yet that those who had helped to bring about the revolution now rejected its popular consequences. The leaders of the SPD, many of them young clergymen like Markus Meckel, favoured taking up this stance on principle which expressed their sense of responsibility. The holy spirit was more important than the general feeling in the country: in a democracy – and the GDR was facing its first democratic elections ever – this attitude was a recipe for disaster. Christof Geisel has aptly characterised the former opposition to the régime as "the last strong-hold of GDR patriotism" and the finale as "the short path from illegality to marginality".[59]

The "Alliance for Germany" avoided all such pitfalls even though it still had misgivings about German membership in NATO, not so much on prin-ciple but because it would not be swallowed by Moscow and thus would delay unification. On the whole, however, the Alliance presented itself as their master's, i.e. the Federal Chancellor's voice, and proclaimed only one message in a variety of different slogans: "Germany Comes", "Freedom and Prosperity for all" (slogan of the CDU in the 1950s), "A United Germany Must Not Be Neutral", "Currency Union only together with Social Market Economy", "Our Motto is: National Solidarity" and so forth. Leaflets in the layout of West German tabloids carried only shots of Kohl (together with Gorbachev; with Bush; in front of the Brandenburg Gate, and cheered in Dresden), not a single picture of one of the Alliance's leaders. Since the opposition liked to expose the Federal Republic as the uncaring capitalist state the Alliance pledged their word that no one in need had to fear a reduction of social benefits. Then there was the reminder that, under the leadership of the CDU, West Germany had shown the way after 1945, had demonstrated how a country could be rebuilt from scratch through hard work and initiative. This was exactly what people wanted to hear, to believe and to vote for: a better life and no further messing about. The result of the elections on 18 March 1990 was a landslide victory for the Alliance, especially for the CDU: Alliance 48.15 per cent (CDU 40.91 per cent) as against 21.84 per cent for the SPD, the predicted front runner.[60] Nobody denied that it was a vote for speedy unification beginning with monetary and economic union. It was understood throughout the world that this about-turn of all predictions was Kohl's personal achievement. Even Rudolf Augstein, editor of *Der Spiegel* and long-term critic of the Chancellor, said so but could not help putting it in this way: "It was above all his very personal success – the citizen of the GDR wanted the great fat man as the guarantor of the prosperity miracle".[61] Never mind that Churchill, in his year of triumph, could not be described as slim or slender either. Augstein's condescending attitude was, it is sad to say, not uncommon among the educated middle classes in West Germany. It was an indication that 40 years of separation had produced different mentalities that were not easy to overcome.

The outcome of the elections on 18 March was not only the result of an aggressive PR strategy on the part of the Alliance and their West German partners. In equal measure it was due to the fact that the SPD in East and West did not see which way the wind was blowing. The party had become a victim of political correctness. Before 1933 Saxony and Thuringia had been the birthplace of German industrialisation and the cradle of Social Democracy. In the late 1940s and 1950s the West German SPD (eclipsed in the GDR) had been the champion of national unity and as such in opposition to Chancellor Adenauer who was accused of letting the East Germans down. All these credentials were wasted within a few months. How could that have happened? The failure of the party at this crucial juncture in German history has now been studied in depth by a young German historian who gave his book the telling title: "*Uneinig in die Einheit*" (*Disunited into Unity*).[62] To understand why the party did badly in the elections one has to consider the long-term impact of *Ostpolitik* on the SPD's notion of détente. For the architects of *Ostpolitik*, like Egon Bahr, who saw himself as a German Kissinger, the German Question was a matter of Realpolitik and nothing else: how to foster détente while guaranteeing international stability. It could only be solved by dealing and deals with the governments in power; rebellious dissidents or worse, demonstrators, i.e. potential mob violence, would only jeopardise international security which was of overriding importance.[63] In the 1980s the SPD tried to soften the ground further by establishing contacts with the SED which meant to keep aloof from all "trouble-makers", such as the small and apparently irrelevant circles of human right activists. For the SPD leadership under Oskar Lafontaine and Hans-Jochen Vogel, including former chancellors Willy Brandt and Helmut

Schmidt, this was the guideline to which they stuck up to and beyond the last moment. The news about the foundation of an Eastern SPD, set up by malcontents among the Church's pastors, was an unwelcome surprise. During the first months, the founding fathers, or rather youngsters, tried to keep a distance from their elders in the West whose record of collaboration with the SED was no recommendation: quite deliberately they chose a different name (SDP instead of SPD). However, with the approach of the elections and the need for help they made their peace with the established sister-party. On 13 December a joint committee of the two parties had been set up; a month later at their party congress in Berlin the SDP reinvented itself by adopting the name SPD. In a sense it was a fateful decision because from now on they were identified with the opponents of Chancellor Kohl, especially with Lafontaine, the SPD's candidate for his office, and Werner Momper, Governing Mayor of West Berlin who would have nothing to do with the SPD in the other half of the city. Lafontaine was no friend of a speedy currency union, which would only be a change for the worse by exposing the economy to Western capitalism. Nor did he declare himself in favour of outright unification: nobody could be in doubt, listening to his speeches, that the Prime Minister of the Saarland cared more about European unity than about German unification. To make things worse: in Ibrahim Böhme the SPD chose as their candidate a "sunny boy" with no professional standing or political convictions. At their party congress in Leipzig in late February he pleaded in all seriousness for a reconciliation with the SED, a party of which he had been a past member, as he admitted. He was a charismatic communicator and for a while the darling of the Western media before he was exposed, though after the elections, as a Stasi informer. Western politicians like Norbert Gansel, Erhard Eppler and Johannes Rau, Prime Minister of Northrhine-Westphalia, who were close to the grassroots and were better informed about the real situation thanks to many private contacts in the GDR, especially within the network of the Protestant Church, could not make up for those who were seen to represent the SPD at the top. Not even the popular Willy Brandt on the campaign trail would be able to reverse the trend. He was too statesman-like and rejected accession according to article 23 because it would give East Germans and Germany's allies no say in the matter. In conclusion: for the loss of the elections the SPD had only itself to blame for its lack of empathy with the concerns of ordinary citizens. Ever since Brandt's famous words on 10 November, a day after the Wall had been breached, "*Jetzt wächst zusammen, was zusammengehört*" (What belongs together will now grow together)[64] had to compensate for the sad record of his party.

Notes and references

1 His prognosis in April 1989 was met with polite chuckles by German officials, Vernon A. Walters, *Die Vereinigung war voraussehbar: Hinter den Kulissen eines entscheidenden Jahres* (Berlin, 1994), p. 27.

2 See Jens Hacker, *Deutsche Irrtümer. Schönfärber und Helfershelfer der SED-Diktatur im Westen* (Berlin, 1992), pp. 352–82 and pp. 422–36.

3 Wolfgang J. Mommsen, "Wandlungen der nationalen Identität der Deutschen" (1983), in *Nation und Geschichte* (Munich, 1990), p. 76.

4 Joachim Fest, "Von der Unverlorenheit der deutschen Frage", *Frankfurter Allgemeine Zeitung*, 28.9.1982. Fest had not studied history but written by far the best biography of Hitler, at a time when biographies were out of fashion among the German academic community.

5 Quoted by Philip Zelikow and Condoleezza Rice, *Germany Unified and Europe Transformed* (Cambridge MA, 1995), p. 34.

6 Helmut Kohl, *Erinnerungen 1982–1990* (Munich, 2005), vol. 1, p. 889.

7 Klaus Schroeder, *Der SED-Staat. Partei, Staat und Gesellschaft 1949–1990* (Munich, 2000), p. 277. Between 1984 and 1988 the annual number of legitimate migrants amounted to 40,000.

8 See Andreas Grünberg, *"Wir sind das Volk". Der Weg der DDR zur deutschen Einheit* (Stuttgart, 1990), p. 21. This is a very useful booklet for pupils. See the best account and interpretation of events in English. Konrad Jarauch, *The Rush to German Unity* (Oxford, 1994).

9 Reaction of the Politburo to the crisis, Günter Schabowski, *Das Politbüro. Ende eines Mythos* (Hamburg, 1991), pp. 50–70.

10 Interview with *Süddeutsche Zeitung*, 19–20.5.2007.

11 *The Times*, 28.8.1989. See also Lothar Kettenacker, "Britain and German Unification", in Klaus Larres (ed.), *Uneasy Allies. British–German Relations and European Integration since 1945* (Oxford, 2000), pp. 99–123.

12 Richard Kissler and Frank Elbe, *Ein runder Tisch mit scharfen Ecken. Der diplomatische Weg zur deutschen Einheit* (Baden-Baden, 1993), pp. 28–44. Frank Elbe was head of Genscher's office. See also Dietrich Genscher, *Erinnerungen* (Berlin, 1995). In 2007 German TV produced a "docu-drama" on this episode.

12a Not mentioned in his recently published memoirs which contains only a superficial account (17 pages out of 400) on German unification. Eduard Schewardnadse, *Als de Eiserne Vorhang zerriss – Begegnungen und Erinnerungen* (Drisburg, 2007).

13 *Guardian*, 22.8.1989.

14 Gerhard Rein (ed.), *Die Opposition in der DDR. Entwürfe für einen anderen Sozialismus* (Berlin, 1989), pp. 13–15. For the opposition in 1989/90 see also

1. EKB, vol. VII/1and 2, esp. Rainer Eckert, "Die revolutionäre Krise am Ende der achtziger Jahre und die Formierung der Opposition" (pp. 667–757) with a most extensive bibliography at the end. He analyses all groups and parties.

15 Documents in Rein, pp. 84–104. The first move had been made as early as 24.7.1989.

16 For the precise course of events, see the account of the Leipzig historian Hartmut Zwahr, *Ende einer Selbstzerstörung. Leipzig und die Revolution in der DDR* (Göttingen, 1993), pp. 79–102.

17 See Schabowski, pp. 71–112. See also the interview with Erich Honecker after his fall, Reinholt Andert and Wolfgang Herzberg, *Der Sturz. Erich Honecker im Kreuzverhör* (Berlin, 1991). For Honecker the real culprit was Gorbachev.

18 Wolfgang Schneider (ed.), *Leipziger Demontagebuch* (Leipzig, Weimar, 1990), p. 60. These photos represent by far the most authentic portrayal of the autumn revolution. Therefore plenty of use has been made of them in this account.

19 Grünberg, p. 41. In English, "Hey Krenz, you merry old warrior / I don't believe a word you say / You cheered the tanks in Beijing / You showed your teeth during mass murder / And your false laugh. Franz Cremer [= East German sculptor] / Moulds you into a monument of hypocrisy / You are the Stasi metastasis / In the sick body of our state party".

20 Ibid., p. 39 and weekly chronicles in Schneider (ed.), Demontagebuch.

21 Schabowski, p. 113.

22 Konrad H. Jarausch and Volker Gransow (eds), *Uniting Germany. Documents and Debates, 1944–1993* (Oxford, 1994), p. 70.

23 Ibid., pp. 70–73, "loud applause", it says in brackets.

24 Schneider (ed.), *Demontagebuch*, p. 90.

25 Hans-Hermann Hertle *et al.* (eds), *Das Ende der SED. Die letzten Tage des Zentralkomitees* (Berlin, 1997).

26 Schabowski, p. 137. According to William R. Smyser, *From Yalta to Berlin. The Cold War Struggle over Germany* (Berlin, 1999), p. 342. Krenz said literally, "Das wird ein Knüller für uns" ("that'll be a real hit for us").

27 See Smyser, pp. 340–46.

28 Jürgen Habermas, philosopher of the Frankfurt school, later accused the East Germans of "DM nationalism": "Yet again, German Identity – A Unified Nation of Angry DM-Burghers", in Harold James and Marla Stone (eds), *When the Wall Came Down. Reactions to German Unification* (London, 1992), pp. 86–102.

29 See Schneider (ed.), *Demontagebuch*.

30 See the Appeal "For Our Country", 26.11.1989, by leading East German intellectuals, reform communists and dissidents: Jarausch/Gransow (eds), p. 85. They received support from certain West German intellectuals such as the SPD Governing Mayor of West Berlin, Walter Momper (Daniel Friedrich Sturm,

Uneinig in die Einheit. Die Sozialdemokratie und die Vereinigung Deutschlands 1989/90, Bonn/2006, passim).

31 Schneider (ed.), *Demontagebuch*, p. 176.

32 See official minutes in: Hanns Jürgen Küsters and Daniel Hofmann (eds), *Dokumente zur Deutschlandpolitik. Deutsche Einheit. Sonderedition aus den Akten des Bundeskanzleramtes* (Munich, 1998), pp. 513–15 (from now on: *Deutsche Einheit*). It was the second exchange between the two leaders. See also Kohl, vol. 1, pp. 951–53.

33 Jarausch and Gransow (eds), p. 83.

34 *Deutsche Einheit*, p. 58 (translation L.K.).

35 Schneider (ed.), *Demontagebuch*, p. 118.

36 Grünberg, p. 81.

37 Jarausch and Gransow (eds), p. 90.

38 Dirk Philipsen, *We are the People. Voices From East Germany's Revolutionary Autumn of 1989* (Durham, NC, 1993), p. 143. This volume contains first class source material in English for students of this period.

39 See Schroeder, pp. 335–44.

40 Helmut Herles and Stefan Rose (eds), *Parlaments-Szenen einer deutschen Revolution: Bundestag und Volkskammer im November 1989* (Bonn, 1989), p. 193. As to the Stasi and its last stand, see Armin Mitter and Stefan Wolle (eds), *Ich liebe euch doch alle! Befehle und Lageberichte des MfS. Januar bis November 1989* (Berlin, 1990).

41 This apt expression was first used by Timothy Garton Ash in a British newspaper.

42 *Der Spiegel*, 1989/47 ("Pleite der Marx-Wirtschaft") , quoted by Grünberg, p. 67 (translation L.K.).

43 See n. 26.

44 See chapter 6.

45 Kohl, vol. 1, p. 1020.

46 Horst Teltschik, *329 Tage. Innenansichten der Einigung* (Berlin, 1991), p. 90. The diaries of Horst Teltschik, the foreign policy adviser of the Chancellor, are perhaps the most important source for the unification process.

47 Jarausch and Gransow (eds), p. 96.

48 See e.g. the memo by Peter Hartmann who advocated a fast-moving development, 29.1.1990, in *Deutsche Einheit*, pp. 727–35.

49 Jarausch and Gransow (eds), p. 105 f.

50 This is what Kohl said to his Home Secretary in January 1990: Wolfgang Schäuble, *Der Vertrag. Wie ich über die Einheit verhandelte* (Stuttgart, 1991), pp. 20–21.

51 See ibid., p. 24.

52 Teltschik, p. 39.

53 Kohl, vol. 1, p. 1045.

54 See introduction, a summary of the decision-making process in the Chancellery, *Deutsche Einheit*, pp. 84–96.

55 See Dieter Grosser, *Das Wagnis der Währungs- , Wirtschafts- und Sozialunion. Politische Zwänge im Konflikt mit ökonomischen Regeln* (Stuttgart, 1998), pp. 189–97.

56 Nachtrag zum Bundeshaushalt, 7.2.1990, in *Deutsche Einheit*, pp. 766–70.

57 East German reactions to Bonn's offer, 13 Febraury 1990, in Jarausch and Gransow (eds), pp. 112–114. See also Grosser, pp. 198–204.

58 Ibid., p. 117.

59 Christof Geisel, *Auf der Suche nach einem Dritten Weg. Das politische Selbstverständnis der DDR-Oppositionin den 80er Jahren* (Berlin, 2005), pp. 139–62.

60 For the election campaign and the result, Grünberg, pp. 109–32 (with a lot of visual material). See also Jarausch, pp. 181–97.

61 *Der Spiegel*, 1990/12 ("Kohl's Triumph"); quoted by Grünberg, p. 124 (translation, including all slogans, L.K.)

62 Daniel Friedrich Sturm, *Uneinig in die Einheit. Die Sozialdemokratie und die Vereinigung Deutschlands 1989/90* (Bonn, 2006). The following is a summary of his research.

63 See Andreas Vogtmeier, *Egon Bahr und die deutsche Frage* (Bonn, 1996), pp. 333–78.

64 Sturm, p. 208.

CHAPTER 6

The Diplomatic Process

The East-German *Volksdemokratie* was brought down by its own people who did not want to be dictated to any longer, by ordinary citizens who either turned their backs on the GDR or demonstrated in the streets of Leipzig expressing their desire to be again *ein Volk*. However, the German Question was not for the Germans to determine alone, as they had in 1871. The Four Powers who had accepted unconditional surrender of the Third Reich in 1945 were, according to international law, responsible for Germany as a whole and still exercised, at least in theory, supreme power in its former capital. The diplomatic process was positively influenced by a strange phenomenon of which historians are seldom aware: the international community found the division of Germany, enforced by a concrete wall across its capital, more incomprehensible, more absurd, than most West Germans who after 40 years got used to this unnatural state of affairs. On the occasion of a German general visiting Washington in early 1989, Rozanne Ridgway, assistant Secretary of State, remarked to a colleague that unification was "the subject that all Americans are interested in and no German cares about".[1] However, it is also true to say that Germans abroad wished to convey the impression that they had learnt their lesson and did not nourish unrealistic hopes. The West Germans were not pressing the issue since they knew that it was a matter of international law as well as of international understanding. No one knew this better than Helmut Kohl who was both a politician and a historian by profession. It was his good fortune that it was the *Bundeskanzleramt* (Chancellery) and not the *Auswärtige Amt* (Foreign Office) under Hans-Dietrich Genscher that was in charge of German affairs as a result of the Basic Treaty of 1972.[2] For the GDR, West Germany was a foreign country and thus the domain of its Ministry of Foreign Affairs. Both Hans-Dietrich Genscher and Markus Meckel, foreign minister during the final phase of negotiations, were East Germans and as such inclined not to insist on conditions that might have endangered eventual unification. For the Chancellor, however, who more than any of his predecessors felt committed to the legacy of Konrad Adenauer,[3] the long-term security of Germany, above all its being firmly embedded in the Atlantic Alliance and the European Community, was more important than speedy unification. Again and again he reiterated his position in his talks with President George Bush and other NATO partners: German unification was the order of the day, but not at any price. It was this crucial understanding that explains the unremitting support he received from the Americans who in turn persuaded the British and French to go along with what in their eyes was a deeply worrying prospect. There was another guiding principle that determined the Chancellor's approach to the final settlement of the German Question. That was to keep negotiations strictly within limits, i.e. within the realm of the Four Powers who were responsible for Germany as a whole. In other words, he wanted to avoid having to negotiate a peace treaty with all the CSCE members, 45 years after the Second World War. On this point, too, Kohl enjoyed the full backing of the White House.

For the sake of his narrative the historian has to pursue one development at a time, even though he is fully aware that other currents have a bearing on his story. Obviously, the rapidly deteriorating situation in the GDR coupled with the incessant mass exodus of its people provided the decisive impetus to the progress of negotiations. However, once the prospect of German unification had been firmly placed on the international agenda it generated a momentum of its own.

The first sentence of an important work on the origins of German unification mark I reads: "At the beginning there was Napoleon".[4] In order to explain the course of events leading to German unification mark II it would be equally justified to write: "At the beginning there was Gorbachev". It is a characteristic feature of German history that at almost every crucial juncture it has been shaped by foreign influences. This is true of Germany's territorial status, in particular, and may have to be explained by its geographical position in the very midst of Europe. In terms of modern historiography giving credit to a single person for achieving a historical breakthrough may seem a little old-fashioned. But so was the final settlement of the German Question, which was a left-over from the Cold War period, if not from the nineteenth century. Gorbachev's "new thinking", inspired by his quest for "glasnost" and "perestroika", implied reforms both in the domestic and foreign policy arena that were dictated by the economic burden of the armament race. Here he had come to an understanding with

US President Reagan which signalled the end of the Cold War. The phrase he used to describe his new ambitions in foreign policy was the need to create "a common European house". Both Moscow and Washington knew that the gulf dividing Europe was nowhere more glaring than on German soil.

When Chancellor Kohl visited Moscow in late 1988, nobody was thinking of German unification in territorial terms. Kohl wanted to preserve the "substance of the nation".[5] If the *Staatsnation* had been broken up, then the *Kulturnation* was still worth maintaining. This concept, in many ways reminiscent of the period before 1871, may have been disputed by the SED in their nation-building effort, but it did not threaten the GDR and was therefore compatible with Gorbachev's vision of "a common European house". Horst Teltschik, Kohl's influential foreign policy adviser, later confirmed that by not questioning the territorial existence of the GDR, the Chancellery hoped the SED might be persuaded to launch a process of reforms, not unlike those in Poland and Hungary.[6] The government's position had been formulated by President Richard von Weizsäcker in 1985 in this way: "The subject of unity confronting us today primarily relates to the whole of Europe. It no longer revolves around national frontiers and territories. It is not a matter of shifting frontiers, but of depriving them of their divisive impact on people".[7] For Kohl it seemed to be obvious that the German Question could only be solved within the context of an undivided Europe. If he insisted on the right of self-determination, as laid down in the Helsinki Final Act, he now accepted that it was up to the East Germans to decide their own future and that Bonn had to accept their vote. This was the essence of *Ostpolitik* brought up to date. This was also the basis of a common understanding between Bonn and Moscow. After all, Gorbachev had no intention of abolishing the GDR or the Soviet Union, for that matter, when he demanded a renewal of socialism. Self-determination in his view did not necessarily imply a vote for unification with the capitalist West. His diplomats knew that East German dissidents, who put great store on his reforms, had no such plans. However, reforms in the Eastern bloc could no longer be dictated by the Kremlin. Nor did Gorbachev wish to do so. In fact he had abandoned the ominous Breshnev doctrine that had served to justify the invasion of Czechoslovakia in spring 1968 in order to quell Prague's fight for freedom. Moscow had signed the Helsinki Agreement which committed all members to refrain from the threat or use of force in relations with other countries whatever their political system. From 1988 onwards he kept dropping hints that he was no longer prepared to interfere in the domestic affairs of other Warsaw Pact countries. In his speech to the Council of Europe in July 1989 he defined his idea of the "common European home" by saying that the social and political order of European countries was "entirely a matter for the people themselves and their choosing".[8] It was an unmistakable invitation to his Warsaw Pact partners to put their houses in order and not to expect to be kept in power by the Red Army. However, Honecker and his old guard misread the signals: while Gorbachev meant to encourage reforms that he judged to be vital for the survival of the GDR, they felt that they were now free to steer their own course. In fact, the more they emancipated themselves from Moscow, the closer the abyss of their eventual fate. Nevertheless, they tacitly assumed that the Soviet leader would not dare to leave them in the lurch during any crisis that would endanger the very existence of the GDR as a socialist German state.[9] Only a few months before his fall Honecker believed that he was master in his own house, threatened neither from foes nor friends. There is no doubt that a sense of false security on the part of the East German leadership was one of the most important contributing factors in the process of German unification. For any signs of potential danger the SED Politburo looked to Bonn and Moscow, but never to their own folk. The human rights activists appeared to be a negligible minority with no support from abroad and little at home, the masses being docile sheep pressed into many flocks[10] and kept in check by the watchful eye of the Stasi. After all people ought to have learnt the painful lessons of East Berlin (1953), Budapest (1956) and Prague (1968), which had demonstrated what would happen should they dare defy the authorities.

The story of what actually happened in the summer and autumn of 1989 has been told in the previous chapter. Governments in both parts of Germany were totally unprepared to handle the diplomatic fallout of these events. Yet it was this very numbness and inactivity on both sides that accelerated the disintegration of the GDR. With Honecker in hospital and Bonn's political establishment on summer leave, the historical current of events gained a momentum of its own. The exodus of refugees via Hungary and Czechoslovakia grew into a stampede followed by Monday demonstrations in Leipzig and the explosion of independent political groups which demanded an end to one-party rule. Kohl's initial restraint for fear of a backlash, his anxious refusal to exploit the situation, helped convince the international community that they were witnessing a genuine movement for democracy. However, at the same time it dawned upon the governments of the Four Powers responsible for the German Question that they could not remain passive while events with such potentially far-reaching consequences were unfolding.

Fortunately for Germany, the US government, which was furthest away from the field, had been the first to grasp the overall significance of the development in central Europe. With the approaching end of the Cold War, they reasoned, the German Question was bound to rear its head once again, because the post-war division of Europe and the division of Germany were inseparable matters. The only bone of contention between Washington and Bonn had been the modernisation of short-range nuclear missiles. When that issue had been buried at the NATO summit in May 1989 in favour of negotiations on conventional arms control, the President's political standing in Europe had improved considerably and he was now in a position to tackle the German Question. After all, an enlarged Germany would still be no larger than the US state of Montana,[11] thus there was no reason to become unduly concerned about it, so long, and this was the crux, as the country remained within the Western orbit. In his seminal speech at Mainz during his visit to Germany in late May 1989, President Bush elaborated on Gorbachev's rhetoric and said that "there cannot be a common European home until all within it are free to move from room to room". His most resounding and much quoted demands were "Let Europe be whole and free" and "Let Berlin be next".[12]

Only a couple of weeks later Gorbachev arrived in West Germany, surprised at the enthusiastic welcome by the German population wherever he appeared. Yet the ground was well prepared. He let it be known that 1,000 tanks were to leave East Germany by the end of 1990. Shortly afterwards he announced the unilateral reduction of 500 short-range nuclear warheads, coupled with an offer to talk on radically reducing conventional weapons. On the eve of his visit, some of his advisers were quoted in the British press as saying that they would not rule out German unification provided certain conditions were met.[13] Ordinary Germans sensed that the Soviet leader embodied the hope that, with the end of the Cold War in sight, the division of both Europe and Germany would soon end. As, indeed, did Chancellor Kohl, who managed to establish a personal relationship with his guest through a *tête-à-tête* at midnight on the banks of the River Rhine, which served as a reminder of the current of history and the inevitability of German unification.[14] Gorbachev lived up to the occasion when he endorsed, once again and this time in a joint declaration with Kohl, the principle of self-determination and the right of all nations to choose their own political system. The German Question was for Clio to decide. "I think everything is possible", he said, but "time itself must deal with it."[15] His tour of the country and its places of technological excellence convinced him that closer economic co-operation with the Federal Republic was more advantageous to the Soviet Union than its ideological ties with the GDR. According to the official history of German unification the visit marked "a turning point in German–Soviet relations".[16]

The swelling exodus of young East Germans during the holiday season via Hungary, Poland and Czechoslovakia called for action by West German diplomats. These refugees, often young families, were stuck in West German embassies in East Berlin, Prague, Warsaw and Budapest and demanded safe conduct to the Federal Republic.[17] Yet at the time hardly anybody anticipated that this kind of haemorrhage would prove terminal for the GDR. Bonn's attitude to the refugee crisis is succinctly summarised by Zelikow and Rice: "Reform in the GDR was the goal; unification was still a mirage."[18] Repercussions were more far-reaching at home than in the international arena because SED and the government remained unresponsive: they felt, so to speak, no need to call the ambulance. The régime's blatant loss of authority empowered those who had wished to express their pent-up frustrations for some time. They started filling the streets of Leipzig every Monday in ever growing numbers.

It was the fall of Honecker[19] on 17 October, and the hectic damage-limitation exercises of his successor that seemed to put the German Question "back on the international agenda". Soon this phrase was to become highly controversial. Kohl had used the phrase on 22 August, while Genscher tried to dampen public speculation about unification and stick to the course of urging reforms. What was at stake, Western governments kept saying, was the liberalisation of the GDR according to the demands of the East German human rights activists. This was also the position of the British Foreign Office which, at that time, hoped and worked for an "Austrian solution" without running the risk of alienating the Germans by openly discouraging reunification: a separate state, democratic but independent.[20] On the whole, the British press seemed to be less troubled about the prospect of German unification. When several British journalists were invited to address an audience of 200 VIPs in Bonn on the German Question they were almost amused to find that the Germans seemed "somewhat taken aback that instead of expressing angst, we each of us, in our different ways looked forward to a united Germany".[21] The standard phrase they encountered in their conversations with German officials and journalists was that unification "won't happen in our lifetime". Two weeks before the Wall came down unification was still a taboo in German diplomatic circles. Instead, Hans-Dietrich Genscher propagated his idea of a confederation, subsumed in some pan-European order.[22] Willy Brandt went even further in his denial of unification when he met Gorbachev in October 1989: "Reunification means a return to the past which is both impossible and undesirable."[23] For independent minds abroad, not shackled by official briefings, the merger of the two German states, kept apart during the Cold War, appeared much more natural than for the over-anxious Germans themselves who had fully internalised what they assumed to be widespread foreign fears of another *quasi*-nuclear fusion in the midst of Europe. And it is not that they were wrong: wherever Gorbachev turned up in Western Europe politicians secretly beseeched him to stop the train careering towards unification.[24] However, this advice proved to be counter-productive because the Soviet leader gained the impression that he was expected to play the villain of the piece and thus compromise his relations with the FRG.

The political takeover by Egon Krenz, once nominated by Honecker as his successor, did not have the hoped-for effect of calming down the widespread unrest in East Germany. Krenz reassured Gorbachev, whose backing he had sought before the coup, that he would hasten to introduce far-reaching reforms, above all the lifting of travel restrictions. Demonstrations would remain peaceful but the police would keep a watchful eye on Berlin and make sure there was no mass rush to the Wall. Western Allies were increasingly apprehensive about a revolutionary upheaval in the GDR. The "official mind" now advocated a reformed East German state as demanded by the new democratic groups springing up in East Germany: it was the common platform on which Britain, France, Italy and the United States could agree, and it seemed to be the only way to restore stability. To coordinate policy among allies and maintain security is, after all, the standard approach of foreign offices to any crisis. James Baker, the US Secretary of State, in an attempt to reassure Moscow and to appease London and Paris, now preferred to speak of "reconciliation" between the two German states rather than of "reunification", assuming that the GDR would survive as a separate state after the removal of the Communist system. His speech was the result of a controversy within the State Department between the policy planning staff, which pleaded for the retention of *Ostpolitik*, and the European bureau's recommendation to go along with the Chancellor's change of track, as urged by the US embassy in Bonn.[25] The three Western ambassadors in Bonn did not believe that Krenz would be able to master the situation when they met with Rudolf Seiters, head of the Chancellery, who openly admitted that with each step towards freedom in the GDR, the division of Germany became less tenable.[26] Throughout October, the rapport between President Bush and Chancellor Kohl grew closer and developed into an explicit policy of unification. After a crucial phone call from the Chancellor protesting at widespread stories about reunification leading to a neutralist Germany, Bush went out of his way to say in an interview with the *New York Times* that: "I do not share the concern that some European countries have about a reunited Germany".[27] He emphasised his belief in Germany's commitment to and recognition of the Alliance and reassured his allies that a consensual solution to the German problem would be found. From that day on Washington's position was clear to everybody inside and outside the administration. None of the major Allies would now openly oppose the eventual goal of unification, only the approach was still up for debate.

Europe's unease about the prospect of a united Germany in the midst of Europe did, of course, not vanish overnight. It was most candidly voiced by former Prime Minister Edward Heath who commented that "naturally we expressed our support of German reunification, because we knew it would never happen".[28] At a dinner in Paris after the fall of the Wall Margaret Thatcher, the Prime Minister, gave Kohl more or less the same message when he dared to remind her of NATO's support for reunification in 1970.[29] She tried desperately to slow down the "German juggernaut" by wooing Gorbachev and hoping to revive the *entente cordiale* with France. She actually posed as Gorbachev's defence council in the Western world arguing that he could not sustain the loss of the GDR. Mitterand was more prudent, sympathising with her in private but not in public and thus earning the verdict in her memoirs of "a tendency to schizophrenia". When he observed that the Germans were a people in constant movement and flux she actually produced a map from her famous handbag "showing the various configurations of Germany in the past which were not altogether reassuring about the future". According to Jacques Attali, one of Mitterand's closest advisers, she pointed to Silesia, Pomerania, and East Prussia and said: "They'll take all that and Czechoslovakia". From her point of view a reunited Germany was "simply too big and powerful to be just another player within Europe" and that the country was "by its very nature a destabilising rather than a stabilising force in Europe".[30] However, to her chagrin, Mitterand adopted a more relaxed and philosophical attitude: further European integration rather than Palmerstonian Realpolitik seemed to be the best way to contain the new Germany which, not unlike Gorbachev, he left to history to evolve according to its natural pace. The influential *Economist* did not agree with this analysis and predicted: a stronger European Union would not restrain Germany but be dominated by it.[31] These were remnants of both wartime and Imperial thinking when Britain faced a hostile European continent and, to her constant surprise, still ruled faraway India. In a later telephone conversation with President Bush, Thatcher claimed in all seriousness that "the Germans would get in peace what Hitler could not get in the war".[32] Her prejudiced views on Germany were not shared by British historians who had studied recent German history and historiography: scholars such as Paul Kennedy and Hugh Trevor-Roper who pointed out that this time

Germany was being "united from below, not from above", by "peaceful pressure, not force of arms" and that "there was a fundamental change in the German mentality since 1945".[33] The problem was that British mentality, reinforced rather than traumatised by the war, had not been transformed to the same extent. The Foreign Office, meanwhile, was much more circumspect and deeply unhappy with Mrs Thatcher's ungracious and rather populist views on the German national character at a crucial juncture in Anglo–German relations. Later, during the only debate on this issue in Parliament, Douglas Hurd, the Foreign Secretary, claimed that the government was "glad that the years of painful division are coming to an end".[34] That was not the whole truth but a welcome relief from tensions that had been welling up between Bonn and London.

The situation inside the Kremlin was even more muddled than in the capitals of the West because there was agreement that reforms in the GDR were the only chance for it to survive; but there was no consensus whether or not to dictate what was to be done. Gorbachev and his foreign minister, Eduard Shevardnadze, clearly refused to apply old-style methods of coercion which many of their advisers felt were called for.[35] Moreover, Soviet officials were so accustomed, as one observer in their ranks put it, "to equating the 'will of the party' with the 'will of the people' that they could not adequately grasp the potential for the popular overthrow of a socialist government".[36]

And yet, carefully phrased statements and diplomatic niceties all went overboard thanks to the historical hurricane brewing up in the streets of East Germany. What was being projected into some distant future happened the next if not the same day. The fall of the Wall on 9 November 1989 caught everybody by surprise. The Federal Intelligence Service (*Bundesnachrichtendienst/BND*), placed under the Chancellery, did not predict it.[37] As an indicator of change the soothsayers, be they academic experts or secret agents, were focusing on the shifting power structure of the régime, rather than the mood of the people. In his state of the nation speech the previous day Kohl had addressed the refugee crisis by saying that the flight of these predominantly young fellow countrymen was "a vote with their feet" – by then a standard phrase in the West – "for freedom and democracy".[38] In fact, these people had wished to achieve unification on their own terms. In his talks with Lech Walesa the following day, on his state visit to Warsaw, the Chancellor tried to play down the crisis. The Polish trade union leader, more attuned to the voice and power of angry masses, was not convinced and argued that things could develop much faster than predicted. Only minutes after these talks Günter Schabowski, the new spokesman of the GDR government, faced the international press and, by referring to the immediate lifting of travel restrictions, dropped a bombshell of world historical dimensions. The Berlin Wall came tumbling down that very night.

What followed internally has been dealt with in the previous chapter. Here we have to concentrate on the diplomatic fallout that began with the difficult manoeuvre of interrupting a state visit the following day. The new Polish Prime Minister Tadeusz Masowiecki who pretended that nothing much had happened was not pleased. The plane of the Federal Air Force taking the Chancellor to Germany could not fly over the GDR nor land in Berlin according to international law. Flying via Sweden it landed in Hamburg where US Ambassador Vernon Walters provided a military aircraft to the German capital. Standing on the balustrade of Schöneberg townhall the same night amidst cheering crowds, Kohl received an urgent phone call from Gorbachev: could the Chancellor refrain from stirring up emotions and promise the prevention of chaos. What about reports that angry crowds were about to attack installations of the Red Army?[39] It was only later that Kohl learnt Gorbachev had been deliberately misinformed by opponents of his policy within the KGB and the Stasi who hoped to stage a military intervention. With another old-style leader at the helm of the Soviet Union they might have succeeded. Kohl gave his word that such anxieties were totally unjustified: the atmosphere was that of a family party, nobody was thinking of inciting people to a revolt against the Soviet Union. With such briefings Gorbachev let the GDR leadership know that this time, contrary to 17 June 1953, no Soviet tanks would intervene. The new would-be reformers were left to their own devices.

Kohl knew that henceforth he had to coordinate every further step with the Four Powers responsible for Germany as a whole. Immediately upon his return to Bonn, Kohl informed them of recent events and offered his assurances that he would work towards calming the situation.[40] Margaret Thatcher was most apprehensive and suggested a meeting of the heads of state and government of all 12 EC countries. Her approach seemed to be: self-determination without unification. Mitterrand's reaction was much more diplomatic and friendly. He fully understood that this was a historical moment for the German people. Gorbachev was most concerned about stability so that the new East German leadership would have a chance to bring about a thorough transformation of society. For them to succeed close cooperation between Bonn and Moscow was essential. Of course, he still hoped that speedy action would save the GDR whereas Kohl knew perfectly well that every ounce of freedom was likely to shift the balance in favour of unification. Unreserved, even enthusiastic congratulations came from President Bush and the Spanish Prime Minster Felipe Gonzáles.[41]

Only now that the Wall had fallen so suddenly did it dawn upon Bonn's political establishment that it had made no provisions for such circumstances. There were virtually no plans for dealing with imminent reunification of the two estranged partners. The truth is that all Federal governments since Brandt had sincerely embraced the implications of détente, which meant that they refrained from double-play, and from making secret plans for a takeover. "What governments and planning staffs do not anticipate they do not provide for", we are told by the authors of the official history of German unification. "Who knows which conditions would prevail in a certain situation?"[42] This state of affairs, one might say, of political innocence, is a crucial explanation for both the diplomatic success of the coming months and the mistakes made during the merger process in the years to come. This chapter is devoted to the success story. The Four Powers had all reason to believe that Bonn was as flabbergasted by what had happened as the rest of the world. The Chancellor now had to perform a difficult balancing act: not to alienate the Four Powers who urged him to stop the political rollercoaster and yet not to let down people in East Germany who had switched their slogans from "We are the people!" to "We are one people!" First he just waited for the East German government to move and initiate reforms while German diplomats tried to persuade their host countries that the division of Germany and that of Europe were interrelated and could only be overcome by one and the same process. This formula was sufficiently vague to satisfy everybody except the Russians. The Chancellor was tempted to go slow, to "sit it out", as he was always accused of doing by his opponents. However, on 21 November Horst Teltschik, his foreign policy adviser, was approached by Nikolai Portugalov, a staff member of the CPSU Central Committee concerned with Germany, who handed him a handwritten paper. Teltschik was "electrified", as he wrote in his memoirs, especially when he was told that Moscow was considering all possible options and was not averse to a confederation of the two states.[43] It was a wake-up call for Bonn, the realisation that the Soviet government was ahead in anticipating the "unthinkable". Now the Chancellor was told by his advisers that there was no time for procrastination. He had to come up with his own plan if he did not wish to risk others stealing his thunder.[44] This was the background to his "Ten Point Programme" which, after being drafted in utmost secrecy, he announced in the *Bundestag* on 28 November as part of his budget speech.[45] President Bush was the only person who was notified of the new concept in advance. The Chancellor did not even take his own foreign minister into his confidence even though Hans-Dietrich Genscher would soon have to bear the brunt of foreign reactions.[46] The plan was a kind of road map describing the gradual approach to the final goal: "treaty community" (*Vertragsgemeinschaft*) between the two German states via "confederative structures" to an eventual "federal system" for all Germany. Kohl stressed that this development had to be closely linked with further progress on the European Community, the CSCE process (Helsinki) which would weld the two parts of Europe together and rapid progress in arms control: in other words, German unification as a vehicle to overcome the division of Europe. For good reason, as it turned out, the Chancellor did not commit himself to a definite timetable within which to reach the final destination. What was of overall importance was that German unification had been put firmly on the international agenda.

The response of parliament and press in Germany was unequivocally positive while the reaction abroad was much more muted, especially in Britain and Italy. However, Gorbachev was not at all pleased, which came as a surprise to the Chancellery because it was, after all, Portugalov who had prompted Kohl's rush into action. Moreover, Bush and his advisers who had met the Soviet leader in Malta had formed the opinion that he was "malleable" on the German Question.[47] Back in Moscow Gorbachev and Shevardnadze adopted a different tone and dismissed the "Ten Point Programme" as an unacceptable "diktat" when they discussed the matter on 5 December with Genscher who was dispatched on an appeasement mission to the capitals of Europe.[48] Washington was slightly worried that Germany's continued commitment to NATO had not been mentioned. The NATO summit in Brussels in early December provided the perfect opportunity to put the alliance back on track: Kohl pledged his unswerving loyalty to the alliance and President Bush reiterated his support for the Chancellor's policy by making it abundantly clear that NATO had supported German unification for the last four decades. How best to achieve this goal was, from now on, the only option. In his memoirs Kohl is full of praise for the President for whom the division of a country was just unacceptable. Bush's calculation was, he writes, that "if he was to act as Germany's advocate regarding her historical claim he could be sure that we would do our best to keep the reunited country within NATO".[49] This was exactly the strategy which Kohl pursued, not only for the sake of German unity, but also as an end in itself.

The next "tribunal like interrogation" Kohl had to face about his initiative was the EC summit in Strasbourg on 8/9 December 1989, which he remembers as one of the most unpleasant meetings with colleagues.[50] Apart from Spain and Ireland none of the European neighbours was looking forward to a united German in their midst. His line of argument was always the same: that all Germans have a legitimate right to self-determination, and that German unification and European integration had to be seen as one and the same process. In other words, the Germans would never push their luck without consulting their partners. It was a great success of German diplomacy on that occasion that the final communiqué had adopted the crucial sentence of the letter regarding German unity attached to the Moscow treaty of 1970: "We strive to strengthen peace in Europe in which the German people would regain its liberty in an act of self-determination".[51] This statement left the door open to further development without being too specific as to its precise course. It allowed the British to keep hoping for an "Austrian" solution, with the Kremlin's backing. The German delegation also managed to persuade the Commission to work out a strategic concept of how to approach the unification process. This was to be done under the guidance of its president, Jaques Delors, "a loyal friend of the Germans", as Kohl emphasised, who later pursued the speedy incorporation of the new federal states into the European Community. The Chancellor knew, of course, that to the French Europe was as important as NATO was to the Americans. He therefore went out of his way to dispel their worries that a united Germany would grow cold on Europe. There can be no doubt that, to an extent, Kohl "bought" French consent with a firm commitment to abandoning the cherished Deutschmark in favour of a common European currency, sooner than the state of European integration at that time suggested. However, it would be wrong to assume that a common currency was not in any way in Germany's interest. Germany was, after all, by far the most export oriented country in Europe. In the fields of foreign policy, security and the economy further European integration was and still is clearly in Germany's "national interest". But no politician would dare to put it in such terms. The political class in Germany is only too aware that after two attempts at dominating Europe by force, it is bound to face the continued latent anxiety of its neighbours.

For Moscow the time had come to call the Four Powers responsible for Germany into action by suggesting a meeting of ambassadors in the building of the former Control Council, allegedly with a view to discussing the potentially explosive situation in Berlin. Margaret Thatcher was only too eager to comply with this request, whereas Genscher and Baker were agreed "to resist Soviet calls for four-power intervention in German politics".[52] The US ambassador stuck to the official agenda and made sure the discussion was confined to practical matters concerning Berlin. Under pressure from the German Foreign Office no further meeting of this kind, reminiscent of post-was conferences, was convened. At the next NATO meeting, Genscher vented his anger and told his colleagues that such rendezvous were incompatible with Germany's membership in the Alliance and in the councils of Europe. While before Bonn never tired to stress that it had no intention of going it alone, these were the first indications that the German government was equally determined to see to it that the fate of the nation would not be decided by the victorious powers on their own.

In his memoirs Kohl takes full credit for his "Ten Point Programme". However, he did have second thoughts as to whether he had gone too far when he realised how much he had upset Gorbachev. As a fence mending exercise he sent a lengthy letter to the Soviet leader protesting his innocence and explaining his intentions.[53] He began by confirming the validity of all previous German–Soviet agreements from the Moscow treaty of August 1970 up to the most recent communiqué of 13 June 1989 at the end of Gorbachev's visit to Germany. The common ground of all their efforts had been the maintenance of stability in Europe, which was now at risk. Kohl insisted that the current turmoil had not been generated by Bonn but by the GDR government and its reluctance to introduce radical reforms. He then pointed to the number of refugees causing serious problems in both German states, but again was adamant that this unprecedented exodus had not been encouraged by his government. The peaceful demonstrations of those who refused to leave their country, he argued, had at no time erupted into violence, not least thanks to appeals from the West. His "Ten Points" were no timetable for certain actions to be taken (which, of course, they clearly were!) but an attempt at de-escalation by persuading people to stay and to work for a better future. Kohl then conveyed the impression that he approved of the new East German proposal of a "treaty community" which would generate "confederal structures". In the end, however, he did not deny that the final goal was German unity according to the statement of the letter attached to the Moscow treaty of 1970: striving for "a state of peace in Europe in which the German people will regain its unity in freedom" – by now a standard reminder in many of Bonn's official communications. He concluded his letter by saying that he would welcome the opportunity to discuss these matters with the Soviet leader face to face, at a meeting which would also serve to improve trade relations between their two countries. Throughout 1989/90 Kohl used to address the special national interests of each of the Four Powers whose consent was indispensable: the prospect of German industrial investment in a reformed Soviet Union had the same quality as the profession of loyalty to NATO for the USA and, in order to please Paris, European monetary union over the objections of the *Bundesbank*. The problem was that Kohl had nothing tangible to offer

Mrs Thatcher except the wholly unsatisfactory promise to be good. Indeed, soon enough, in her notorious interview with *Wall Street Journal* on 25 January 1990 the Prime Minister was to refer to Kohl and Genscher as though they were selfish schoolboys: it had to be "drummed into their heads" that the long-term interests of Europe, above all Gorbachev's continued tenure in office, was far more important than their narrow nationalistic aspirations. These comments marked the lowest ebb in Anglo–German relations during the whole period. The Chancellor decided not to engage in a public debate but to ask Horst Teltschik to impress upon the British ambassador how he felt about Mrs Thatcher's uncalled-for opinions in view of his avowed determination to achieve unification within the European process.[54]

The reception he received on his visit to Dresden shortly before Christmas made a deep emotional impression on Kohl and convinced him that now the train towards unification could not be stopped. However, he meant what he said in his letter to Gorbachev and was eager to keep the lid on a potentially explosive situation. His speech in front of an excited flag-waving crowd shouting "Helmut! Helmut!" provided ample proof of his pledge. So worried was he that people would suddenly launch into the banned first verse of the national anthem (*"Deutschland, Deutschland über alles, über alles in der Welt"*) that he arranged for a choirmaster to start singing the old church hymn *"Nun danket alle Gott"* (Now thank we all our God). Fortunately there was no need to execute this emergency plan. In his address Kohl went out of his way to refer to history's traumatic legacy and to plead for sympathy with Germany's neighbours and their anxieties. The final goal of national unity, which he would never lose sight of, could only be achieved by a policy of constant patience, prudence and moderation.[55]

So far the Soviet government had been observing the pace of events in East Germany and on the diplomatic front without developing a coherent strategy. In concert with Britain and France, Gorbachev was hoping to prevent, or at least to slow down, what appeared to be the drift towards an inevitable West German takeover. However, the rapid disintegration of the GDR, both of its economic foundations and its power structures, forced Gorbachev and his advisers to abandon their stalling tactics in favour of a more constructive approach in line with Soviet interests.[56] These objectives were only slowly shaping up within a government not used to free exchange of views. They were to safeguard security *vis-à-vis* NATO, to incur material advantages, as long as they were still on offer, and to make sure the West did not pass the buck of principal opposition to Moscow, thereby compromising future German–Soviet relations. Gorbachev had just returned from the Lithuanian trouble spot when he convened a meeting of his crisis staff on

Germany for 26 January. A most recent and revealing summary of this inner circle debate is reproduced in Kohl's memoirs without any source given.[57] Henceforth, the Kremlin gave up any hope of restoring the authority of its East German satellite state and decided to influence the course of events through close cooperation with Bonn, based on the fact that Russian troops were still based on German territory. It was now not a matter of preventing unification but of regaining control of a process which, so far, had been the outcome of revolutionary turmoil on the streets of East Germany. Moscow was now called upon to reassert the international dimension of the German Question in coordination with the other three powers responsible for the country. Moreover, the Russian public had to be prepared to accept the inevitable. One of Gorbachev's advisers, Alexander Jakovlev, suggested that the Russian people should be reminded that it had, after all, been Stalin who had declared himself in favour of German unity, and that since 1946 his government had worked consistently for a Germany that was united but also neutral and demilitarised. For the historian, it is interesting to note that in a crisis situation like this, politicians tend to hold on to outdated interests and ideas, without realising that times have changed. For Gorbachev, a reunited Germany's continued membership of NATO was still out of the question, incompatible with the existence of Soviet troops on East German territory. A simultaneous withdrawal of all foreign troops from Germany, including US forces, seemed to be a perfectly plausible condition for Soviet approval of German unification. A one-sided withdrawal of the Red Army would amount to a loss of face which Gorbachev could not survive. While the three Western powers as well as the Federal government were insistent, though not for the same reasons, on Germany being firmly anchored in NATO, Moscow and the East German political establishment, old and new, wanted a demilitarised Germany as the paragon of peace. The looming power struggle around this issue could only be solved behind closed doors, not in the streets of Leipzig or at the "Round Table", the newly established governing body in East Berlin. Kremlin experts were sufficiently briefed and realistic to know who could and who should not work out a sensible compromise. It should be the Four Powers together with the two German states, rather than a peace conference or the Conference on Security and Cooperation in Europe (CSCE) with its more than 30 member states. A small circle of decision-makers including the two German governments was a cru-cial precondition for a speedy result. According to Kohl's memoirs, the idea of the *Two plus Four* negotiations was thus the brainchild of Soviet thinking.

However, Zelikow and Rice came to the conclusion that the *Two plus Four* concept was the result of a controversial debate between the NSC staff, to which they themselves belonged, and Dennis Ross and Robert Zoellick, two close advisers of James Baker. Everybody knew the President had settled on a policy of rapid unification without yet working out a coherent strategy of how to achieve this goal. His experts, including the authors, favoured a *de facto* fusion of the two German states before any outside pressure could be organised. The Four Powers would then be obliged to give their blessing to the outcome. Indeed, this would have been a solution that Bush and Kohl might have secretly banked on but which was the worst case scenario for all other major players in this game. They were the only leaders in the West who regarded the demonstrators in East Germany, pushing the issue of unification relentlessly, as their true allies. For Ross and Zoellick this looked like the abdication of politics and was fraught with risks. They wished to put the train, apparently careering out of control, back on track, if need be on a fast track. The points had to be set in a way that the Four Powers and the two German states would be coupled to make sure they would move in one and the same direction. Right from the beginning there should be no doubt about the final destination: German unification. There was one more "irreducible" condition: "The East German delegates must come from a freely elected government".[58] At the time of submitting their memo these officials did not know that their opposite numbers in Moscow had arrived at the same conclusion as to the necessary platform for negotiations. They assumed the Soviets might agree to this kind of committee but not to its terms of reference. However, it was not plain sailing for the *Two plus Four* plan, not even within the State Department, where some officials felt it might lead to excessive delays and that *Two plus Zero* would still be the best option. But then Zoellick came up with his trump card when he argued that the Germans might be obliged to work out a private deal with Moscow: "If the Germans work out unification with the Soviets, NATO will be dumped and become the obstacle." That was indeed the most ominous scenario in the eyes of Germany's neighbours. German journalists were saying at the time that once again Europe was being haunted by the "ghost of Rapallo". All of a sudden, NATO had changed its *raison d'être* inasmuch as the alliance now seemed indispensable as a check both on the Red Army and a reunited Germany, which might otherwise be tempted to develop her own nuclear weapons. Zelikow and Rice tell us that "every European head of government Bush spoke to wanted U.S. forces to stay in Europe, and to stay in strength". To refer to Germany as a potential threat was an open secret though not to be mentioned in public communications. It goes without saying that Kohl and Genscher were fully aware of these anxieties: they addressed them in various ways knowing that they played into their hands at the same time, especially after they had learnt that even the Warsaw Pact foreign ministers of Poland, Czechoslovakia and Hungary had advocated NATO membership for a united Germany.[59] Historians will have to wait for another few decades to learn first hand about all the arguments of Western diplomats in their efforts to persuade the Soviet government to drop its opposition to NATO as a safe haven for Germany. By the end of January 1990 there were only three major players left: The United States and the Soviet Union, both wooing the Federal Republic to play ball with them. Even before negotiations had started in earnest *Two plus Four* had in fact mutated into *Three plus Zero*.[60] Washington saw to it that France and Britain would come on board, Moscow was in charge of East Berlin, and both felt responsible for Poland's long-term security within the post-war borders of Europe. After the first free elections in East Germany, Hans-Dierich Genscher took the pastor turned foreign secretary under his wing: his new East German colleague Markus Meckel whose mission it was to establish peace on earth in Europe.

Yet in spite of a flurry of diplomatic communications no one of the six knew what the others really had in mind or who would be part of the inner club. Kohl could not be sure that Gorbachev and his close circle of advisers had already accepted German unification in principle and were now only concerned with its modalities. For months he tried to elicit an invitation from Moscow. His foreign minister was busying himself with ideas of how to reconcile American and Soviet positions on Germany's membership in NATO. So he suggested, without consulting the Chancellor, that the Western alliance would not expand into East German territory and that NATO and the Warsaw Pact would develop "cooperative security structures". The Americans suspected Genscher would go too far to meet Soviet concerns and preferred dealing with the German Chancellor, whose transatlantic loyalty was never in doubt. At times President Bush was better informed on Kohl's plans than the German foreign office, which was often at loggerheads with the Chancellery, especially with the energetic Horst Teltschik, who was not a diplomat by temperament but got on well with American and Soviet officials. He was the *bête noire* of the German AA, who regarded him as much too pushy. Hans-Dietrich Genscher favoured a more cautious approach. His private secretary Frank Elbe describes him at that time as "a giant insect stretching out its feelers to check the environment only to retreat at the slightest obstacle".[61] A frank exchange of views with James Baker in Washington in early February 1990 cleared the ground: Genscher took note that the Bush administration had opted for *Two plus Four* as the forum to settle all outstanding external aspects of the German question. He was probably less pleased to be informed by his American colleague that the

Chancellor had received the much coveted invitation to Moscow and was again marching ahead.[62] In the meantime Kohl had set up the *Kabinttsausschuss Deutsche Einheit* (Cabinet Committee on German Unity) consisting of six working groups, which would coordinate all domestic and external issues of unification. It was to push the *AA* further to the sidelines.

Before Kohl set off to Moscow on 10 February 1990 Gorbachev had received two visitors who put him in the picture: Hans Modrow, the new East German Prime Minister, gave a gloomy account of the increasingly disastrous situation in his country. Foreign Secretary James Baker briefed him on the American plans for a *Two plus Four* process as the only sensible way to settle the external aspects of German unification, which was now to happen sooner rather than later. At a time when the idea had been overtaken by events, when Bonn suggested a currency union to stop the flood of refugees, Modrow seems to have adopted Kohl's phased plan for unification in three stages (Ten Point programme). In accordance with Soviet thinking he also visualised a neutral Germany. It was exactly that kind of Germany that James Baker depicted as potentially dangerous: a loose, possibly nuclear cannon between East and West as it were, and therefore to be rejected by all means. Gorbachev had an open mind and was not as troubled by the prospect of a united Germany as Britain and France, but he did not want to commit himself as to the final military status of the new Germany. While Baker tried to sell him Genscher's idea of no eastward extension of NATO "jurisdiction", Washington was already thinking of watering down this formula in order to incorporate the whole of Germany into the alliance. American officials supported Gerhard Stoltenberg, the German minister of defence, who insisted that NATO should cover the whole of Germany, whatever the legal position of German troops in East Germany. He had been embroiled in a public controversy with Genscher who did not even want to see any German soldiers in the former GDR.[63]

The preparations for Kohl's visit to Moscow had not only been smoothed in diplomatic terms. During his June visit Gorbachev had casually enquired whether the Federal Republic was prepared to help out with food deliveries if the supply situation in Moscow and Leningrad worsened during the winter. In January, the inhabitants of these cities were indeed in desperate straits and the Chancellery was approached by one of Gorbachev's aides who wished to know whether they could still count on Bonn's promise. Indeed, they could: on 9 February, exactly one day before Kohl's departure, an agreement was signed which set in motion a gigantic relief action supplying – ironically from NATO depots – thousands of tons of meat, butter, cheese and even textiles and other consumer durables.[64] The German saying for using a sprat to catch a mackerel is perhaps more appropriate in this case: *mit der Wurst nach dem Schinken werfen* (to use the sausage in order to gain the ham). Germany's generosity was to be well rewarded the following day when Kohl and Gorbachev sat together for more than two-and-a-half hours with only their closest advisers present.[65] Kohl gave a detailed account of the alarming development in the GDR, of the emigration of predominantly young and skilled people seeking a better life in the West, 380,000 in 1989, and more than 50,000 in January alone. German unification had become a matter of crisis management. That is why he, the Chancellor said, had decided on a speedy economic and currency union so that people would be persuaded to stay. That is why it was indispensable to bring elections forward to 18 March. Unification was in the offing, the question now was to find a common solution for the external aspects. The new Germany would comprise the FRG, the GDR and Berlin, no more. There was no reason for anybody to be suspicious about the Oder-Neisse border. Neutrality, Kohl explained, was unacceptable to him, it was, moreover, *eine historische Dummheit* (a historical stupidity) as Germany's special status after 1918 had proved. However, he was prepared to meet Soviet security concerns and would therefore suggest that NATO would not be extended to the territory of the former GDR. After further questions and answers Gorbachev, according to Teltschik who took minutes, then bent forward and pronounced the decisive sentences: He was not troubled by the prospect of German unification. It was up to the Germans to decide for themselves which way to go. The Germans in both East and West had already shown that they had learnt the lessons of history and that no future war would originate from German soil. Kohl and his advisers could hardly grasp the significance of that statement which marked the crucial "breakthrough". The Chancellor just confirmed in his own words that henceforth only peace would emanate from Germany. He then went on to play heavily on Soviet hopes and fears. The united Germany offered more economic advantages than the old GDR whose obligations regarding the supply of manufactured goods to the Soviet Union would be met by the Federal Republic. For the time being the Red Army could remain in their East German barracks. The new Germany would dispose of fewer, rather than more, conventional forces and of no nuclear arsenal of its own.

It seems the unwelcome prospect of a neutral Germany getting herself atomic weapons was employed by Western diplomats to convince the Russians that NATO was the best place to keep Germany under closer supervision. Far from being indignant, Kohl and Genscher encouraged this kind of unfriendly logic in order to reach their goal, which implied the continued stationing of foreign troops on German soil. It is worth recalling at this stage that Weimar Germany had regarded the presence of foreign troops as an unacceptable infringement of its sovereignty. Times had changed, and the Germans with it. It was just that Soviet troops on German territory was incompatible with the country's continued membership of the Western Alliance. After he had obtained a clear mandate for unification following the 18 March elections, Kohl told the Soviet ambassador that his government would not mind the presence of Russian troops for a transitional period.[66]

Though he would not commit himself on the thorny question of NATO, Gorbachev expressed understanding for the Germans seeking to avoid isolation and exposure. He could not risk saying any more without endangering his position at home. No objections were raised to the *Two plus Four* procedure, which Baker had suggested on his previous visit to Moscow. Kohl summarised the results of his talks at a press conference, announcing that Gorbachev had given him the "green light". To Teltschik, who was even more jubilant than the Chancellor, the Kremlin had shown more willingness to cooperate than could have been hoped for. However, Genscher and his advisers were less sanguine about the outcome and felt that Gorbachev had only expressed his personal views, not the considered policy of his government. Cautiousness was the hallmark of the *AA* at the time. German diplomats were right in the sense that Soviet ambassadors in the capitals of the West hastened to qualify the Chancellor's glowing account by stressing that German unification, though accepted in principle, had to be firmly linked to the "overall European development".[67] Zelikow and Rice tell us that henceforth Washington and Bonn were increasingly worried about Gorbachev's position at home. How long would he enjoy the loyal support of veteran Soviet officials? This was exactly the anxiety Margaret Thatcher had been expressing for some time. In her eyes overcoming the Cold War was far more important than settling the unpleasant German problem: that the two were intrinsically linked she would not see or did not want to admit.

The best way to strengthen the Soviet leader's position was to develop NATO's cooperative structures and to get on with negotiations on the reduction of conventional forces in Europe. The next occasion to discuss these matters was NATO's annual meeting in Ottawa in the second half of February 1990, the first and only meeting of the foreign ministers of both the Western alliance and the Warsaw Pact. The original agenda was to discuss the problem of "open skies", a long-standing issue among the Superpowers. It was now eclipsed by the German Question and the problem that only a small group of NATO states should be invited to discuss its final settlement. Then there was concern about the future level of conventional forces in Europe. According to Zelikow and Rice the President and his foreign secretary wanted "to avert any public perception that U.S. and Soviet troops should be treated alike. It was their belief that the Soviet troops must leave and the American soldiers must stay".[68] However, this was not Margaret Thatcher's view. She actually suggested to Bush that Soviet troops be allowed to stay indefinitely on German territory.[69] The Germans would thereby be restrained and Gorbachev would find it easier to accept unification. She maintained that Genscher had no problems with this idea. Whatever the substance of this claim it was bound to increase American suspicions about what they termed "Genscherism", an inclination towards appeasement *vis-à-vis* Moscow. When Kohl was invited to Camp David in the second half of February Genscher was not. At the Ottawa conference a compromise was found which allowed both powers 195,000 troops in central Europe, with an extra 30,000 American soldiers at the periphery.[70]

The unexpected result of the first free elections provided the new Prime Minister Lothar de Maizière with a clear mandate for speedy unification as promised by Kohl during the election campaign in the East. Previously the diplomatic consultation process had been delayed in anticipation of elections producing a legitimate spokesman for the East Germans. Now the domestic fusion of the two states could not go ahead any longer without due regard to its diplomatic repercussions. It was in the interest of both the German and US governments to synchronise the two developments in order to make sure they would reach the finishing line together. However, one could not be certain that the other members of the *Two plus Four* club were driven by the same ambition. They knew that the marriage would, as it were, only be recognised by society if they gave their blessing by registering its legality. The German foreign office, which so far had been in the shadow of the Chancellery, was now called upon to get its act together. Frank Elbe tells us what Bonn hoped to achieve by a settlement of the external aspects: equal status of participants, no peace treaty, surrender of the Four Power rights, sovereignty of the united Germany, membership of NATO with no special strings that would discriminate Germany, withdrawal of Soviet forces and a final settlement of the border issue with Poland.[71]

Up to the East German elections James Baker had to fight for acceptance of the *Two plus Four* procedure on two fronts: several NATO members, notably Italy and the Netherlands, were not at all content to sit on the sidelines. And the whole process was also proving controversial within the US administration. The NSC staff felt that it would give the Soviet government too much leeway – quite apart from Britain and France who might use it for their own ends. They depicted a worst case scenario, which in retrospect did indeed pose a serious threat: "Allied with a leftist East German government, Moscow might try to force the choice between unity and NATO before the West German electorate in a volatile election year."[72] As late as 6 March, Gorbachev told the press that participation of a united Germany in NATO was "out of the question".[73] It was a near miracle that the fear expressed by the NSC did not come true. It could possibly be due to the successful lobby-work of Western diplomats in Moscow. The NSC staff's advice was to give the domestic development a head start and to limit the scope of the *Two plus Four* talks, leaving as much as possible to a sovereign German decision. Since at this stage the *Two plus Four* platform could not be torpedoed any more this was then more or less the brief of the American delegation which would, in any case, have liked to see it more as a forum for consultation than for negotiation. The agenda was the shortest possible – the restoration of full sovereignty of the united German state including the surrender of Four Power rights based on the tacit assumption that Germany was then free to choose her preferred alliance.

The EC special summit in Dublin at the end of April was a demonstration of goodwill for Kohl. The outcome of the East German elections seemed to have clinched the issue of German unification, even for Margaret Thatcher who now brought herself to congratulate Kohl and make amends for her not too diplomatic stance in the past.[74] Henceforth it was only a matter of when and how. Meanwhile, the Chancellery and the *AA* had been competing with each other in generating concepts that would soften Moscow's attitude to NATO membership. The two offices approached the problem from different directions. Genscher went for a multilateral solution by trying to develop cooperative structures between the hitherto hostile alliances, which would – eventually and inevitably – appear to be superfluous. He wished to make sense of Gorbachev's idea of a "common European house" by transforming it into a system of collective security. The Americans realised that NATO had to change its strategy, but did not want to abandon the alliance altogether. Again Genscher had overstepped the margins only to retreat and go along with NATO's "new thinking". Kohl and Teltschik preferred a bilateral, and in the end more rewarding approach, assuring the Americans of their unflinching commitment to NATO and at the same time offering the Soviet Union a special treaty that would put their relationship on a completely new and mutually advantageous platform. Soviet officials liked both proposals but seemed to be even more thrilled by the prospect of a new partnership with Germany which promised material benefits.

After preliminary talks among officials, mainly concerned with procedural questions, the *Two plus Four* forum of foreign ministers met in earnest on 5 May 1990 in Bonn, the anniversary of the very day the Federal Republic had shed the occupation statute in 1955. It was the occasion for the German *Auswärtiges Amt* to stage its own show and impress on public opinion that they, too, were involved in the most important political business in the history of the Federal Republic. From this first meeting it was clear that Moscow was under enormous domestic pressure due to the looming German unification, which seemed to be evolving before the eyes of a powerless Soviet government. According to Shevardnadze recent opinion polls in the Soviet Union had revealed that about 97 per cent of Russians could not visualise Germany as part of the Western alliance. He would not dispute the German right to self-determination, but the closing chapter of a terrible past should be seen to be "honourable and fair".[75] He therefore suggested decoupling the external from the domestic transformation. In other words, the Soviet government wanted more time to come to terms with the new security situation in Europe following German unification: if NATO were to undergo a fundamental change German membership would no longer be "out of the question". Separate talks between the US and Soviet foreign ministers revealed that in the meantime Moscow no longer objected to the presence of American soldiers in Europe.[76] Bush and Kohl, who preferred phone call diplomacy to public performance, were satisfied with the result of the first *Two plus Four* meeting even though they both rejected the Soviet decoupling proposal. The German press, according to Elbe, played up the difference of opinion between *AA* and Chancellery in their reaction to Shevardnadze's timescale for the external aspects of unification. Genscher, in his anxiety not to jeopardise the final outcome, expressed general understanding for the Soviet position whereas Kohl simply insisted on synchronising the two processes. The two were not as far apart as it appeared. In fact, it was a clever double-act: Kohl encouraging the East Germans in the streets while in close contact with Bush and Gorbachev; Genscher keeping his foot on the brakes, thus reassuring Germany's neighbours. The new East German foreign minister, Markus Meckel from the recently founded East German SPD, proved to be Genscher's junior partner in daring to express even more sympathy for the Soviet dilemma. He argued that the democratic revolution in his country had not been staged in order to lead the new *Länder* into NATO. The latter, he said, would have to change substantially if Germany was to remain a member "for the time being".[77] In matters of security the new East German government was still indebted to the pacifism of human rights activists even though these had fared badly in the last elections.

Bush and Kohl got the message from this first exchange of views and responded in their own ways: the one by addressing Soviet security concerns, the other by opening his purse. The Americans had already helped the first conference of foreign ministers to a good start by announcing that they would abstain from modernising their short range missiles programme and their nuclear artillery. Now the American President pushed ahead with a new strategy for the Western alliance, which was to be decided at a special NATO summit in the summer. It was in his meeting with Kohl, scheduled at the last minute, that the Soviet foreign secretary broached the delicate subject of financial credits that – and that's where the problem lay – were to be guaranteed by the Federal Government. The Soviet Union was facing a crisis of confidence on the financial markets because she was unable to meet her obligations. Gorbachev's whole reform programme, known as Perestroika, seemed to be at stake. The Chancellor sent his confidant Teltschik and two leading German bankers on a secret mission to Moscow where they were met by top officials as well as Gorbachev. The pilots of the military plane would only know their destination shortly before take-off and the names of their passengers not at all. While the AA and the rest of the world were left in the belief that the future of Germany was being decided at the conference table, the wheels of diplomacy were in fact being greased with the world's most effective lubricant – hard cash. Shevardnadze gave his consent by laughing when Teltschik explained that the Chancellor understood the financial support to be part of the package which would help to solve the German Question.[78] However, quite apart from this specific constellation there were good reasons to approach Bonn in this delicate matter. The Federal Government was Moscow's chief creditor to the order of DM 6 billion, followed by Japan (DM 5.2 billion) and Italy (DM 4.3 billion) with Britain in only sixth place (DM 1.5 billion), in spite of a prime minister who posed as Gorbachev's chief council in the West. The Chancellor agreed to a short-term credit of DM 5 billion guaranteed by the government and pledged to back long-term credits of 15–20 billion, to be raised on the international market. There are always at least three aspects inherent in any foreign policy decision: national interests, due regard for the concerns of allies and taking along the political establishment and public opinion. What counted for the Soviet government was the combination of German financial support and the prospect of a comprehensive treaty that promised long-term economic benefits.

For some time the Soviet government hoped the final settlement with Germany would take on the form of a peace treaty. The chief issues of peace treaties in the past concerned territory and reparations. However, Bonn made it abundantly clear that this approach, 50 odd-years after the end of the war, was not acceptable. What the Bonn government dreaded above all were demands for restitution payments by a great number of nations that were at war with Germany by 1945. The greatest loss Germany had suffered as a result of the war was the cession of one-quarter of its territory east of the Oder-Neisse border. For the generation of Kohl and Genscher, it was the logical punishment for a war launched with the aim of acquiring *Lebensraum* in the east. Germany's eastern border was no issue in 1990; it had been recognised by both the GDR and the Federal Republic and it was never in dispute among the great majority of West and East Germans. It made sense that this commitment should be confirmed by the new united Germany. Since the treaty concluded with Poland in 1970 had only been binding for the FGR, it did not affect the rights of the Four Powers responsible for Germany as a whole.[79] For legal reasons, it was argued by German diplomats, a final settlement could only take place after and not before unification. Yet Warsaw was very nervous, insisting on a treaty beforehand and lobbying her allies, mainly France and Soviet Russia, to support her claim. In the spring of 1990, Kohl got into a tight corner by calls from all sides to yield to the Poles or to hold on to the legal position. The Chancellor had the greatest difficulty in persuading the right wing of his party to toe the line.[80] After all, who could afford to alienate the powerful refugee organisations who constituted a large voting bloc, especially within the CSU? Then there was the hidden danger of reparations, which might be brought up once the border issue was out of the way. After unification the German government was in a much stronger position to refute such claims, which appeared to be unjustified in view of the loss of large tracts of German territory. Eventually, after much international pressure and haggling, a compromise was worked out. Two resolutions of the *Bundestag* and the *Volkskammer* were passed to the effect that a united Germany would once more recognise the inviolability of the Oder-Neisse border. This pledge was then incorporated into the crucial treaty of 12 September 1990. The final accord was reached on 14 November, with a treaty confirming the validity of previous agreements made by the GDR (1951) and the Federal Republic (1970).

In a society like Russia with no free press or free elections public opinion polls did not count for much. What mattered was the pseudo-parliament of the Supreme Soviet and top officials on whose loyalty Gorbachev depended. For them to swallow the idea that the new Germany should be part of the enemy camp, he had to show that unification was a means of overcoming the Cold War and bringing the division of Europe to a close. Genscher was only too aware of Gorbachev's dilemma. Frank Elbe lists the arguments that were employed by German diplomats to meet Soviet security concerns: German unity would help to deepen the CSCE process and improve Soviet

Russia's relations with the EC. NATO and the Warsaw Pact would cease to be hostile camps and would cooperate in the interest of a peaceful future. For Genscher, further disarmament was "the heart of German unification and European union".[81] The new Germany would dispose of fewer rather than of more conventional forces than the old *Bundeswehr*. Instead of pouring her resources into a wasteful armament race, the Soviet Union could now think of building up a consumer industry within a reformed economic system. The potential of a united Germany, motivated by goodwill, was a greater asset than her relations with the two states in the past. In other words, German diplomats tried to convince their opposite numbers that the Soviet Union would end up as the true beneficiary of German unification. It was not just a charade of specious arguments. The reception of Gorbachev in June 1989 indicated that for most Germans a reformed Russia was a candidate for reconciliation. The author remembers a Bavarian small town speech in the mid-1980s by the late Franz-Josef Strauss, Germany's Cold War warrior *par excellence*, when he referred to his grandfather's and father's attitude towards France, the "hereditary enemy" (*Erbfeind*), "now a thing of the past", only to conclude that one day the Germans would experience the same metamorphosis *vis-à-vis* Russia.

With German unification agreed in principle there were by May 1990 only three contentious issues left to be settled: full membership of Germany in NATO, the precise date for the termination of Four Power rights and finally the limit of German troops. Within two-and-a-half months agreements were reached on all three subjects, not however by officials in the various *Two plus Four* meetings, set up for this purpose, but through a flurry of high level talks among Bush, Gorbachev and Kohl, as well as between their foreign secretaries Baker, Shevardnadze and Genscher. To understand the stupendous success of Western diplomacy it is necessary to draw attention to the fast disintegration of the Soviet Empire in Eastern Europe: the GDR, the former bulwark of Soviet power, was about to be dissolved, the Warsaw Pact was in terminal decline and the Soviet Union itself faced fundamental reforms amidst economic and political turmoil. The Soviet leader's top priority was to save the Soviet Union through far reaching reforms (perestroika) supported by substantial help from the West, i.e. cuts in defence expenditure owing to further disarmament as well as financial and economic aid. The terms of German unification were by now of secondary importance, a means to an end rather a matter of Soviet security. But Gorbachev also knew that for the Russian public and his own advisers, German membership in NATO was by no means a foregone conclusion. In the end it turned out to be more of a domestic than a foreign policy problem.

Gorbachev's dilemma became crystal clear during his visit to Washington at the end of May. There is no better record of his talks with President Bush than that given by Zelikow and Rice. The main purpose of his visit was a trade agreement with the Unite States which had been on the cards for some time. He also wished to explore the chance of further financial credits. Kohl had warned the President that "a stingy policy deny-ing financial credits to Gorbachev could push him out of power, replaced by a military-dominated ruler".[82] He was also prepared to offer substantial German troop reductions to ease Gorbachev's position at home. Bush's chief concern, however, was to nail him down to the concession of Germany's self-determination in matters of security. Face to face with the Soviet leader he reviewed a nine-point plan for addressing Moscow's security concerns about German unification which Baker had already presented on his previ-ous visit. The Americans knew exactly what they wished to achieve, the Russians did not because there was no agreed briefing paper to which Gorbachev felt bound. The US catalogue comprised a variety of proposals regarding reduction of conventional and nuclear forces as well as a totally new strategy for NATO in alliance with the CSCE. As to Germany, the President proposed: settled borders, no nuclear, biological or chemical weapons and no stationing of NATO troops in East Germany for a transi-tional period. Economic support for perestroika was left to the two German states to work out with Moscow. To Bush's surprise, Gorbachev conceded for the first time that the US presence was welcome because it helped to stabilise the continent. But NATO had to change, he argued, because otherwise his own people would not come to terms with the new situation. He came up with a suggestion, already introduced by Soviet diplomats, namely the membership of the united Germany in both alliances. On other occasions the West was asked to consider a status for Germany in NATO similar to that of France, i.e. being part of the political alliance, but not of its military command structure. With the backing of Kohl, the American President insisted on full membership without reservation, or as it was then put *keine Singularisierung*. All of a sudden, Bush confronted the Soviet leader with an argument that had been employed at lower levels in the *Two plus Four* nego-tiations. Under the CSCE principles agreed at Helsinki all states should have the right to choose their own alliances. Should that not logically also apply to Germany once it had become fully sovereign? Apparently Gorbachev nodded and admitted that this was the case. Bush, prompted by his startled advisers, then formulated a position to which the Soviet President seemed to agree: "The United States unequivocally advocates Germany's membership in NATO. However, should Germany prefer to make a different choice, we will respect it". This was, in fact, the final breakthrough, six weeks before Kohl and Gorbachev met in the Caucasus to come to a definite understanding about the loose ends. Soviet diplomats accompanying Gorbachev were as flabbergasted as their American colleagues, but more in the sense of being shocked at what they had just witnessed. Zelikow and Rice describe the extraordinary situation when they quote a colleague: "There was a palpable feeling – conveyed through expression and body language – among Gorbachev's advisers of almost physically distancing themselves from their leader's words."[83] The latter quickly gathered his wits and asked Valentin Falin, head of the Central Committee's International Relations Department, to put the orthodox Soviet case why Germany's NATO membership was unacceptable. Falin maintains in his memoirs that Gorbachev's nodding was meant for him to launch into his presentation.[84] More convincing is what he says about a long telephone conversation with his boss shortly before the meeting in the Caucasus. Gorbachev apparently said: "I am afraid, the train has already departed."[85] The Soviet leaders must have been aware of the departure for some time. But he wished to convey the impression that he was the station-master who had given the signal. From now on the White House knew for sure that they had to help the Soviet reformer to get over his domestic hurdles. That is why, at the end of the visit and after further lobbying by Kohl, the American President was prepared to sign the coveted trade agreement with the Soviet Union.

Western diplomats were in real fear of an impending power struggle behind the Kremlin walls that Gorbachev might not survive and which would bring "the German train" to an abrupt halt. Kohl saw "the storm clouds gathering" and was afraid "he would not bring in the harvest in time".[86] Financial aid on a large scale was too risky because nobody could be sure whether this would not be money down the drain – it could wait until a reformed economy had prepared the terrain. A more promising alternative was to strengthen Gorbachev's position at home by transforming NATO beyond all recognition as he himself had asked for. The West was particularly anxious for Gorbachev to survive the next party congress of the CPSU in July. NATO's scheduled meeting might be too late. At a meeting of NATO's foreign secretaries in Turnberry (Scotland) in early June, James Baker called upon his colleagues to redefine their previous assumptions about the enemy in a revolutionary way. Genscher came to his support by saying that, henceforth, NATO's business should be to make peace rather than prevent war. The result was the "message of Turnberry", which declared that there was now the chance for fundamental changes in Europe and for the creation of a new peace order based on freedom, the rule of law and democracy. "We extend to the Soviet Union and all other European countries the hand of friendship and cooperation."[87] Even more important was the outcome of NATO's special summit in London,[88] scheduled for 5–6 July, which contained more substantial pledges. The declaration stated that NATO and Warsaw Pact states were "no longer adversaries"; former enemies were invited to open permanent liaison missions at NATO headquarters and to conclude non-aggression treaties; far-reaching cuts of conventional forces, including a substantial reduction of German troops, were promised as well as a new military strategy that would replace existing scenarios. In security terms Gorbachev's vision of a "common European house" with all CSCE members under one roof was taking shape. Meanwhile, the CPSU Congress was taking place in Moscow (1–11 July) – the most testing days Gorbachev and his closest collaborators were to experience in their political lives.[89] Conservative elements had rallied for a last stand to take their progressive leadership to account. They accused them of selling-out socialism and their East European allies, while Shevardnadze pointed out that military parity with the West had cost Russia 700 billion rouble over the past 20 years. The division of Germany, he argued, was artificial and unnatural. The rebellion of the hardliners was to no avail. The Soviet leaders won the ballot, this time based on a much wider electorate, with flying colours. Both he and his foreign secretary later admitted that NATO's willingness to cooperate had been of crucial importance for their political survival. Thus furnished with a new mandate, Gorbachev was ready for a final settlement with the German government.

The meeting on Gorbachev's home territory in the Ukraine (where he had begun his spectacular career) had been arranged for some time. During the party congress Falin gave the German news agency an interview expressing hopes for these talks in view of the personal rapport between the leaders but confirming once more Moscow's well-known position that NATO membership for a united Germany was unacceptable.[90] This announcement only served to dramatise the decisions which had, in fact, long been expected. What was striking was the setting. After the decisive concession had been made in Moscow behind closed doors, the two leaders and their entourage took a flight to Archys in the Caucasus, engaged in small talk with peasants and then retired to a mountain lodge to thrash out the last remaining issues – these scenes could have been designed by a film director. Virtually everything except for the limit of German forces and the timescale for the withdrawal of the Red Army had been settled beforehand. Kohl's eight-point communiqué for the press on the questions that had been settled,[91] was almost identical with the final treaty regarding the international aspects of German unification two months later:

1   Germany to comprise the Federal Republic, the GDR and Berlin and no more;

2   complete termination of Four Power rights;

3   free choice of alliance;

4   a bilateral treaty to be concluded between Germany and the Soviet Union about the withdrawal of the Red Army within three to four years;

5   no NATO command structure in East Germany for the duration of the presence of Soviet troops but full protection of Germany under articles 5 and 6 of the NATO treaty;

6   the maintenance of Western garrisons in Berlin for as long as Soviet troops remained in East Germany;

7   Germany's offer of a limit of 370,000 soldiers in the course of the forthcoming CFE negotiations in Vienna;

8   Germany's pledge never to produce, own or dispose of nuclear, biological or chemical weapons and to remain an adherent to the non-proliferation treaty.

After the accord in Moscow and in Gorbachev's datscha the final lap of the *Two plus Four* talks seemed to be a mere formality. All that was left for the officials to do was to couch these points in the proper phrasing of inter-national law and to have it ready for signature when the ministers met for a last time in Moscow on 12 September. However, on the evening of that day the British delegate threw a spanner into the works, or so it appeared to the German delegation, by insisting on the need for NATO manoeuvres in East Germany following the withdrawal of Soviet troops. Having made one concession after another, the Russians objected to non-German troops in the former GDR, especially to large-scale manoeuvres. Even though John Weston had the backing of his US colleagues, Genscher and his team were very upset, all the more since Douglas Hurd, the Foreign Secretary, had promised not to cause further trouble.[92] When Shevardnadze threatened to cancel the signing ceremony in the Kremlin the next day, Genscher woke up James Baker in the middle of the night to enlist his help in salvaging the situation. At the last minute a compromise was worked out which left it to the German government to define the term "deployment". Again the British, in trying to prove their loyalty to the Americans, were exposed as trouble-makers. It was a fitting end to the whole unification process in which the West had gambled for nothing less than complete victory in the Cold War. By that time the Gulf crisis, following Saddam Hussein's invasion of Kuwait, had eclipsed the German Question on the international agenda. However, Soviet leaders were no strangers to the rules of diplomatic poker. It was not until after the amicable agreement on the essentials in the Caucasus that the Russians presented their bill for the costs of maintaining and eventually relocating the Red Army divisions in East Germany. After much haggling and shortly before the deadline, Gorbachev and Kohl settled on DM 12 billion and a 3 billion interest free loan.[93] At the time this looked like a lot of cash, but compared to the burden of sustaining the East German population on a West German level for the next decade, this was to prove little more than a pittance. What mattered most – Russia did indeed withdraw her forces from East Germany in 1994. Moreover, on 9 November 1990 both countries signed a treaty pledging closer cooperation in a variety of areas,[94] which signified that the new Germany, soon to be referred to as the Berlin Republic, had acknowledged her new geopolitical position in the heart of Europe although she had not changed her political alignment to the West. In the same way as Britain regards herself as the honest broker between the United States and the European Union so is Germany likely to play a similar role *vis-à-vis* Russia.

Notes and references

1   Philip Zelikow and Condoleezza Rice, *Germany Unified and Europe Transformed* (Cambridge, MA, 1995), p. 26.

2   See above, p. 74.

3   See the first volume of his memoirs (Helmut Kohl, *Erinnerungen 1982–1990*, Munich, 2005), esp. p. 862. It is particularly in his relations to France and Israel that he refers to his predecessor and role model Adenauer.

4   Thomas Nipperdey, *Deutsche Geschichte 1800–1866. Bürgerwelt und starker Staat* (Munich, 1989), p. 11.

5   See Matthias Zimmer, *Nationales Interesse und Staatsräson. Die Deutschlandpolitik der Regierung Kohl 1982–1989* (Paderborn, 1992), pp. 86–92.

6   Interview with Horst Teltschik in June 1992, Zelikow and Rice, p. 34f.

7   Quoted ibid., p. 60.

8   Quoted by William R. Smyser, *From Yalta to Berlin. The Cold War Struggle over Berlin* (London, 1999), p. 328. See also the most comprehensive study on how

Moscow wrestled with the German question: Rafael Biermann, *Zwischen Kreml und Kanzleramt. Wie Moskau mit der deutschen Einheit rang* (Paderborn, 1997).

9 See Wjatscheslaw Kotschemassow, *Meine letzte Mission* (Berlin, 1994), p. 170. The Soviet ambassador to East Berlin tells us that he was never officially asked for military support but he knew that individual members of the Politburo expected not to be left alone in a critical situation.

10 See Mary Fulbrook, *Anatomy of a Dictatorship. Inside the GDR 1949–1989* (Oxford, 1995), pp. 58–77.

11 Apt remark made by Elizabeth Pond, *Beyond the Wall: Germany's Road to Unification* (Washiongton, DC, 1993).

12 See Zelikow and Rice, pp. 24–32.

13 The *Independent*, 13.5.1989 ("One Germany wouldn't worry Moscow") and 7.6. 1989. Also *Daily Mail*, 3.7.1989 ("Soviets won't stop a united Germany").

14 Kohl, vol. 1, p. 889.

15 Quoted by Smyser, p. 58.

16 Hanns Jürgen Küsters and Daniel Hofmann (eds), *Dokumente zu Deutschlandpolitik. Deutsche Einheit. Sonderedition aus den Akten des Bundeskanzleramtes 1989/90* (Munich, 1998), p. 38. From now: *Deutsche Einheit*.

17 See initial correspondence reproduced in: *Deutsche Einheit*, doc. 1–36.

18 Zelikow and Rice, p. 79.

19 Honecker rang the Soviet ambassador with whom he used to be on good terms to say goodbye admitting that he, too, had voted for his dismissal (Kotschemassow, pp. 170 and 176).

20 Zelikow and Rice, p. 97. Based on interviews with FO officials in June 1992 and a FO paper "The German Question" shared with the US.

21 Peregrine Worsthorne in: *Daily Telegraph*, 25.10.1989, also Peter Jenkins in the *Independent* of the same day.

22 Hans Dietrich Genscher, *Erinnerungen* (Berlin, 1995), pp. 652–61.

23 According to minutes of the Soviet Politburo released after 15 years: *Der Spiegel* 2006 (46), 13.11.06, p. 134.

24 See ibid.

25 Zelikow and Rice, p. 397, n. 93.

26 *Deutsche Einheit*, p. 52.

27 *New York Times*, 25.10.1989; quoted by Zelikow and Rice, p. 94. Telephone conversation between Kohl and Bush, 23.10.1989, *Deutsche Einheit*, doc. 64.

28 *Der Spiegel*, 1989(39) (25.10.1989).

29 Kohl, vol. 1, p. 984.

30 Margaret Thatcher, *The Downing Street Years* (London, 1995), pp. 790–98. Jaques Attali, *Verbatim* (Paris, 1995), vol. 3, p. 369 (8.12.1989). See also Lothar Kettenacker, "Britain and German Unification, 1989/90", in: Klaus Larres (ed.), *Uneasy Allies. British German Relations and European Integration since 1945* (Oxford, 2000), pp. 99–123.

31 Inge Lehmann, *Die deutsche Einigung von außen gesehen. Angst, Bedenken und Erwartungen in der ausländischen Presse* (Frankfurt a.M., 1996), p. 422. See also Lothar Kettenacker, "Zwangsläufige deutsche Dominanz? Über Konstanten britischer Europaperzeptionen", in: *Tel Aviver Jahrbuch für deutsche Geschichte* 26 (1997), pp. 235–49.

32 Quoted in: Zelikow and Rice, p. 207.

33 *Sunday Correspondence*, 18.3.190 and *Daily Telegraph*, 24.3.1990. See also the "seminar" on the German national character which the Prime Minister convened in Chequers in March 1990: Charles Powell, "What the PM learnt about the Germans", in: Harold James and Marla Stone (eds), *When the Wall Came Down* (London, 1992), pp. 233–39.

34 *House of Commons Debates,* vol. 166, col. 1088–90 (22.2.1990).

35 See esp. the memoirs of Valentin Falin, the Soviet ambassador in Bonn, during the years of Brandt's *Ostpolitik* (*Politische Erinnerungen*, München, 1993, pp. 466–500). About the decision-making structures in Moscow: Biermann, pp. 37–84.

36 Zelikow and Rice (p. 85) quoting Igor Maximychev, deputy of Vyacheslav Kochemassov, Soviet ambassador in East Berlin and according to Biermann in daily contact with Honecker.

37 Richard Kiessler and Frank Elbe, *Ein Runder Tisch mit scharfen Ecken. Der diplomatische Weg zur deutschen Einheit* (Baden-Baden, 1993), p. 45; also: *Deutsche Einheit*, p. 59.

38 Kohl, vol. 1, p. 958. English text: Konrad H. Jarausch and Volker Gransow (eds), *Uniting Germany. Documents and Debates, 1944–1993* (Oxford, 1994), pp. 74–77.

39 Ibid., p. 969.

40 Minutes of telephone conversations with Bush, Thatcher and Mitterrand: *Deutsche Einheit*, doc. nos. 81, 82 and 85.

41 Not mentioned in this context in *Deutsche Einheit* but singled out for praise in his memoirs (p. 978).

42 Küsters and Hofmann, in: *Deutsche Einheit*, p. 59 (translation L.K.).

43 Horst Teltschik, *329 Tage. Innenansichten der Einigung* (Berlin, 1991), pp. 42–46.

44 In his memoirs Kohl does not mention Portugalov who prompted him to take the initiative.

45 See Kohl, vol. 1, pp. 988–1019 (title of this chapter "Offensive"). English text: Jarausch and Gransow (eds), pp. 86–89.

46 Genscher supported the plan in public but it was regarded as a rash decision inside the *AA* and contributed to the tensions between Chancellery and *AA*. See Kissler and Elbe, pp. 49–55.

47 Zelikow and Rice, p. 130.

48 Kiessler and Elbe, p. 69; Teltschik, p. 68 (5.12.1989).

49 Kohl, vol. 1, p. 1007.

50 Ibid., pp. 1010–1016.

51 Quoted in: *Deutsche* Einheit, p. 72.

52 Genscher, p. 695.

53 *Deutsche Einheit*, doc. No. 123 (6 printed pages!).

54 Teltschik, pp. 115–17; Kohl, vol. 1, p. 1042–43.

55 Kohl, vol. 1, pp. 1020–32 (title of this chapter: "Crucial Experience").

56 See Biermann, pp. 320–419.

57 Kohl, vol. 1, pp. 1048–51 (perhaps minutes from his later friend Gorbachev). See also: Zelikow and Rice, pp. 160–64 (based on the memoirs of Soviet diplomats).

58 Zelikow and Rice, pp. 165–72.

59 See Helmut Kohl, *Erinnerungen* (vol. 2, Munich, 2005), p. 106.

60 This is also borne out by the entries in the index of *Deutsche Einheit* generally referring to Kohl's telephone calls and letters: a considerably higher number for Bush and Gorbachev than for the other three players.

61 Kiessler and Elbe, p. 78.

62 Zelikow and Rice, p. 177.

63 See Teltschik, pp. 151–53 (19.2.1990).

64 Kohl, vol. 1, pp. 1069–70; Teltschik who was first aproached by Soviet ambassador Yuly Kvitsinsky, p. 100 (8.1.1990) and p. 114.

65 Minutes in: *Deutsche Einheit*, doc. No. 174 (10.2.1990); Teltschik, pp. 137–43.

66 Teltschik, p. 180 (22.3.1990).

67 Zelikow and Rice, p. 190.

68 Ibid., p. 191.

69 Ibid., p. 207.

70 Kiessler and Elbe, pp. 99–105.

71 Ibid., p. 106.

72 Zelikow and Rice, p. 209.

73 Ibid., p. 225.

74 See Teltschik, p. 211–12. Kohl on his difficult relationship with Margaret Thatcher who had invited him to the *Königswinter Conference* to Cambridge at the end of March: vol. 2, pp. 58–65. He says she never forgave him when she had called on him in 1984 at his Austrian holiday resort and he had escaped to a local café rather than engage in further conversation with her.

75 Kiessler and Elbe, pp. 119–32.

76 *Deutsche Einheit*, p. 162.

77 Minutes of the first meeting in: *Deutsche Einheit*, doc. no. 268. For GDR's unrealistic position during the *Two plus Four* negotiations see also Kissler and Elbe, pp. 189–201. For Meckel's hopes and ambitions regarding a new European peace order see the report of his West German adviser: Ulrich Albrecht, *Die Abwicklung der DDR. Die "2 plus 4 Verhandlungen". Ein Insiderbericht* (Opladen, 1992).

78 Teltschik, pp. 230–35.

79 See note of the Federal government to the Three Western Powers, 19.11.1970 (*Documentation Realting to the Federal Government's Policy of Détente*, published by the Press and Information Office, Bonn, 1978, pp. 31–34).

80 The controversy is best explained by Küster and Hofmann in: *Deutsche Einheit*, pp. 120–27.

81 Kiessler and Elbe, p. 140.

82 Zelikow and Rice, pp. 271–85 (here: p. 274, interpretation of what Kohl said, not his own words). See also minutes of the telephone conversation between Kohl and Bush, 30.5.1990, in: *Deutsche Einheit,* doc.no. 293.

83 Ibid., p. 278.

84 Falin, p. 493.

85 Ibid., p. 492.

86 Kohl, vol. 2, p. 116.

87 Kiessler and Elbe, pp. 153–54. Zelikow and Rice (p. 307 and n. 45) report that Genscher had been pushing for the most conciliatory tone.

88 Zelikow and Rice, pp. 221–24.

89 See Smyser, p. 390. See also Biermann, pp. 665–76.

90 Teltschik, pp. 297–98.

91 Most specific report (including press release) in: Teltschik, pp. 316–42. See also Kohl, vol. 2, pp. 162–85 as well as the book by the government spokesman: Hans Klein, *Es begann im Kaukasus. Der entscheidende Schritt in die Einheit Deutschlands* (Berlin, 1991).

92 Kiessler and Elbe, pp. 209–14. Zelikow and Rice (pp. 259–63) insist that the new phrasing was in no way different from the previous agreement.

93 See Teltschik, pp. 357–63. See also: Kohl, vol. 2, pp. 209–17.

94 *Vertrag über die Entwicklung einer umfassenden Zusammenarbeit auf dem Gebiet der Wirtschaft, Industrie, Wissenschaft und Technik zwischen der Bundesrepublik Deutschland und der Union der Sozialistischen Sowjetrepubliken*, 9.11.1990, in: Bulletin der Bundesregierung, No. 133 (15.11.1990), pp. 1382–87. See also Kohl, vol. 2, pp. 258–66. As to the prospects of these relations see the speculations by Nikolai Pawlow, *Die deutsche Vereinigung aus sowjetischer Perspektive* (Frankfurt a.M., 1996), pp. 243–52.

CHAPTER 7

The expensive takeover business

The result of the first free elections was a clear mandate for fast-track unification (§ 23 Basic Law) as advocated by the "Alliance for Germany". However, it did not produce an overall majority for the latter which scored 48.15 per cent and secured 194 seats out of 400. The Liberals, prompted by the West German FDP to get their act together, had no problem in joining the new government since their proposal for a plebiscite on the question of unification had already been realised by the elections. But they could supply only 21 seats, not enough for the two-thirds majority required for any changes to the constitution. In fact, by 4 April the Round Table had published a new draft constitution that incorporated all the demands of the human rights movement for a democratic renewal of the GDR or, alternatively, for a new all German constitution. Its civil rights went far beyond those laid down in the West German Basic Law, guaranteeing, *inter alia*, work, accommodation and education. The draft also revealed a strong inclination towards pacifism: "The country's coat of arms is a depiction of the motto 'Swords into Plowshares'."[1] It was the last political manifestation of the civic movement which had spearheaded the revolution only to be dismissed by popular vote. The SPD was faced with a dilemma: while it had been supporting the indirect approach to unification via a new constitution it was now called upon to make the best of the new situation by joining the government of Lothar de Maiziere who had accepted, in principle, Kohl's offer of a monetary and economic union. Winding down the GDR on the best terms available, which meant adding a social dimension to the union, required a strong government that would have the backing of a large majority of the new democratic parliament. Divided in itself between the executive committee and the parliamentary party, the SPD also received confusing signals from its Western sister party.[2] Fifty SPD deputies from the

Bundestag, through a telegram, as well as the Young Socialists, advised against a grand coalition which, so they argued, would have to cope with Kohl's false promises. Eventually the new members of the *Volkskammer* reasserted their authority, helped by the exposure of party chairman Ibrahim Böhme as a Stasi spy, and decided to join the government on favourable terms. Markus Meckel's ambition to become foreign minister, and the desperate pleas for common sense by Richard Schröder, who chaired the parliamentary party, made sure that constructive pragmatism triumphed over antagonistic posturing.

However, this did not mean that idealism had died. The *Volkskammer*, now dominated by conscientious theologians, was keen to demonstrate to the world that the GDR, too, had learnt the lessons of history. On 12 April "the first freely-elected representatives of the GDR" acknowledged the historical responsibility of their country for the crimes committed by Germans during the Nazi period, especially against the Jews and the people of the Soviet Union, as well as for the suppression of the "Prague Spring" in 1968 by Warsaw Pact troops. They also confirmed "the inviolability of the Oder-Neisse border with the Republic of Poland".[3] A week later, Lothar de Maiziere, the newly elected and, as it turned out, last prime minister of the GDR, delivered his government's statement: in the same spirit and this time addressed to his fellow countrymen in the West, appealing to their sense of national solidarity by reminding them that it was the East Germans who had paid the price of war. After acknowledging the "many wonderful signs of friendship, helpfulness and openness" he also revealed his concern "to see a trend of decreasing willingness to sacrifice and to show solidarity".[4] The main message was his government's firm pledge "to implement unity via a path based on an agreement under article 23 of the Basic Law", preceded by "a monetary, economic and social union". The latter was indeed the next big issue that the new government had to tackle. And it could be argued, that on this issue, the SPD managed, once again, to shoot itself in the foot.

The offer of a currency union was one of the answers to the impact of mass migration on the strained resources of the Federal Republic. By the end of 1989 everybody knew that the damage being done to both German societies could not be sustained for long. In this most volatile situation, Oskar Lafontaine, leader of the opposition to the Bonn government, came up with the idea of closing the gate once more by terminating the common citizenship in order to prevent the thousands of refugees from having "access to the social security system of the Federal Republic".[5] This was a longstanding demand of the SED which Bonn had always refused with reference to the

Basic Law and which, in the last resort, had produced the present crisis and thus a unique historical chance. Was it an act of political suicide that the SPD should go on to appoint a man as their candidate for chancellor who was prepared to play off the West Germans against their fellow countrymen in the East? Oskar Lafontaine (born 1943) and Gerhard Schröder (born 1944) belonged to that generation of West Germans who were born during or after the war, were often active in the student movement of 1968 and felt most uneasy about the sudden upsurge of national sentiment in the East because they cared more about the views of their French neighbours and about Europe at large than about the German nation state, which many of them had long since written off. The East German theologian Richard Schröder remembers that while Hans-Jochen Vogel (born 1926), his opposite number as leader of the parliamentary party in Bonn, discussed every move with him Lafontaine showed "no interest in talks with us".[6] I never forget what a friend of mine, a teacher from Freyburg Saale, who went out of his way to take part in the Leipzig demonstrations, had told me in 1990: "In ten years time you would not have wanted us any more!"[7] I was shocked but could not disagree since I knew how many of my West German friends, much as they welcomed the East Germans' struggle for freedom, felt lukewarm about the prospect of unification.

Fortunately, the SPD was not completely dominated by what journalists referred to in the 1980s as the *Toscana Fraktion* and Lafontaine's suggestion turned out to be no more than the provocative stimulus to a serious debate on how to cope with the mass migration of East Germans. Towards the end of 1989 the leaders of the parliamentary SPD in Bonn, notably Wolfgang Roth and Ingrid Matthäus-Meier, along with other experts in the field of economic and financial affairs, came up with the idea of a currency union of sorts. They had the backing of the SPD's MEPs. By mid-December the inner circle of the government had already come to the same conclusion.[8] The ongoing mass exodus and the impending collapse of the GDR led Bonn's political class to the inescapable conclusion that only the Deutschmark would stop them from migrating to the land of the Deutschmark! Kohl's advisers had realised that offering monetary and economic union was indeed a sensible alternative to sending an immediate aid package to the East German government, not yet legitimised by free elections. However, the Chancellor was still reluctant to agree to what was, to all intents and purposes, an anticipation of unification. He was only prepared to commit himself publicly on 6 February on the eve of his visit to Moscow when he had reason to assume that Gorbachev had already consented to unification in principle.[9] After consulting Cabinet and party, he declared that he would offer the GDR immediate negotiations on a currency union. Modrow's forthcoming visit to Bonn was scheduled for 13 February.

According to Dieter Grosser, this offer was "one of the riskiest decisions Kohl had ever taken".[10] The title of his study, the most comprehensive of its kind on the subject, tells it all: "Daring Monetary, Economic and Social Union. Political Constraints in Conflict with Economic Rules". Indeed, most of the economic experts in the land, with Karl Otto Pöhl, head of the *Bundesbank*[11] (Federal Reserve Bank), in the forefront, were strongly opposed to what they felt was an irresponsible gamble, a step that should have been taken only after a transitional period of rising productivity and as the crowning end of economic harmonisation. But these were extraordinary times. Kurt Biedenkopf, a leading economist and former rival of Kohl, expressed the mood of the CDU in the *Bundestag* better than anyone else at the time, by saying: "Revolutions have no place in textbooks."[12] Monetary Union proved to be the decisive asset of the "Alliance for Germany" during the forthcoming election campaign even though the exact exchange rate had not yet been fixed. This offer was all the more effective as Oskar Lafontaine, Kohl's challenger for the chancellorship in the forthcoming federal elections, publicly warned against a currency union that had not been agreed with Brussels. He argued that, since the nation state had become obsolete, German unification could only be achieved as part of further progress towards an ever closer European Union.[13] This was not the message to convince East Germans to vote for the SPD in the spring of 1990. And many among their own ranks in the East tried to keep their West German comrades at bay. Once part of the government, the East German SPD had to play a useful role during the forthcoming negotiations about the monetary and economic union which, after all, should also cover all matters of social security.

In his government statement, de Maiziere had asked for a 1:1 exchange rate, despite the real rate on the black market being at least 5:1, if not higher.[14] The exchange rate and the question of property rights proved to be the most explosive issues during the negotiations. Experts of the Federal Reserve Bank feared for the stability of the Deutschmark while East Germans dreaded the return of Germans reclaiming their confiscated property in the East. That a treaty covering so many sensitive issues was negotiated and signed within six weeks was only possible because the "real existing socialism" of the GDR was to be replaced, lock stock and barrel, by West Germany's successful Social Market Economy.[15] It would be wrong, though, to speak of a 'diktat', because Bonn had to pay a heavy price for the bankrupt's assets, in the end a price much higher than anticipated at the time, which could only be rationalised in terms of historical justice and national solidarity. Nevertheless, coming cap in hand to their wealthy West German cousins had been a most humiliating experience for all East Germans involved in these negotiations. The data about the true and depressing state of the economy, allegedly the tenth strongest in the world, proved a surprise to Bonn, which demonstrates how deficient its intelligence on the GDR had been, in spite of a legion of "experts". The real picture was one of low productivity in both industry and agriculture, high debts run up by state-owned concerns (VEBs) and housing associations and, last but not least, enormous loans from foreign banks. The reaction to the *Bundesbank*'s proposal of a 2:1 exchange rate was widespread protest. More than a hundred thousand demonstrators took to the streets of East Berlin, fearing for their savings and the dream of catching up with West Germany's standard of living.

Norbert Blüm, Bonn's minister of labour, who had a pronounced social conscience and was de Maiziere's most important ally in the West, dismissed all objections raised by economists on purely financial grounds. By 2 May, after much haggling about the treatment of savings accounts, a compromise had been reached: wages, salaries and pensions to be exchanged 1:1; savings were to benefit from this most favourable rate according to age groups (from 2,000 Marks for youngsters to 6,000 Marks for old age pensioners); all additional capital, whether reserves or debts, to be dealt with on the basis 2:1 (foreign loans 3:1). However, West German negotiators thwarted a last minute attempt by the GDR's last government to raise wages and pensions in order to offset the higher prices for previously subsidised commodities like food and rents. The various armed forces of the GDR, the instruments of oppression like army, border police and members of the Stasi, forfeited their special provisions to which they had been entitled, only to be incorporated into the general pension system. Yet Bonn was most generous *vis-à-vis* old age pensioners: their entitlement was raised to 70 per cent of earnings after 45 working years and adjusted to the growth of general earnings (*dynamische Rente*) with minimum pensions increased at once from 330 Marks to DM 495. All this, Ritter states, amounted to a substantial improvement for the great majority of old age pensioners who up to the present day belong to the most contented sections of East Germany's society.[16] Kohl, who admits that they had "no master plan for German unity", would have preferred to delay the costly "Social Union",[17] if it had not been for the expectations of his East German voters and Norbert Blüm who pricked his conscience.

The other bone of contention was the property issue. Here Moscow, prompted by the outgoing Modrow government, felt compelled to warn

Bonn against any attempts to question the redistribution of landed estates ordered by the Soviet Military Administration after 1945. Kohl's government went along with this ruling, even though it was later disputed in the courts by former aristocratic landowners.[18] In their negotiations about monetary union, officials decided to shelve the thorny issue of confiscations before the GDR came into being. There was general agreement, however, that the land reform between 1945 and 1949 could hardly be rescinded. As far as expropriations, ordered by the GDR at a later stage, were concerned, Bonn insisted on the principle "restitution before compensation". In the years to come this decision led to obstacles in the path of investment and thus contributed to the delayed recovery. Again this rash decision indicates that in the course of 40 years and in spite of all national rhetoric West German governments had never made serious preparations for the nitty-gritty of Day X: unification had been a case of collective repression until the poor cousins suddenly knocked at the door.

The coalition government in East Berlin was committed to introducing the new currency union before the summer recess of the *Volkskammer* so that East Germans could set off for their first free holidays with the cherished DM in their pockets. The signing of the treaty on 18 May by Theo Waigel, the West German minister of finance, and his East German opposite number Walter Romberg (SPD) went ahead without further ado. Not so its ratification by the *Bundestag*, where divisions within the SPD took on the character of a political farce. Hans-Jochen Vogel, who had the backing of the parliamentary party for the treaty, went on a pilgrimage to Saarbrücken to beg Lafontaine to change his mind. But to no avail. The "candidate" felt he could not lead an election campaign against Kohl without distancing himself from the latter's policies. By taking this stance, Lafontaine has earned himself the criticism that he saw the events as a matter of electioneering and not the most momentous decision-making process in the Federal Republic's history. "Never in my 64 years", Vogel was reported to have said on his way back, "have I experienced a week like that."[19] At their meeting on 20 May the Minister-Presidents of the SPD-run *Länder* agreed that the treaty should only be accepted on the condition of certain amendments: it was a purely face-saving formula for the sake of party unity. The SPD leadership in the East implored their West German colleagues to abandon their delaying tactics. Yet the gulf within the party could not be bridged and grew ever wider, thus demonstrating how deep the reservations about the idea of a nation state ran in Germany's oldest political party. The arguments employed by Lafontaine against the currency union, which to his mind, was "rash, over-hasty and therefore wrong"[20] came (though based on economic grounds) very close to those used by the PDS, the former GDR's ruling party of which he is now (2008), under its new name (*Die Linke*), the co-chairman. However, it must be said that he did not miscalculate the changing mood of his West German fellow countrymen: by May 1990 only a minority (28.5 per cent) were prepared to make financial sacrifices for German unification. Only six weeks earlier, 61 per cent had accepted the need to make considerable economies. This was not just another proof of the volatility of the *vox populi*. It is sad to say that both major parties had their eyes as much on the federal elections as on the terms of unification: Kohl by refusing to reveal the financial liability of unification – he was not prepared to confront the nation with a Churchillian "blood, sweat and tears" speech – and the Social Democrat Lafontaine by appealing to the hedonism of his fellow countrymen. The SPD leader knew that he could not take it upon himself and the party to wreck the union treaty and thus the prospect of early unification. His manoeuvring was arguably too clever by half and proved highly damaging for his party's electoral chances. The treaty was saved thanks to Hamburg's vote in the Upper Chamber (*Bundesrat*) – so that the SPD could not be associated with what Lafontaine kept referring to as "chaotic consequences". Hans-Jochen Vogel tried to mediate between the majority of MPs, who backed the treaty, and the party's leadership, including the "Young Socialists", who opposed it in its present shape. To overcome the deadlock, the two governments decided to consent to certain unimportant amendments, hoping that the Eastern SPD would persuade Lafontaine and his allies to abandon their opposition. This plan did work: on 14 June, the leadership of both parties eventually agreed to vote for the treaty. In the course of the debate Willy Brandt pleaded for a united stand on the German Question and threatened to lay down his honorary chairmanship. "We must see to it", he is quoted as having said, "that we don't put the interest of the party before that of the German people."[21] However, the party remained divided to the end. When the final vote was cast in the *Bundestag* on 21 June, 444 voted in favour, against an opposition of 60, of whom 25 were members of the SPD. In the *Bundesrat*, all SPD-led *Länder* voted in favour of the treaty except for Saarland (Lafontaine) and Lower Saxony (Gerhard Schröder). On the same day, the *Volkskammer* had passed the treaty by a majority of 302 to 80 with only one member of the SPD voting against his party – former chairman and Stasi spy Ibrahim Böhme, who thereafter vanished from the political scene.

Monetary and economic union had been an emergency measure to halt the mass migration and prevent further chaos. It did not determine the legal procedure under which the merger of the two states would actually take place. It was a matter of great political and psychological importance whether the GDR was to be absorbed into the Federal Republic (as the Saarland had been in 1956) as the result of a regional plebiscite and in accordance with *Grundgesetz* § 23 or whether a new state would be created on the basis of a new constitution provided for by § 146.

As mentioned above, the Round Table, by spring 1990 more the organ of the civil rights movement than the electorate, had already developed a draft constitution, with the explicit approval of the SPD delegates. On the eve of the first free elections the SPD was still divided, with a majority of the Eastern grass roots inclined to go along with the fast-track solution of § 23, which proved to be the great asset of the "Alliance for Germany". The SPD (West), still wrestling with monetary union, favoured the organic approach via § 146, which seemed to offer the chance of "deepening and extending the democratic substance of the new Republic".[22] Willy Brandt, always an advocate of "daring more democracy", declared himself in favour of a plebiscite in both parts of Germany "for national-psychological reasons". Sturm makes a very pertinent point that sums up the complex situation between the two parties, in many ways even between the two societies: "The SPD argued that the procedure via § 23 would deprive the East Germans, enabled through § 146 to make their own contribution, of their right to self-determination. Now, the SPD (West) tried to impose this approach on its sister party."[23] The unspoken assumption "We in the West know best what is good for you political greenhorns in the East" was a kind of leitmotiv of unification.

The conservative government saw no need to meddle with the Basic Law, which had stood the test of time. But Interior Minister Wolfgang Schäuble, an efficient administrator, realised early on that state structures had to be adjusted and that this required careful planning. From mid-February a group of 20 advisers began to work towards a legal blue-print for unification. Later, after the free elections, news about another treaty would smooth the passage of monetary and economic union and was bound to forestall calls for a new constitution. Bonn wished to send out signals saying "A fast-track solution via § 23 does not mean that you have no say in these matters". It was an important message. Ordinary people in East Germany did not mind that the currency union had all the hall-marks of a West German takeover. However, the GDR's new political class resented it deeply: in international law the GDR was still an independent, and for the first time, truly democratic state. Once the procedure according to § 23 had been established by free elections it would have been feasible and perfectly legal if the *Volkskammer* decided by majority vote to resurrect the old *Länder*, incorporate them into the Federal Republic and leave it to the *Bundestag* to introduce a bill that would regulate the details of transition (*Überleitungsgesetz*). This sword of Damocles hung over all negotiations conducted by de Maiziere's government in the summer of 1990. The government had to steer a course between two extreme procedures: a new state after long constitutional deliberations, or a kind of shot-gun marriage by a blitz vote in parliament. To avoid the impression that the country was about to be swallowed up by the Federal Republic, a proper unification treaty was indeed required. It would need to be freely negotiated and to settle all outstanding matters left over from the first treaty. After all, monetary union had left the government with no other option than to join on the most favourable terms.

In East Berlin preparations for such a treaty started much later than in Bonn because the first treaty was still on people's mind and de Maiziere and his colleagues preferred a longer transitional period, knowing full well that they were all working towards their own redundancy. Moreover, de Maiziere felt the need to put his own house in order before a unification of the two states could be approached.[24] However, Schäuble's opposite number, Günter Krause, leader of the CDU in the *Volkskammer*, was more pragmatic and keen to reach an early understanding. After an exchange of draft papers, the two delegations met for the first time on 6 July shortly after the currency union had come into force.[25] De Maiziere insisted on the term "*Einigungsvertrag*" as though two equal partners were about to work out a merger agreement. "The division could only be overcome by sharing"[26], he declared thus expressing a widespread feeling in East Germany. However, while ordinary citizens had in mind the sharing of wealth, he also believed that a new state would emerge and that its proper purpose and symbolic representation, such as its name, capital, flag and anthem, were up for an agreed revision. He was soon to be disillusioned when Schäuble reminded him of the true state of affairs: The Federal Republic was welcoming its fellow countrymen as in the past with open arms, ready to help, but the Basic Law was not to be remodelled as a result. After the first clash of opinions and an understanding to postpone the delicate question of the future capital, negotiations proceeded surprisingly well. Soon it turned out that Schäuble would have more problems with his own people than with Krause, especially with the mostly SPD-run *Länder*, which resented not having been involved in the first treaty and were only too aware that they had to share the financial burden with the reconstituted *Länder* in the East. While each delegation consisted of nearly 50 participants, the West German one represented altogether more diverse interests. But the East German negotiators were in a particularly weak position because they were faced with an unknown body of new legislation and had no mandate for a veto.

The first and most difficult question was: would the laws of the GDR remain in force for the time being, save for a certain number of federal laws or vice versa. Schäuble, too aware of Bonn's complex legislation after 40 years, pleaded for a generous transitional period. Not so his colleagues, the ministers of justice, finance and labour who were concerned about the equality and security of the law throughout the land: the reintroduction of the rule of law meant to them that the same law should prevail throughout. Surprisingly, the East German government gave in, and when the two delegations met again in early August it was decided that Federal Law should be the norm, with an annexe of specified exceptions.[27] However, Schäuble could at least convince the East German delegation that this was not the time to solve questions which for some time had been controversial in the Federal Republic or to extend the whole range of social benefits.

The decision to agree to the introduction of Federal Law might have been influenced by the fact that by the end of July the GDR was virtually broke. The government was in near panic when it turned out that the money supplied by Bonn for the transition, DM 14 billion in all, had already been spent and pensions could not be paid. A month before, de Maiziere had warned against the undue haste of marriage preparations. Now in August, he and Krause rushed to the Chancellor's holiday resort in Austria to suggest an early date for both unification and federal elections (14 October).[28] The idea, also first favoured by Schäuble, that unification should be confirmed by separate elections, i.e. a popular vote by the East Germans for the new *Bundestag*, was now abandoned in favour of a last say by the *Volkskammer*. This scenario occurred earlier than expected when the modalities for the federal elections came up for debate. The two governments agreed that the first joint elections should take place on 2 December on the assumption that the GDR would cease to exist on that day. However, SPD (East) and FDP did not go along with the prime minister's commitment and pressed for early unification. As a result, the FDP left the government. To avoid a total break-up of the coalition, it was agreed to decouple unification from the election date. But the election treaty also entailed problems that caused a great deal of controversy among parties and constitutional lawyers in the West. Did the 5-per cent blocking clause, once designed to ban tiny parties and potential troublemakers, apply to the new territory as a whole, as demanded by the SPD, or to its separate constituents? In the latter case, the PDS, successor party to the SED, would have a fair chance of being represented in the new *Bundestag*. A clear majority in both parliaments voted for a treaty that laid down the same date for the first federal elections (2 December) and the same voting mode for the whole country, thereby keeping the old communists out of the new parliament (22–23 August). That was not the end of the matter because the Federal Constitutional Court was later to intervene and suspend the law for the benefit of the smaller parties in the GDR (29 September) – for the first all-German election the 5-per cent blocking clause would apply to both parts of the country separately and parties were allowed to join forces in parliament (*Listenverbindung*).

In East Berlin attention was focused on the unification date. It was in this context that a motion was proposed in the *Volkskammer* to bring it forward to 3 October. The result was announced in the early morning of 23 August at 2.45 a.m. Of 363 deputies 294 had voted for the motion by the CDU/DA, SPD (East), DSU and FDP. Only two members of the SPD voted against and two abstained.[29] In many ways it was, in spite of all the confusion at the time, the most historic moment of the whole process of unification, because the *Volkskammer*, the first freely elected parliament of the GDR, had voted for the extinction of its own state. Ever since Chancellor Kohl had come to power, he had argued that it was up to the East Germans, not to those in the West, to decide whether they wished to live in one country. It is important to reiterate that according to the Basic Law, the Federal Republic had no choice but to recognise them as fellow citizens, whether individually, as in the past, or collectively as from 3 October, 1990. Fortunately, it had not come to a separate ballot on the issue because a plebiscite in the West might have been a strange if not shameful affair, with many influential leftwing intellectuals as well as those concerned about an economic downturn in the West, voting against unification.

Strictly speaking, the *Einigungsvertrag* had now become superfluous, because the newly elected all-German parliament could regulate all necessary adjustments by way of a *Überleitungsgesetz* (law for managing transition). However, in the meantime, the unification treaty had made considerable progress – quite apart from its psychological impact, which was to demonstrate that the last government of the GDR had come through to fight for the interests of its people. We must therefore turn to the last stages of these negotiations which, after all, were concerned with nothing less than unwinding the fabric of a twentieth century state, including legislation, administration, state assets, international treaty obligations, culture, social questions, etc. East Berlin was particularly interested in the clarification of financial questions, social issues and changes to the constitution. While Bonn's technocrats busied themselves with legal procedures, their colleagues in the East were worrying about very specific problems. Just to give a few examples picked from one of the first papers handed to Schäuble:[30] What about Kohl's promise to help with employment? Would women in the GDR be able to retain their *Haushaltstag* ("home work day") they had been entitled to, their maternity leave, their child allowance, their right to secure nursery school places? Would divorce and abortion laws be adjusted in line with the stricter federal standards? Would school certificates and university degrees be recognised? Would "Carl Zeiss Jena" retain its famous company name or would it be transferred to its sister firm in Oberkochen, West Germany? And so forth. In the end, the treaty, covering nearly 1,000 pages including all annexes, settled even questions like the right of East Germans to stay overnight in their beloved allotment datschas. West German officials, mostly lawyers by profession, hoped that most of these questions would be covered by existing laws and regulations without allowing for too many exceptions. However, there were certain sticking points which had to be worked out in detail in order to reach a consensus – between the two governments as well as within de Maiziere's coalition government. The SPD's frustrations about the unification treaty, negotiated by Krause, leader of the parliamentary CDU, rose steadily to the point of open criticism by Werner Romberg, Minister of Finance, who confronted the prime minister with a treasury crisis. When the latter dismissed him on 16 August, the remaining ministers belonging to the SPD left the government. De Maiziere, who took over foreign affairs from Marcus Meckel, was now fully in control, no longer burdened by a coalition partner in cahoots with the SPD (West), which always had an eye on the forthcoming federal elections. Nevertheless, he could not do without the votes of his former partners if he wished to achieve the required two-thirds majority for the unification treaty. The SPD (East) was tempted to scuttle the whole treaty, opt for early unification and leave it to the *Bundestag* to sort out the mess, possibly a new parliament dominated by the Social Democrats who would then do their best to reward their East German voters. This at least was the line taken by Oskar Lafontaine, who encouraged his fellow Social Democrats in the East to raise their demands. It was, in many respects, a repeat performance, reminiscent of the negotiations on monetary union. In the end, the SPD in both states could not afford to be seen boycotting a freely negotiated treaty that paved the way to a unified country. All they could bargain for were better conditions for their East German clientele.

On 24 August, a day after the *Volkskammer* had voted for early unification, a draft treaty on all its essential conditions was ready for signing. Indeed Schäuble, who had worked hard for a fair deal, believed it could be initialled that very day. But he had not reckoned with the opposition at home and its electioneering tactics. The SPD (West) could not enter the election campaign without showing itself to have made a significant contribution to the unification process. Hans-Jochen Vogel, its chairman, told the Chancellor in no uncertain terms that the draft in its present form, negotiated without consulting the major parties, would not do. Kohl agreed to convene a summit of party leaders. The first of four such meetings took place at the Chancellery on 26 August. The SPD expected clarification on the following issues: property rights, satisfactory financial provisions for *Länder* and local governments, acceptable rules on abortion and certain improvements to the Basic Law. Vogel's bargaining position was not particularly strong, however, because nobody truly expected the SPD to turn down the unification treaty. Moreover, Schäuble proved to be a skilled negotiator in that he fixed a final date for signature in advance and decided to leave tricky issues to the all-German legislator, i.e. the new parliament, to resolve. At the last minute, the FDP, with the backing of the SPD, raised objections to the consensus reached on abortion, so that the signing process had to be put off for another two days. Eventually, Schäuble and Krause signed the final version in East Berlin at 1 p.m. on 31 August. Not surprisingly, further amendments were agreed upon before the two parliaments gave their final approval on 20 September (*Bundestag:* 442:47; *Volkskammer:* 299: 80).

So much for politics, but what about the problems that stood out as the major obstacles to an early understanding? These issues are significant for two main reasons. They are the first indications – more were to follow – of the gulf which had been widening between the two German societies for the previous 40 years. They are, moreover, evidence for the need of an overhaul of the Federal Republic's constitutional set-up which raises the question: Was the unification process a missed opportunity for reforms that had been long overdue? No doubt the SPD would have answered affirmatively. There was general agreement that the preamble of the Basic Law had to be revised, now that the German people had achieved the unity and freedom for which they had been fighting for the past 200 years. Paragraph 23, which provided for the accession of further territories to the area where the Basic Law was in force, had also become obsolete. More than any treaty with Poland, these revisions confirmed that the new Germany had, as it were, reached its final destination and had no intention of regaining territories east of the Oder-Neisse border. The cancellation or retention of paragraph 146, which provided for a new constitution and thus the creation of a new state, was a much more controversial matter. German political culture has always been tinged with an element of Utopia. It was the political Left in both German states that had been particularly affected by this penchant, in spite of the experiences of two dictatorships in the twentieth century, which, it could be argued, should have inoculated them against this tendency. Drawing lessons from the Nazi period, the Federal Republic's Basic Law, promulgated in 1949, had expunged all decision-making by plebiscite, allowed for by the previous constitution (Weimar). However, during the civil rights movement in the autumn of 1989, grass-roots democracy (*Basisdemokratie*), under the banner "We are the people", had triumphed over a dictatorship "in the name of the people" (*Volksdemokratie*) and seemed to have earned itself a place in the new constitution. Nevertheless, the very same people had also urged its new government, including the SPD, not to put too many obstacles in the path of early unification, of reconstituting the nation. It was therefore the SPD's sister party in the West that took up the demand for more democracy, for a more social democracy to be precise. Schäuble, who wished to keep revisions of the Basic Law to the absolute minimum, realised that in order to achieve the required two-thirds majority, he would have to meet the opposition halfway. He would need to retain a revised paragraph 146, i.e. the vague prospect that a new constitution, to be decided by the German people in a free vote, could not be ruled out in the future. That concession, however, would not satisfy the SPD's chairman Vogel, who insisted that the unification treaty should contain a more specific commitment. In the end, Schäuble got his way by suggesting a compromise that followed his guiding principle: the contracting parties recommend that the future parliament should be called upon to deal with all problems, highlighted by unification, which required revision or amendment of the Basic Law, within two years. He thus managed to put off solving the disagreement to a future date. It worked, perhaps not least because, at this point in German history, none of the parties were able to predict what issues might preoccupy the *Bundestag* in months and years to come.

Another bone of contention was the future capital. In the eyes of Lothar de Maiziere Berlin was the cornerstone of German unification, since it symbolised so uniquely the period of separation. It was his *conditio sine qua non* that the treaty named Berlin as the capital of a united Germany. Though he himself had no problem with Berlin becoming the capital, Schäuble knew that Bonn had staunch supporters within all parties, quite apart from the thousands of civil servants who had settled there. Moreover, all *Länder* governments except one, of course, were united in their opposition to Berlin which, over the years, had become a financial millstone around their necks. It now emerged that the Bonn Republic had engendered an emotional attachment never achieved by the Weimar Republic. The small provincial town on the Rhine represented a thoroughly peaceful and harmless Germany, almost reminiscent of the period before 1871. In Bonn

(*Bundestag*), consensus depended on a viable future (in terms of investment and compensation) for the old federal capital (Bonn): in East Berlin
(*Volkskammer*), it depended on a firm pledge to make Berlin again the
capital of a united Germany. Schäuble, aware that a face-saving formula
was called for, came up with the idea of naming Berlin as the capital while
leaving it open whether it would also be the seat of government. To prevent
another dubious compromise, the *Bundestag* decided that parliament and
government should not be geographically separated. Nobody dared to ask
how a capital should be defined, if not by the seat of government. However,
the *Länder* would not be appeased by Schäuble's splitting exercise. Again,
Lafontaine was prepared to scuttle the treaty if the *Länder* were to be denied
their say in the matter. Opposition within the upper chamber (*Bundesrat*)
was eventually overcome by minor changes to the protocol that ensured
that the *Länder* should be involved in a future decision even though it was,
constitutionally speaking, none of their business where the *Bundestag* would
meet in future.

Three further issues proved to be most contentious: how to deal with
property titles;[31] differing laws on abortion; and the huge archive of Stasi
files, which affected the identity of so many GDR citizens. Apart from the
general unease about employment prospects under capitalist conditions,
no issue caused more anxiety among East Germans than the uncertainty of
property rights, which concerned almost half of all commercial businesses
and an equal percentage of agricultural lands. Nazis and Communists had
confiscated the property of millions of Germans who were driven into exile
and death. What about their property rights, and those of their descendants
now that the rule of law was about to be restored? When the problem was
first discussed in connection with monetary union it became obvious that it
defied any simple solution. Both Modrow and de Maiziere could count on
Moscow's support. The Soviet government made it abundantly clear that
unification was at risk unless the legality of land reform carried out after the
war under its authority be recognised. Schäuble was not inclined to disagree
with this position. However, as so often, he was challenged from within his
own ranks, in this case the Liberals, the CDU's coalition partner, who voted
for restitution of all confiscated land. On 14 March, the Cabinet Committee
on German Unity agreed to take the following line whenever the problem
was mentioned in public: The principle of private property remained sacro-
sanct and should be restored in the GDR as far as possible and according
to the rule of law. Only those cases should be open to claims in which
the GDR government had used coercive measures to confiscate private
property. However, social and economic conditions generated over 40 years

could not just be rescinded, as that would have meant replacing one kind of injustice with another. The definitive decision to recognise the redistribution of land after 1945 was taken by both foreign secretaries in a joint letter addressed to the Soviet government in mid-June. At the same time an understanding had been reached on all other property questions, especially as regards land and buildings, which were to be dealt with on the basis of "restitution rather than compensation".[32] Parliament was asked to find some kind of redress for landowners affected by Soviet measures after the war. Apparently nobody thought of introducing long leases for land or property since this system had not been as common as in Britain.

During the summer, when the effects of monetary union were starting to be felt, it dawned on officials that their guiding principle might impede necessary investments. It was therefore decided to include a law which permitted compensation of property claims if they threatened to hamper investment and employment. The East Germans would, of course, have preferred compensation as a general rule because it seemed to imply that the government would then have to pay the bill. Late in the day, the SPD-run *Länder* adopted this interest and demanded that the same principle, i.e. compensation rather than restitution, should apply to all cases of expropriation whether before or after 1949. When he met the Chancellor on 26 August, Vogel argued that this was the only way of guaranteeing social peace in the East. However, the government was not inclined to abandon an agreed position previously approved by the SPD. Nor were Kohl and Schäuble prepared to give in to last minute attempts by deputies of their own party who wished to reclaim all private land lost after the war in the Soviet zone of occupation.

Termination of pregnancy was a particularly delicate issue between the two governments, which were both dominated by the Christian Democrats. In the GDR where women's rights were taken more seriously than religious reservations, the legality of abortion depended on the time-scale (*Fristenregelung*), while in the West medical and social indications were decisive (*Indikationsregelung*). Since the two procedures could not be reconciled, it was agreed that, for the time being, both should be legal. The debate then focused on the question whether residence or the place of abortion, would entail exemption from legal action. Schäuble persuaded his party and the East German government to adopt the principle of residence, which meant that a woman from the West would be committing an offence should she have her pregnancy terminated in the East. This time, the West was on the defensive and tried to fend off the more liberal GDR position. However, shortly before the treaty was to be initialled, the FDP questioned the consensus and pleaded for the alternative principle, i.e. that a woman of the Federal Republic would go unpunished if she had her abortion carried out in the East. The Liberals, who had the minister of justice and the SPD on their side, hoped to use the unification treaty to liberalise West German legislation. They were also in favour of extending the transitional period on abortion laws to five years. Schäuble and his conservative CDU would not tolerate more than two years before the *Bundestag* should determine the rule throughout the country. The Chancellor was adamant that the government should represent a united front as far as the unification treaty was concerned. The length of the transitional period, which affected the constitution and thus required a two-thirds majority, was now introduced as a bargaining counter. The Conservatives were prepared to accept the *Tatortprinzip* (place of abortion as criterion) which the more liberal-minded had preferred anyway, so long as the Liberals accepted a shorter transitional period. They did, as did the SPD after lengthy internal debates and a final change of wording which shows that in Germany jurisprudence and theology have much in common. The final draft of article 31 now referred to "pre-natal life" instead of "unborn life" (CDU/CSU) or "life *in statu nascendi*" (SPD).[33]

If for nothing else, the GDR may well be remembered as the most extensive and absurd surveillance state in history. The Stasi was the past that would not go away, even after the dragon had been slain. What to do with its agents, formal and informal, and how to handle the enormous archive (later specified) that had been saved from final destruction – were two questions which preoccupied the minds of civil rights activists above all others. The two governments took a more detached view. Ordinary Stasi officials, who had spied on their own people, were pensioned off – though without their special bonuses – so they would not cause trouble in the future. A different category were the real spies, those agents, whether from East or West Germany, who had provided the Stasi with intelligence gained abroad or in the Federal Republic. Bonn was inclined to let them off the hook declare a general amnesty and destroy all files. This was understood by the public to mean that all Stasi officials would be exempt from legal action. The emotional uproar in the East was such that negotiations on a limited amnesty had to be abandoned and the whole problem was deferred to after 3 October, in the hope that the climate would by then have cooled. And it did cool down. "There has been no 'victors' justice", as one of the foremost British experts on the GDR observed.[34] The proceedings against some of the top leaders, like Krenz, Mielke and Schabowski, mainly because of the murders of escapees, were more of a nominal nature, for the purpose of maintaining the rule of law. In 1999 the prosecutor's office in Berlin

(*Staatsanwaltschaft II*) closed down, after having looked into 22,000 cases and recommending criminal indictments in 1,065 of them. In many if not most cases the defendants were not sentenced or got away with very light sentences.[35]

The debate on how to deal with the Stasi files proved to be even more difficult. After all, six million East Germans and no less than two million West Germans were affected by these files, as interior minister Peter-Michael Distel had revealed in April. While civil rights activists were proud to have saved the bulk of this material from the shredders, Distel would have preferred to finish the destructive work of the Stasi. Many politicians and officials in the West, including the Chancellor,[36] took the same line, because they were worried about the explosive nature of these papers and their potential for abuse. Post-war governments in the Federal Republic were rather relieved to learn that all membership cards of the Nazi party were in the hands of the American Army. However, now a powerful lobby of human rights activists claimed that without these archives no justice could be done to the victims of the SED. Nor would it be possible to come to terms with 40 years of dictatorship or indeed learn the lessons of that experience. In other words, the Stasi files were seen as the most important historical records of the GDR, in that they might explain why a régime, which in the end collapsed overnight, could have survived for so long. Schäuble and Krause, the two negotiators, wished to lay down the restrictive use of this sensitive material, which should be deposited with the Federal Archives and be supervised by the Federal Data Protection Commissioners. The *Volkskammer*, suspicious that the West might get its hands on these files, quickly passed a law on 24 August regarding "the safekeeping and use of all the personal data of the Ministry for State Security", which were to be deposited at special archives affiliated to the new *Länder*. Schäuble and Krause refused to incorporate this law into the unification treaty, because splitting up the Stasi material and the responsibility for its use did not make sense. Finally, it was agreed to put Joachim Gauck[37] in charge, by appointing him to the position of "Special Commissioner of the Federal Government for the Administration of Documents and Data belonging to the former Ministry of State Security". In fact he was promoted from an office he had held before on behalf of the GDR government to the same function on a Federal level, though now equipped with generous funds and a huge staff of experts. Henceforth, his archive, which would soon employ more than a thousand people, would be referred to as the "Gauck Bureau".

In order to join the Federal Republic according to paragraph 23, the GDR government had to reconstitute the original five *Länder*, which had been replaced by 15 districts in the early 1950s. To facilitate the process, the new *Länder* were formed out of these administrative districts with a final redrawing of the border lines after regional plebiscites. After unification, the territory of the former GDR was officially referred to as the five "New Federal *Länder*" (NBL): they are "Mecklenburg-Vorpommern", with its capital Schwerin, "Sachsen-Anhalt" (Magdeburg), "Brandenburg" (Potsdam), "Thüringen" (Erfurt) and, by far the most populated unit, "Freistaat Sachsen" (Dresden). East Berlin was just reunited with the Western part of the city from which it had been separated in 1948. It would have made much more sense to recreate larger and more viable units. But, as in so many other areas, the pressure of time scuppered all attempts at reform. The complicated procedure for territorial restructuring as laid down by the Basic Law was another impediment. Moreover, the civil rights activists were glad to see the SED centralism being replaced by a rebirth of historical tradition. The attitude of the old *Länder* to the newcomers reflected the growing unease among West Germans towards their "poor relations". That at the time most of the old *Länder* were ruled by the SPD, a party traditionally on the side of the underdog, made no difference. Looking on the new *Länder* as poor petitioners, they were unwilling to share federal funds such as their percentage of the turnover tax. The less well-endowed *Länder* of the Federal Republic, which benefited from a compensation system (*Länderfinanzausgleich*), feared becoming worse off financially. To be spared any such losses, the *Länder* agreed to set up a "German Unity Fund" by means of a loan to be financed by the Federal Government and the *Länder* in equal shares. The prospect of unification did not produce a new sense of national solidarity, a readiness to give and share, as might have been the case had division been overcome by the mid-1950s. The Federal Republic had prospered to such an extent that its citizens had shed their national feelings until unification became a con-stitutional requirement from which there was no release. The old *Länder*, as well as the West German population, tried to maintain their standard of living as far as possible. However, it must be said that as far as the rebuilding of a democratic and administrative infrastructure was concerned, the old *Länder* were ready to give the newcomers a helping hand.

When EU Commissioner Vasso Papandreou wished to know whether the Federal Republic had adopted any social institutions of the GDR, Bernhard Jagoda, permanent secretary of the ministry of labour, could not think of a single example.[38] Not that the GDR had nothing to show for in terms of social achievements; women's rights, for instance, had been particularly well protected by the state. However, the pressure of time and the "window of opportunity" opened by Gorbachev left no chance for a simultaneous reform of the Federal Republic's welfare system, with or without the adoption of certain GDR institutions. Gerhard A. Ritter, to whom we owe the most comprehensive study of the crisis of the German welfare state between 1990 and 1995, came to the conclusion that during the unification phase "there was no genuine chance for major reforms".[39] Indeed, he goes further by interpreting the successful efforts at grafting the West German model on the East as "evidence of its capacity and efficiency under difficult circumstances".[40]

German unification was the result of crisis management prompted by mass migration followed by the implosion of the GDR. What had begun as euphoric revolution in the streets of Leipzig and elsewhere had turned into a technocratic takeover business in the hands of hundreds of West German officials. Not surprisingly, this transformation, done at breakneck speed, caused a great deal of frustration among East German dissidents and civil rights activists, who harboured hopes for a new, more democratic German state. According to Konrad Jarausch, the unification treaty was better than its opponents admitted and worse than its advocates maintained. The final verdict of his perceptive study is a very balanced one:

The wish that East and West would meet halfway ignored that dictatorship and democracy are essentially incompatible; the expectation of an agreement between two equal partners overlooked the collapse of the GDR; the hope that unification would be preceded by reforms which were overdue did not reckon with parliamentary majorities.[41]

Having said all this, it must not be overlooked that the precise date of unification had been determined by the *Volkskammer*, not the *Bundestag* or West German officials. It was the East Germans who willed and craved for unification after having endured 40 years of boredom and repression. On the part of the Federal Republic, unification was primarily perceived as an extension of the democratic welfare state to that part of Germany, which for purely geographical reasons had been subjected to a dictatorial régime enforced from abroad. The political establishment of the governing parties (CDU/CSU and FDP) and their political clientele welcomed the rebirth of the nation state, though not as a reincarnation of Bismarck's achievement. It is therefore fitting that 3 October has been turned into Germany's official holiday. It is equally symptomatic that 3 October 1990 has been celebrated as a popular festival around the Brandenburg Gate with official speeches and fireworks but no pomp or circumstance.

Notes and references

1 Konrad H. Jarausch and Volker Gransow (eds), *Uniting Germany. Documents and Debates 1944–1993* (Oxford, 1994), p. 137.

2 Daniel Friedrich Sturm, *Uneinig in die Einheit. Die Sozialdemokratie und die Vereinigung Deutschlands 1989/90* (Bonn, 2006), pp. 332–45.

3 Jarausch and Gransow (eds), pp. 138–39.

4 Ibid., p. 140.

5 Quoted by Gerhard A. Ritter, *Der Preis der deutschen Einheit. Die Wiedervereinigung und die Krise des Sozialstaates* (Munich, 2006), p. 191.

6 Sturm, p. 390.

7 Interview with the author on the occasion of his friend's visit to Oxford in the summer of 1990.

8 See Wolfgang Schäuble, *Der Vertrag. Wie ich über die Einheit verhandelte* (Stuttgart, 1991), p. 21.

9 Helmut Kohl, *Erinnerungen 1982–1990*, vol. 1 (Munich, 2005), pp. 1057–59.

10 Dieter Grosser, *Das Wagnis der Währungs-, Wirtschafts- und Sozialunion. Politische Zwänge im Konflikt mit ökonomischen Regeln* (Stuttgart, 1998), p. 177.

11 See David Marsh, *The Bundesbank: The Bank that Rules Europe* (London, 1992). But not any longer, one might say today.

12 Quoted by Grosser, p. 183.

13 Ibid., pp. 189–90; also Sturm on Lafontaine at the SPD Party Congress in Berlin (18–20.12.1989), pp. 237–253.

14 English translation of speech in Jarausch and Gransow (eds), pp. 139–42.

15 Negotiations described in Hanns Jürgen Küsters and Daniel Hofmann (eds), *Dokumente zur Deutschlandpolitik. Deutsche Einheit. Sonderedition aus den Akten des Bundeskanzleramtes* (Munich, 1998) pp. 139–53 (henceforth: *Deutsche Einheit*); also Grosser, pp. 277–329.

16 See Ritter, *Preis der deutschen Einheit*, pp. 195–238. For a summary, see also his previous work, Gerhard A. Ritter, *Über Deutschland. Die Bundesrepublik in der deutschen Geschichte* (Munich, 1998), pp. 221–24.

17 Helmut Kohl, *Erinnerungen 1990–1994* (vol. 2 Munich, 2007), pp. 122–28.

18 See *Deutsche Einheit*, p. 142.

19 Sturm, p. 404.

20 Ibid., p. 408.

21 Ibid., p. 414.

22 Quoted by: Konrad H. Jarausch, *Die unverhoffte Einheit 1989/90* (Frankfurt a.M., 1995), p. 263.

23 Sturm, p. 423.

24 This was the impression which Schäuble (p. 34) had gained.

25 For the decision-making process see: Wolfgang Jäger, *Die Überwindung der Teilung. Der innerdeutsche Prozeß der Vereinigung 1989/90* (Stuttgart, 1998), pp. 478–525.

26 Schäuble, p. 124.

27 See Ritter, *Preis der deutschen Einheit*, 241–43.

28 See Jäger, p. 479.

29 See Jarausch, pp. 284–93; Sturm, pp. 419–36.

30 Jäger, p. 483. Schäuble tells us (p. 125) that his government did not turn up with their own draft but expected the GDR to make suggestions by drawing attention to their problems.

31 See Grosser, pp. 330–45.

32 Text of agreement between the two government, ibid., pp. 336–39.

33 Jäger, p. 515.

34 David Childs, "The Changing British Perception of the GDR: a Personal Memoir", in Arnd Bauerkämper (ed.), *Britain and the GDR. Relations and Perceptions in a Divided World* (Berlin, 2002), p. 395.

35 See James A. McAdams, *Judging the Past in Unified Germany* (Cambridge, 2001).

36 Kohl, vol. 2, p. 206. Recently confirmed by Wolfgang Schäuble (Home Secretary at the time). See / Süddeutsche Zeitung, 13.1.2009.

37 Ibid., pp. 215–18. See Joachim Gauck, *Die Stasi-Akten* (Hmburg, 1991); also: Werner Weidenfeld and Karl-Rudolf Korte, *Handbuch zur Deutschen Einheit 1949–1989–1999* (Frankfurt a.M., 1999), pp. 727–30.

38 Ritter, *Preis der deutschen Einheit*, p. 295.

39 Ibid., p. 294.

40 Ibid., p. 298. Ritter's book has been aptly summarised in a review in Süddeutsche Zeitung (on 7 January 2007) "Einigung im Eiltempo. Der Lebensstandard im Osten stieg; das Vertrauen schwand".

41 Jarausch, p. 272.

CHAPTER 8

The long hangover

The diplomatic process was a great success, not least because German unification seemed the only exit strategy for a crisis that had been triggered by the ongoing migration and the manifest bankruptcy of the GDR. However, the rush into unity also accounts for the severe domestic problems that lay ahead. Any company would have shied away from such a risky takeover business. But it is important to remember that unification was a political necessity, not the commercial undertaking that some of its critics suggested. At the outset, Kohl and Modrow had envisaged a slow pace solution, starting with a gradual build-up of federal structures and taking, perhaps, up to five years or more. A longer transition period might have given people, and above all the economy, more time to adjust to the eventual merger. But one of the chief architects of German unification, Home Secretary Wolfgang Schäuble, says: "Who would have hesitated in 1990 would have gambled away the chance of unity, perhaps for ever."[1] Economic historian Dieter Grosser,[2] agrees and argues that another five years of separation may have virtually depopulated the GDR, or have led West Germans to become disillusioned to the extent of abandoning the project of unification, which, to many of them, had seemed an unrealistic one in the first place.

Generally speaking, historical decisions, while often based on other than rational motives, are nevertheless buttressed with rational arguments. To Helmut Kohl and his coalition government, the year 1990 offered a singular opportunity to reconstitute the nation state. Missing it, they feared, could incur the wrath of future generations. They felt, therefore, that any sacrifice was justified in the name of national solidarity and national identity. In the 1950s and early 1960s no government would have hesitated to stress that motive in public, before the electorate. Attitudes, however, had changed. By the 1990s, politicians feared they would lose elections if they demanded people tighten their belts in the interest of the greater national good. Kohl, therefore, persuaded himself and the public that the burden of reunification could be shouldered without raising taxes. It is unfair to insinuate that he deliberately deceived the public as to the real costs of unification, of which others, such as his opponent Oskar Lafontaine, seemed rather more aware. Two illusions were crucial if we are to understand why the government did not anticipate what lay ahead.

First of all, Bonn was in possession of few hard facts as to the true state of the East German economy.[3] Since the days of *Ostpolitik*, serious research on the GDR, such as that carried out by the *Forschungsbeirat für Fragen der Wiedervereinigung*, had been wound down for the sake of better relations with the Honecker régime. It was no longer politically opportune to expose the GDR's mismanagement of the economy, for instance as a result of nationalising another 11,400 private enterprises in 1972. Official statistics were henceforth taken at face value. The 1990 edition of *Baedeker's* travel guide to the GDR, told visitors that the country occupied tenth place among the world's leading industrial economies. Journalists from the West, accredited since the early 1970s, were not encouraged to look behind the façades of buildings and industrial plants and report on the real state of affairs. Not even the *Bundesbank* disposed of safe data on the GDR's national debt or gross national product. The Banks' experts believed that privatising national enterprises would earn them enough money to bankroll the economic transformation, while the last SED government hoped to turn the income from such sales into "people's shares". The journalist Uwe Müller put it this way: "The journey into the adventure called reunification resembled a blind flight in thick fog, inside a plane with no navigational instruments."[4] In other words, though some may have had forebodings, nobody had a clear notion of what it meant to fuse a thriving market economy with a socialist one. There was after all, no precedent that could be studied: It was to be a singular historical experience. No wonder that when, at a later stage, delegations from South Korea arrived to learn their lesson, they would leave Bonn with the realisation that a sudden collapse of North Korea would be an unbearable calamity.

The second major illusion resulted from a false historical analogy to which Kohl, a historian by profession (his PhD had looked at post-war German politics) was particularly prone. He later admitted himself that in this respect at least he had been mistaken.[5] But at the time he held the firm belief that monetary union in 1990 would release the same sort of economic energy as the West German currency reform had in 1948. In that year, West

Germans got their first taste of the Deutschmark, of real hard currency, after years of shortages moderated by the black market. Pessimists like Oskar Lafontaine were told that a new economic miracle was on the horizon. However, the background could not have been more different. After the war, the Americans (while in Thuringia for a short while) and the Russians stripped the Soviet zone of occupation of both brains and assets. Whereas the United States propped up West Germany with Marshall Aid, the Soviets regarded their zone as war booty, so that by 1955 the reparation bill, once submitted to the whole of Germany, had been settled.[6] The study by the British economic historian Alec Cairncross, who came to that conclusion, carries as a dictum a quote from Theo Sommer (1985), editor-in-chief of *Die Zeit*: "The West Germans were lucky. It was the East Germans who paid the full price of Hitler's war." By the end of 1948, 732,000 people had fled the Soviet zone; by 1961, when the Wall was erected, another 2.7 million had followed. These were, in the main, young and highly motivated migrants who, once settled, helped fuel the West German economy. Benefiting from low costs and an undervalued currency, West Germany was soon to supply Western Europe with consumer goods, while the GDR was left to satisfy Soviet demands for industrial equipment. In short, the terms of trade faced by the Federal Republic after 1949 and by the GDR in 1990 were very different. Kohl and his ministers could have told their electorate that West Germany had been the great beneficiary of the Cold War and that it was now pay-back time – whatever the costs of unification it was nothing in comparison to the losses suffered by the East Germans since the Second World War. After 1990, this should have been the key message from the government. Indeed, the entire welfare system should have been overhauled to make it fit to shoulder the burden of unification and of an increasingly global economy.[7] Nothing of the sort happened. Instead, the GDR was swiftly brought into line with the Federal Republic's overregulated administrative and social system. The political management of the economy also continued to follow established patterns without regard for the new situation. Governments, whether run by the CDU/CSU or the SPD, had got used to overcoming a crisis by pumping public money into the infrastructure, rather than launching thorough-going reforms. In a sense, German unification demonstrated how easy it is for societies to become the victims of their past successes. These general remarks are meant to make the developments that occurred after 1 July 1990 – the story of how the economy of the GDR was seized by terminal decline – a little easier to understand.

The adjustment of the administrative structures in the former GDR caused few problems and concerned mainly local government which, in the field of social policy, was now to shoulder responsibilities previously carried by central government.[8] Local self-government had always been the pride of German constitutional history – it had preceded full democracy on the national level by more than a century. It was now reinstalled first by the elections on 6 May 1990 when up to 75 per cent of mayors were replaced by new personnel and then by a new law 11 days later, which restored financial independence and made local government compatible with the Federal Republic. As from 1 July all communities, two-thirds of them with fewer than 1,000 inhabitants, were subsidised by the Federal government. To keep the system functioning, the lower echelons of the bureaucracies remained in the hands of experienced officials of the old régime who were obliged to follow the orders of the new crop of political leaders, often scientists or theologians with a clean record. Since at that time no new *Länder* had yet been constituted, local government was also in charge of education and culture (this process is reminiscent of the way in which West German democracy, after the war, had been rebuilt from the grassroots on the initiative of military government). On that level cooperation between West and East began much earlier and in a more tangible sense than elsewhere. Between summer 1989 and October 1990 town-twinning between both German states rose from 70 to 854. The same process of logistical support was set in motion as soon as and even before the new *Länder* had been reconstituted by law on 22 July. The interior ministers of the West German *Länder* agreed to share responsibility for the new *Länder* between them: Schleswig-Holstein and Hamburg would be in charge of neighbouring Mecklenburg-Vorpommern, Niedersachsen would cooperate with Sachsen-Anhalt, Nordrhein-Westfalen with Brandenburg, Hessen with Thüringen, Baden-Württemberg and Bayern with Sachsen. Hundreds of civil servants from the West turned into commuting advisers who would spend only weekends at home. Not surprisingly, quite a few of those West German "pioneers" rose to prominent positions in the new *Länder*, becoming Lord Mayor (Leipzig) or even Minister-President as did, for example, Kurt Biedenkopf (Sachsen) and Bernhard Vogel (Thüringen). Politicians and officials imported from the West seemed to have the know-how that would enable them to exact the highest subsidies from Bonn. On the whole, they enjoyed a better reputation than West German entrepreneurs who often tried to channel such financial transfers into their own pockets.

Berlin was a special case, not only because it epitomised the Cold War and its decline like no other place in Europe.[9] In administrative respects the fusion of the divided city posed no problems. Article One of the Unification Treaty said that the 23 districts were to form the *Land Berlin*. By January

1991 the city state had a new government (*Senat*) following the first free elections since 1946 on 2 December. However, in party political terms, Berlin remained a divided city for the rest of the century. The elections for the Chamber of Deputies revealed that the socialist PDS gained 31.3 per cent of the votes in East Berlin with only 1 per cent in the Western part. At the federal elections in 1998 the picture had not changed much (30 per cent : 2.7 per cent). Of course, East Berlin, capital of the GDR, contained a high percentage of officials who had been made redundant, thousands of former diplomats, Stasi agents, NVA officers and other stalwarts of the old régime. After all, the entire East German diplomatic corps had been sent home.[10] The same applied to the higher ranks of the NVA, which, within one year, had been reduced from 90,000 to 50,000 soldiers as the East German contingent of a much reduced *Bundeswehr*.[11] Only petty clerks at the lower echelons of local government had been retained. That the officials of the old régime vented their frustrations at the ballot box and not on the streets could be seen as a vindication of the new system – aided, of course, by the blessings of the welfare state.

The question of Berlin's status was an altogether more complicated matter. The Unification Treaty stipulated that "the capital of Germany is Berlin", without specifying what that meant exactly. Would parliament and government have to make a move from Bonn to Berlin? Would the Bonn Republic, which stood for years of solid democracy and political reliability – tranquillity, even – be replaced by the Berlin Republic with its memories of the darkest moment of German history? These questions elicited heated public debate, which deeply affected the identity of the new Germany. Lothar Gall, one of Germany's foremost historians, for instance, pleaded for Frankfurt-am-Main, the city where once the emperors of the old Empire had been crowned and which was now the financial centre of the country, set apart by distinctive high rise office blocs ("Mainhatten") and Germany's largest airport. The advocates of Berlin argued that to reject the city at this stage would be dishonourable, and that it alone offered a bridge between East and West Germany – a place where the two societies, the two Europes, could find reconciliation. The climax of this discussion came during the *Bundestag* debate preceding the free vote on 20 June 1991. It lasted 11 hours and included some very passionate performances on both sides. The result was surprisingly close: 338 to 320 in favour of Berlin.[12] Most deputies of the CDU/CSU and SPD, though not its leaders, had wished to hold on to Bonn – it was the Liberals and the smaller parties such as the Greens, who tipped the scales. The debate itself, more perhaps than the eventual outcome of the vote, was most significant. It was now clear that the new Berlin Republic had severed its roots with Bismarckian state-building. The old GDR had more in common with *Preußen-Deutschland* than the new enlarged Federal Republic, which is an extension of the Rhenish or Bonn Republic. In many ways, one could argue, Greater Germany, in the guise of the Second and Third Reich has been replaced by a combination of Greater Holland (West and North), Greater Saxony (East) and Greater Switzerland (South).

The implementation of the vote for Berlin proved to be a chapter of its own. The original timescale for the move of the government could not be met and was constantly extended. Certain ministries were allowed to remain in Bonn with outlets in the new capital: agriculture, defence, health, research and technology. Kohl had a say on the design of the new chancellery (known as the "washing machine" in the vernacular) but he was unable to commandeer his civil servants to pack up and move from the Rhine to the Spree. Preparations for the move were so slow that the suspicion of secret sabotage cannot be dismissed out of hand. Perhaps a few ministerial officials, attached to their homes in Bonn and surrounding villages, hoped to hold on until their retirement. Mounting costs and the worsening financial situation of the federal budget served as a perfect excuse for procrastination. Only the presidents of the Federal Republic, Richard von Weizsäcker and Roman Herzog, set a good example by moving their official residences to Berlin in the mid-1990s. In the end, it was the new Chancellor Gerhard Schröder who gave the decisive signal when he summoned his new cabinet to Berlin for the first time on 25 November 1998. A couple of years later the Berlin Republic was fully established in the new capital.

So much for high politics – but what impact did unification have on ordinary people? The first wave of monetary union hit the average consumer hard, after subsidies for basic foodstuffs like bread, butter and vegetables were cancelled. From one week to the next bread was six times more expensive.[13] However, industrial products like household commodities and electric appliances were cheaper than before. As happened in West Germany following the currency reform of 1948, shop windows and department stores were suddenly crammed with consumer goods. Motorways into the GDR were blocked with lorries. West Germany's industry had enough spare capacity to supply the whole of the East German population, which found these products more attractive than their own: they were offered for the same price, if not for less, and were generally of better quality or at least better marketed. It is perhaps rather regrettable that during the first weeks and months retailers, not yet privatised, charged higher prices than in the West. Not surprisingly, people often did their shopping across the border, their favourite items being colour TV sets, video recorders and fashionable clothing. It says a lot about past frustrations that they spent most of their new Deutschmark on second-hand cars and package holidays. In July and August, 1990 no fewer than 330,000 new vehicles were registered, nearly a tenth of the existing stock. Naturally the authorities were concerned about living costs. But it turned out that for the average employee's family of four, these costs actually had gone down by 5 per cent over the previous 12 months. The worrying question though was whether the breadwinner would be able to hold on to his or her job in the near future.

The drop in East German production and sales was dramatic.[14] Even industrial companies with capital to invest bought their new equipment in the West while their own products proved uncompetitive in every respect. In the past, state-owned industries had been credited with 4.40 Mark for each DM they gained for their exports, mainly in the field of textiles, furniture and chemicals. To stay competitive, their productivity should have gone up and their prices down. In actual fact the opposite happened. Wages were raised in anticipation of the exchange rate and in view of higher earnings in the West. Managers were not at all prepared for Day X. They were used to looking to the state for help, this time to the white knight in the guise of the Federal government, which was keen to sell all state-owned enterprises. The attitude of West Germans after 1945, of course, had not been dissimilar. From one month to the next they looked, not to the Nazi Party for food and a future, but to the Allied military government, in other words: to the new *Obrigkeit* (authorities).

Trade with Comecon countries offered a temporary respite. Exports were heavily subsidised to meet existing contracts, especially with the Soviet Union. DM 5 billion were made available in the second half of 1990 because Bonn wished to foster this trade and to please Gorbachev.[15] While the going was good, East European countries went on a shopping spree in the GDR. Thus capital goods, even the notorious *Trabant*, joke of a car that it was, continued to be exported to the East. But as soon as trade was to be conducted in hard currencies, this cosy market was bound to collapse. In the long run, the loss of this protected market following the demise of Comecon and the Soviet Union proved to be one of the decisive reasons for the depressed state of the economy in the new *Länder*. German competitors abroad had no reason to worry about East Germany: in the second half of the 1990s it contributed no more than 3 per cent to Germany's exports while the tax revenue per person reached 31 per cent of that of a West German citizen.[16]

Though people enjoyed their new life, they were all too aware of the flip side of freedom – unemployment. Hitherto employment had been guaranteed because, under socialism, productivity and profit did not come into the equation. After 1 July, the GDR was exposed to the harsh climate of capitalism. Industries faced a complete shut-down or a process of rigorous rationalisation to make them fit for privatisation. The rate of redundancies soon rose dramatically. It was clear that the transition to a market economy could never be achieved without financial help from Bonn. The Federal government, officially in charge since 3 October, set itself two tasks: (a) to privatise all state-owned enterprises as soon as possible if a buyer could be found; (b) to mitigate the necessary fallout of that operation by looking after the unemployed so that ordinary people were not worse off than before, at least not in financial terms. If it had not been for the generous West German welfare system, which now covered the new citizens whether old, sick or unemployed, the impact of this unprecedented slump within the precincts of one national economy would have been catastrophic. Now it was more a psychological problem for those affected and a financial burden for the Federal government.

Bonn was determined to create the conditions for a free market whatever the costs, even if it meant partial deindustrialisation. This became the gigantic task of the *Treuhand AG*, a kind of trusteeship that acted as a holding for all of the "people's enterprises" (*Volkseigene Betriebe/VEBs*). The idea of such a holding company had originally been suggested in February 1990 by Wolfgang Ullman, a theologian and one of the civil right activists at the Round Table. The transition to joint-stock companies held out the prospect of a more efficient economy. Some would-be economists among the Social Democrats believed in a country-wide distribution of "people's shares" with a view to turning former propaganda into reality. The Modrow government then set up a new office in order to transform some 8,000 enterprises, hitherto run by state employees, into capitalist businesses managed by the same officials. Privatisation though was not on the agenda. Nevertheless, some stalwarts of the old régime seized their chance to become real capitalists through management buy-outs. But in most cases, altogether more than 3,000 up to the end of June 1990, the transition was a farcical operation that no Western accountant would have underwritten.

With the agreement on monetary union by mid-May, Bonn, now virtually in charge of the GDR economy, suggested new terms of reference and a new outfit for the *Treuhand*.[17] The organisation would have to make a serious effort to privatise industry, not only those small businesses that had been nationalised in the early 1970s and could thus be returned to their previous owners. Yet even de Maiziere's government was reluctant to part immediately with what they saw as national assets. They preferred privatisation "step by step" while Bonn insisted on this transformation being carried out "as soon as possible". Eventually East Berlin accepted all of the West's changes to their draft legislation without causing a row. However, the precise structure of the new *Treuhand*, i.e. how to divide responsibilities for various holdings and companies, remained unclear when the *Volkskammer* was asked to give its blessing. There were still quite a few deputies who had second thoughts and believed the move to represent a sell-out of their country's assets. They accepted that the proceeds from sales should be used to finance the budget and all necessary structural adjustments. But what was left over, they decreed, should be turned into shares that should compensate people for the loss of their savings due to the unfavourable exchange rate (2:1). The law distinguished between firms that could be restored to profitability and those that could not and would have to be closed down. If a business could be sold as it was, it would not be redeveloped. Naturally, in many cases the need to modernise was reflected in the price. Clearly, privatisation and the creation of a competitive market had top priority. However, saving jobs and creating new ones was very important for political reasons. Here a dilemma arose because redevelopment often implied rationalising production by shedding jobs, as indeed was also soon to happen in the old Federal Republic. Businesses did not have the same latitude as government offices, which were also overstaffed (and arguably remain so to the present day) because the taxpayer in the West would meet these expenses anyway. When the new law came into force on 1 July all of the remaining 4,000 firms became joint-stock companies. The *Treuhand* was now in charge of nearly 8,000 former state-owned firms covering more than half of the GDR's territory, and four million employees. The new boss, Detlev Carsten Rohwedder, was an experienced manager from the West, and had been permanent secretary of state in the Ministry of Economics for ten years before becoming chief executive officer of the steel firm Hoesch, which he put back on its feet. The board of the *Treuhand* consisted of the minister-presidents of the new *Länder* as well as representatives of the German Federation of Industry, the Trade Unions and certain banks. As was to be expected, most of the top officials were recruits from the West. It was not until unification was a fact that the new organisation became a half-way functioning body. Soon afterwards, on 1 April 1990, Rohwedder was murdered in an attack by the German terrorist organisation *Rote Armee Fraktion* (RAF). He was replaced by an energetic woman, Birgit Breuel, who remained in charge up to the final days of the *Treuhand* some six years later.

The *Treuhand* was faced with an impossible task: finding buyers for companies that were clearly unprofitable. Hardly any investor would be prepared to take on the large industrial plants with obsolete equipment and an inflated workforce, except for certain companies which, after due redevelopment, held out the prospect of a secure market in the future, such as electricity or food processing (sugar, milk products, cigarettes, etc.). Often enterprises could only be sold if the *Treuhand* offered a low price, paid outstanding debts, made good ecological damages and did not impose hard conditions such as the saving of jobs. According to its guidelines, redevelopment should be left to the new investor who might have his own ideas. In many cases though, some of the costs of modernisation were met if an investor had submitted a convincing concept or if the prosperity of a whole region depended on one big employer. Thus the survival of the once world-renowned firm of Carl Zeiss Jena cost the public no less than DM 3.5 billion – almost enough money to pension off the whole workforce. To prevent total deindustrialisation in the name of capitalism the Federal government decided in 1992 to make more money available in order to save industrial core areas such as the shipyards along the Baltic coast. The latter were sub-sidised to the sum of DM 7 billion so that one-fifth of the former work-force of 50,000 could be retained. At the same time, former *Kombinate* (large conglomerates) were split up into 25,000 small businesses (shops, hotels, restaurants, etc.) which could be sold more easily. When the *Treuhand* closed down at the end of 1994 there were only 65 firms left in its portfolio. Altogether 860 enterprises were sold to foreign investors like Dow Chemicals, and 3,000 were acquired through management buy-outs. Henceforth super-vision of remaining transactions passed to a federal office "for special tasks in connection with unification". Only that branch of the *Treuhand* which was in charge of leasing all land holdings and properties once in possession of state and party was kept in business for the time being. By the end of 1994 the *Treuhand* had spent some DM 320 billion and had netted only 67 billion without being able to prevent the loss of two million jobs, half the previous workforce.

It is not surprising that the *Treuhand*'s activities met with harsh criticism from East Germans, who often felt that what they had spent their lifetimes building up had been sold off to dubious customers within a few years. There is no doubt that, in the short term, unification proved a bonanza for West German entrepreneurs who gained a new home market and picked the few plum parts of the old industries with a view to expanding their busi-nesses or eclipsing potential competitors. For a short while, East Germany indeed became a playground for some of capitalism's more unsavoury

characters – the asset strippers, and those who were happy to pocket subsidies, but less keen on providing a service in return. To some extent this
was unavoidable, given how quickly an entire national economy needed to
be transformed. But these incidents did not help improve people's perception of capitalism, which had been demonised by Communist propaganda
for many years. Officials of the PDS, successor party to the SED, were quick
to say "we told you so! This is what you wanted!"

The decline of the East German economy into long-term depression was
not anticipated. During the first half of the 1990s it looked as though East
Germany would slowly catch up with the West. GDP, which was down by
19 per cent in 1991, rose between then and 1994 from 7.8 per cent to 9.9 per
cent, only to drop again to 2 per cent in 1997.[18] It was only when the impact
of globalisation began making itself felt that it dawned on the government
that *Aufbau Ost* (Reconstruction of the East) would not be accomplished as
soon as all state-owned enterprises were in private hands. Globalisation
forced managers to rationalise production by slimming down the workforce.
As an export nation, Germany had always benefited from a global market.
However, this time the driving forces were the arrival of international
investors in strength and their expectation of short-term profits. German
entrepreneurs started to move their production sites for the manufacture of
cars, household goods and the like to countries beyond the Eastern borders
where wages were much lower. Moreover, countries like Poland, the Czech
Republic and Hungary would soon join the European Union and offer the
prospect of new markets.

The chief incentive (apart from subsidies) to investing in the economy of
the *Neue Bundesländer* (NBL), would have been lower labour costs. However,
the Federation of Trade Unions (DGB) took a keen interest in negotiating
favourable wage agreements for their new recruits in the East, regardless of
lower productivity. Since spring 1990 *IG Metall*, the Metal Workers Union,
had been particularly active in the GDR. Which works committee would not
be tempted by the argument, equal pay for equal work. At a time of radical
change the old management was not inclined to pick a fight with its
workforce. Thus in August *IG Metall* succeeded in negotiating a 30 per cent
rise coupled with a reduction in working hours (to 40) and a concession of
one year's notice if they wanted to reduce the workforce. In other sectors of
industry, such as the building trade, wage increases were much higher still.
All this was to lead to disaster on the labour market. For obvious reasons
employer's organisations were much slower in getting their act together.

The Federal government was in an equally weak position. Bonn could
only improve investment conditions by pumping more money into the

infrastructure and by granting tax relief. East Germany's infrastructure was rotten – public services such as roads, telecommunication, schools and hospitals were run down, housing, especially pre-war blocks of flats, was dilapidated. Bonn's big hope, therefore, was the building sector which, the government hoped, would stimulate the whole economy in the same way as the motor car industry and house-building had done in the 1950s. For a while, this was indeed the case. West German investors, often self-employed middle class professionals, were induced through tax incentives to acquire property in the NBL. But the fat rents investors were promised did not materialise. East Germans could not afford to pay for modernised or newly built flats with all mod cons. Moreover, a fast shrinking population due to ongoing westward migration produced an increasing stock of empty buildings. Young families were tempted by building societies to vacate their prefab flats in the cities for new homes in the countryside. By the mid-1990s the boom in the construction industry was over. Property prices went down, especially in Berlin, and have not fully recovered since. This, however, did not deter the government from continuing to make large sums available for improving the infrastructure such as roads, railways and telecommunication. Local government was showered with money for all sorts of projects like shopping malls, oversized waste disposal plants, indoor swimming pools and other similar projects – not all of which were entirely necessary. In many cases, West German construction firms responsible for some of these white elephants employed migrant labourers, using local trades only as subcontractors.

The East German labour market was the government's greatest worry, because rising unemployment kept up the cost of social benefits – money that it would rather have spent on investment. And for a population which based its self-esteem on a strict Protestant work ethic, the psychological impact of being jobless was devastating. The unemployment rate went up from 2.7 per cent in 1990 to 17.1 per cent by the end of the century, when it reached nearly twice the level of West Germany (9.5 per cent in 2000) – where unemployment had also risen due to the effects of globalisation.[19] In certain areas, the job losses between 1989 and 1996 were more dramatic than in others: in agriculture the labour force went down from 976,000 to 210,000; in industry (manufacturing, building, mining, etc.) from 4.39 million to 2.14 million. Even after shrinking from 2.2 million to 1.4 million the public service sector remained overstaffed. These figures would, of course, have been much higher still, had it not been for non-stop migration to the West. Between 1989 and 1999, 1.7 million East Germans, more than one-tenth of the whole population, moved to West Germany. As only 600,000

West Germans settled in the NBL, the net loss in the East was more than one million. By 2003, the NBL were losing around about 100,000 people a year. Further factors helped to tone down the official figures. Many people living close to the former border decided to commute, for instance from Thuringia to Hesse, spending only weekends at home. Others opted for early retirement, as happened increasingly in West Germany, where industry passed on their redundant workforce to the safety net of social security. The government also sought to alleviate the situation by financing job-creation programmes throughout the NBL, often in co-operation with local government. All these were desperate measures to keep unemployment figures from rising further, since they were regarded as the crucial indicator for the success of *Aufbau Ost*.

The economic depression affected East German women in particular with unforeseen consequences for Germany's demographic development. In the old GDR virtually all men and women capable of gainful employment were at work. Women had enjoyed their social contacts at work and their financial independence from fathers and husbands. This was to change dramatically. By 1993, 70 per cent of men but only 55 per cent of women were still employed. Two-thirds of those registered as unemployed were women (compared to 47 per cent in West Germany). It is perhaps no wonder that the birth rate in East Germany plummeted. It had been much higher than in West Germany because of incentives for young families, such as special allowances and cheap housing. On average, each East Germany woman gave birth to two babies (compared to 1.4 in the West). From 1988 to 1994 the number of children born in East Germany went down from 220,000 to 79,000, which prompted one author to comment that only the Vatican produced fewer offspring.[20] The same author tells us that the town of Zeitz, East Germany could boast Europe's first (1846) and henceforth most established production site for prams (brand name: Zekiw), making 4,000 a day since 1972 and exporting these to 20 countries. In 1998, the firm went bust. In demographic terms the two world wars had less of an impact on the population in East Germany than the consequences of unification. As before, it is West Germany that benefited from this exodus of the young, skilled and dynamic migrants from the NBL which, within three years, lost 8.2 per cent of its population, while the old Federal Republic gained 6.58 per cent. Both cities and small towns were equally affected by this dual effect of migration and a declining birth rate, those in predominantly agricultural Mecklenburg-Vorpommern like Schwerin (minus 23.35 per cent) and Rostock (minus 20.6 per cent) being worse affected than others.[21] A study by the Bertelsmann Foundation into towns with 5,000 inhabitants and more, concluded that by 2020, some East German cities will be reduced to half their original size. Massive westward migration of 18- to 24-years-olds is given as the main reason for this dramatic shrinking process.[22] Young women make up a disproportionately large proportion of those moving, thus reinforcing the demographic trend. In some regions the shortage amounts to 20 per cent.[23] Young men seem to be less qualified, less mobile and more receptive to neo-Nazi propaganda. In other words, the NBL are likely to age faster than the West German *Länder*.

The one big worry that haunts German politicians is that East Germany might not catch up with the West and thus slowly turn into a kind of German "mezzogiorno without the Mafia", a depressed region that will have to be permanently subsidised. Maintaining East Germany on that basis would not just be a matter of choice – Germany's Basic Law obliges the legislator to guarantee the same living standards throughout the country. Even if some commentators might plead for a less stringent interpretation by pointing to regional inequality in other countries, the German Constitutional Court, itself a unique institution in Europe, will see to it that the law is upheld. That is why German governments will not rest until the East is level with the West, whatever the costs. If the NBL do become a haven for tourists and old age pensioners, this might well meet the criteria.

All branches of the East German economy have been shrinking since 1990. The one exception is the service industry, which was rather underdeveloped during Communist time, and which rose from an occupation figure of 619,000 to 1.36 million. As a whole this sector, encompassing banks, insurances, hotels, doctors, lawyers, etc., grew by 60 per cent between 1991 and 1996. It is the service industry that caters for tourists and old age pensioners. The Baltic coast, and the island of Rügen in particular, is the most favoured tourist destination. Many aristocratic families have revisited their old estates east of the River Elbe or in present day Poland. A few of them have bought and restored their old manor houses if they still existed. Many of the smaller eastern towns, lucky enough to have escaped Allied bombing raids, such as Naumburg, Quedlinburg, Meissen, Bautzen or Görlitz, have been lavishly restored and now offer visitors a real feel of a merry old Germany – lost now, in the thoroughly industrialised West. In addition, the environment, totally neglected under the old régime, has been cleaned up. This had been one of the chief demands of the civil rights movement.

Thus the overall picture is not all gloom and doom. During the first four years following unification the living standard of old age pensioners and those still gainfully employed rose in an unprecedented way. The net income of the average employee more than doubled between 1989 and 1994 (from M 1,004 to DM 2,300) and he or she now had a far greater choice of consumer goods on which to spend their wages and salaries. Even when the rising cost of basics such as food, rent and utilities are taken into account that increase still amounts to 70 per cent. Generally, unemployment benefits would also buy more than ordinary wages in the GDR. No doubt, the great beneficiaries of unification were groups that had had no lobby in a dictatorship: pensioners, widows, war victims and people with disabilities, who were now covered by the Federal Republic's generous social security system.[24] However, in spite of favourable wage agreements in 1990, there was still a substantial income gap between both parts of Germany, including that of old age pensioners. Between 1991 and 1994 wages and salaries in the NBL went up from 55.7 per cent to 78 per cent of average earnings in the West.[25] Of course, wealth, too, is most unevenly spread after 40 years of Communist expropriation and deprivation. This applies in particular to the housing market with a much higher percentage of owner-occupation in the old FRG. Salaries and wages have been slowly catching up with those in the West. However, there are still considerable differences in the job market. Not only is the unemployment rate still twice as high in the East, but in 2007 every fifth job was paid less than 7.5 Euro per hour compared with every twelfth job in West Germany.[26]

In retrospect, it is surprising that these discrepancies did not produce greater tensions within society. To a large extent this was due to the fact that government and public opinion lived up to their responsibilities in a parliamentary democracy, in that they did not lose sight of their less privileged minorities. The *vox populi* in West Germany, which complained about the slightly raised tax burden (*Solidarzuschlag*), an increase of income tax of 7.5 per cent in 1994, would not furnish moral guidance. As an experienced politician, Kohl knew what to expect from his West German clientele. That is why he abstained from imposing substantial levies and raised the necessary money on the capital market, with the result that the national debt more than doubled between 1989 and 1996.[27] In terms of financial transfers, by 2004 reconstructing the East had cost the FRG 1,250 billion Euro – which prompted the magazine *Der Spiegel* to ask whether *Aufbau Ost* might not lead to *Absturz West* (crash of the West). It is true that in the meantime the publicly financed infrastructure in many East German cities is superior to that in the depressed regions of the West. Nevertheless, without transfers, the GDP of East Germany would be lower than that of Portugal.[28]

Opinion polls suggest that, on the whole, people felt they were financially better off than they had been. However, at the same time, they were inclined to judge the general situation as most worrying. Obviously this had to do with the constant fear of being made redundant. Moreover, people were not accustomed to a free press, which does not, by any means, tend to paint a rosy picture of reality. They were now faced with a press that bombarded them with alarming data on the economy under the impact of globalisation, while most West Germans knew that as an export nation, they owed their prosperity to expanding international trade since the 1950s. East German reactions to being exposed to the harsh climate of international capitalism will be discussed further in the next chapter.

At the end of this chapter it makes sense to emphasise that the decline of the East German economy is entirely due to 40 years of neglect and socialist mismanagement. Generally people tend to blame others for evident failure rather than existing conditions which require careful analysis. Many West Germans, full of themselves and their achievements since the war, are inclined to ascribe the economic problems in the NBL to their fellow countrymen and their attitude to work. "Passive", "only good at doing what they're told", "lack of initiative and entrepreneurial skills" are only some of the common prejudices. Dieter Grosser makes the point that there was no shortage of people with initiative where conditions were favourable, as in the car industry and related areas (dealers, petrol stations, garages, etc.).[29] The migration of so many young adults, especially women, to West Germany looking for work is another argument against such generalisations. Munich is now thought to be the third largest Saxon city after Dresden and Leipzig. The great majority of East Germans are aware that their problems are not the result of German unification. They would agree that it takes one day to fell a whole forest and half a century for it to grow up again. Honecker's decision to nationalise 11,000 small businesses in 1972 had been such a felling.[30] What is still missing in East Germany today is the industrial infrastructure of south German towns with their family-owned firms providing employment for half the population. Big companies, as for instance, the car industry (VW and Opel) that have made large investments in the East, cannot make up for this structural deficit. Most people in West Germany are employed by medium-sized firms in private ownership. They are the backbone of West Germany's industrial strength. Many more of these firms will have to start up business in East Germany before we can talk of the "blossoming landscapes" Helmut Kohl ventured to forecast in 1990.

Notes and references

1 Wolfgang Schäuble, *Der Vertrag. Wie ich über die deutsche Einheit verhandelte* (Stuttgart, 1991), p. 286.

2 Dieter Grosser, *Das Wagnis der Währungs-, Wirtschafts- und Soziaunion. Politische Zwänge im Konflikt mit ökonomischen Regeln* (Stuttgart, 1998), pp. 495–504.

3 See the somewhat alarmist book by the correspondent for *Die Welt* reporting from East Germany: Uwe Müller, *Supergau Deutsche Einheit* (Berlin, 2005), pp. 30–37.

4 Ibid., p. 37 (translation L.K.).

5 Grosser, pp. 499–500 (Interview with Kohl, 1997).

6 See Alec Cairncross, *The Price of War. British Policy on German Reparations* (Oxford, 1986), pp. 207–17.

7 To some extent Kohl admits this in his memoirs when he talks about the Solidarity Pact introduced in 1995: vol. 2, pp. 551–56.

8 See Wolfgang Jäger, *Die Überwindung der Teilung. Der innerdeutsche Prozess der Vereinigung 1989/90* (Stuttgart, 1998), 454–60.

9 See article by Andreas Kießling with subsequent bibliography in Wener Weidenfeld and Karl-Rudolf Korte, *Handbuch zur deutschen Einheit* (Frankfurt a.M., 1999), pp. 57–71.

10 Only London saw the arrival of a new chargé d'affaires after the free elections: the young Leipzig pastor Ulrike Birkner who, on the recommendation of the Anglican Church, took over only to wind down the East German embassy in Belgrave Square.

11 See Jörg Schönbaum, *Zwei Armeen und ein Vaterland. Das Ende der nationalen Volksarmee* (Berlin, 1992), p. 250. Uniforms were exchanged from 2 to 3 October 1990 "as planned" (p. 56).

12 Deutscher *Bundestag* (ed.), *Berlin-Bonn. Die Debatte. Alle Bundestagsreden vom 20.6.1991* (Cologne, 1991). See also Udo Wengst (ed.), *Historiker betrachten Deutschland. Beiträge zum Vereinigungsprozess und zur Hauptstadtdiskussion. Februar 1990 bis Juni 1991* (Bonn, 1992).

13 For the following details see Grosser, pp. 549–51.

14 See ibid., pp. 451–63.

15 Gerhard A. Ritter, *Der Preis der deutschen Einheit Die Wiedervereinigung und die Krise des Sozialstaates* (Munich, 2006), p. 111.

16 Müller, pp. 81–82.

17 See Grosser, pp. 346–64. See also article on the Treuhandanstalt (with bibliography) in Weidenfeld and Korte (eds), pp. 742–51.

18 See ibid., pp. 464–83.

19 Müller, p. 90; also Ritter with statistical evidence: pp. 116–32.

20 Ibid., pp. 95–114.

21 Apart from the charts given by Müller (n. 16) see e.g. the article in *Süddeutsche Zeitung* (15.6.2005): "Ein Land lernt schrumpfen".

22 *Süddeutsche Zeitung, 6.2.2006.*

23 See article "Geld oder Liebe" in *Der Spiegel* 2007/23 (4.6.07), p. 62.

24 See Ritter, pp. 392–402.

25 Ibid., p. 134.

26 According to the *Institut für Wirtschaftsforschung Halle (IWH), Süddeutsche Zeitung, 26–27.1.2008.*

27 On the *Fond Deutsche Einheit* and the problem of how to finance German unification see Grosser, pp. 365–83.

28 Main story of *Der Spiegel*, 2004/15 (5.4.04).

29 Grosser, pp. 461–63.

30 See the excellent article of Frank Ebbinghaus in *Frankfurter Allgemeine Zeitung* (26.2.1997): "Erzwungene Freiwilligkeit. Die Zerschlagung des Mittelstandes in der DDR Anfang der siebziger Jahre".

CHAPTER 9

A crisis of identity

The euphoria about German unification did not last long. It began to dissipate even before 3 October 1990, the official date of birth of the new Germany, to be followed by a kind of open-ended post-natal depression. This feeling was, of course, much more pronounced in the Eastern half of the country. In the West the impression prevailed that they had inherited a huge but run-down family estate, which proved more of a liability than an asset. It seemed a new corporate identity was needed to carry the financial burden and to overcome the psychological and cultural effects of separation. Imagine the problems in terms of a marriage: a couple separated by circumstances but determined to be reunited discover how different their backgrounds are at the very moment of setting up a common household. In the wake of unification the different identities of West and East Germans were exposed for the first time. The inferiority complex that hitherto had mainly affected the régime, ever since the early years of state-building, now seized the whole population. As time went on, each side became more defensive about its own value system, conditioned by totally different experiences.

From time to time, conservative politicians and intellectuals of the older generation have invoked Germany's common heritage and culture. However, the younger generation in the West, moulded by its formative years in the 1960s, had long lost its emotional attachment to the nation state. They were happy to declare their loyalty to the constitution (*Verfassungspatriotismus*) without much regard for the latter's obligation to feel responsible for the other half of the nation. Not a few left-wing intellectuals, unable to distinguish between national solidarity and nationalism had dismissed the nation as an old-fashioned concept. Some self-styled moral guardians, such as Günther Grass proclaimed that with Auschwitz

Germany had forfeited her right to national self-determination.[1] Occasionally, foreign academics detected a certain arrogance among their German students who felt superior to others in their post-national convictions. If West German youngsters happened to bump into East Germans they would often boast that they felt more at home in Paris or London than in East Berlin or Leipzig. To be recognised abroad as German was an embarrassment. Anne-Marie Le Gloannec is right to suggest that for most German intellectuals "the nation is to be understood solely as a pre-political phenomenon, not a democratic one".[2] For a great many West Germans of the educated post-war generation unification came as a shock rather than as an unexpected stroke of luck.

The first signs of unease occurred when the demonstrators in Leipzig, emboldened by the demotion of Honecker and the fall of the Wall, changed track and started shouting *"Deutschland einig Vaterland"* (Germany united fatherland), referring to the part of the GDR's national anthem that had been expunged. While the slogan "We are the people" had been applauded the slight but significant change to "We are one people" had received a rather cold reception in the West as well as among many civil rights activists who wished to turn the GDR into a model state of moral rectitude. Although Kohl and his government were encouraged by this development many journalists and intellectuals were taken aback by what they regarded as the reappearance of a deadly virus. In fact, the slogan had expressed the authentic voice of the people as Richard Schröder, one of the most perceptive East German intellectuals, tells us. At the time he understood this to mean: "Help us. After all we belong together. We can't pull this off alone."[3]

From the moment the fuse of unification was ignited two distinct expectations began to emerge, each arising from differing perceptions of the other. The majority of ordinary East Germans had never abandoned the idea of the German nation, however, as much as it had been ostracised by the SED. But it was not at all the nation state, the so-called *Bismarckstaat*, as defined by the pre-1939 German élite and by its critics after the war. The German nation symbolised the hope of one day being released from the claws of an oppressive régime and being reunited with the other half of the country which, in the meantime, had achieved freedom and prosperity. Their appeal to a common history was indeed a plea for national solidarity. The West should realise that the costs of unification were in fact reparations due to the war and hitherto paid by only one half of the nation. However, hardly anybody in the West saw the burden in those terms, not least because only a few experts were aware of the real fate East Germans had suffered since the war. When the author began reading history at Frankfurt

University in the early 1960s, there was no course on offer dealing with post-war German history. The great majority of West Germans, born during or after the war, did not much care about their fellow countrymen in the East. In the mid-1950s, concern and empathy for the "brothers and sister in the Soviet Zone" were still running strong in West Germany. Later, many fans of Willy Brandt saw *Ostpolitik* as having settled the German Question once and for all. In their eyes the recognition of Honecker amounted to a kind of political rehabilitation of his régime. In other words, most West Germans were ill-prepared for the rendezvous with history in the 1990s. There was not much compassion for the traumatic experience of change to which the East Germans were subjected after 1990, for their expectations, subsequent frustrations and their feelings of being treated as second-rate citizens. All they were now told was that as a result of unification Germany was now a *Normalnation* (normal nation), one amongst others, with no special claim or mission.[4] Even though this message was exactly what people wished to hear and to believe, there is nothing normal about a state evolved from two dictatorships and still inhabited by two different societies. But this yearning for normality after two world wars and 40 years of division and barbed wire could eventually be the foundation of a nation at ease with itself. West German historians are now reconciled to the idea of the nation-state, which after having deviated in the past from the pre-ordained path to democracy and modernity (*Sonderweg*), has now, nevertheless, arrived at its final destination.[5]

All this soul-searching for the sake of a new national identity following unification, however, was largely an intellectual exercise and did not greatly affect ordinary people in the West who soon returned to their everyday routine. Not so the people in the *Neue Bundesländer* who felt as "strangers in their own country", a phrase that kept coming up in their conversations. It was the East Germans who plunged into a crisis of identity. Before the law they were now citizens with equal rights. But the new law was a complicated and confusing business. Moreover, for them, unification was more than a technocratic process of realignment; it was a highly charged emotional experience which few in the West could really appreciate: the euphoria of having peacefully toppled a repressive régime followed by the humiliating request for help, and being rescued from a fast sinking ship. Safely ashore they were being told what a miserable life they had escaped from and how grateful they should be to their saviours. Not surprisingly, they developed an attitude for which Jens Reich, one of the founders of *Neues Forum*, has coined the term *Trotzidentität* (identity of defiance).[6]

Before venturing into generalisations about a common East German mentality it is important to distinguish between three different groups who are vying for attention and pretend to speak for the rest or at least a substantial part of society:

1   the privileged class of the old régime, often academics, artists and former party stalwarts, who try to save their collective biography from the verdict of history;

2   former dissidents and human rights activists who hoped in vain to save the GDR by reconciling socialism with true democracy;

3   the new political leaders from the same background who had realised that there was no alternative to German unification and had joined the freely elected government of Lothar de Maiziere.

The first group found their new home in the successor party of the SED, the so-called *Partei des Demokratischen Sozialismus* (PDS) which receives its popular clout from seizing upon the original concept of group 2. The second group joined forces with the Green Party in the West (*Bündnis 90/Die Grünen*). Members of the third group are now represented in both the CDU/CSU and the SPD and form the new political and intellectual establishment of the NBL. As such they can claim with some justification that they are the true spokesmen for the silent majority of East Germans. This is particularly true of two men of common sense (a rare quality in Germany) who have proved to be the best mediators between the two societies: Joachim Gauck, for many years head of the office in charge of the Stasi archives, and Richard Schröeder, former leader of the parliamentary SPD in the *Volkskammer* and now one of East Germany's most prominent academics and publicists. Both are men of the Protestant Church as are quite a few recruits from the dissident movement. The Church though, having lost its special role before and during the *Wende*, was not happy that so many ministers had left their flock for politics.

The argument that East Germany was "colonised", put forward frequently by those who saw the demise of the GDR as a tremendous loss (coupled often with the end of their professional career), is greatly exaggerated. But this does not invalidate subjective perceptions. A great many top positions in the public domain have been taken over by West Germans, from heads of *Länder* and local governments and law courts to civil servants and academics. The purge affected all universities and research institutes; professors were "evaluated" and those in the humanities were frequently replaced by young

West German academics often at the beginning of a modest career in the West.[7] In banking, industry and commerce it was more or less the same picture. There was no reshuffle of personnel in the opposite direction. The West German establishment remained immune to experts from the East with a few exceptions in the medical and natural sciences. The exchange of élites was much more thorough-going than in the early years of the Federal Republic when the newly established *Auswärtige Amt* was packed with former Nazi diplomats and the law courts were in the hands of former Nazi judges.[8] But the justification for these differences is more pragmatic than ideological. The Federal Republic could not have been built up to the efficient state system it was to become without the unstinting support of the professional classes, who were glad to be re-employed. Their embarrassment at having served a morally discredited régime was the best guarantee for their loyalty to the new democratic state. This was not the case after the demise of a dictatorship that was both less harmful and less popular than the Third Reich, and in a situation where virtually the whole of East Germany could be fed and administered by surplus capacity from the West. Nevertheless, wherever people looked around they met with new faces, new regulations, and new institutions. Naturally they could not help feeling that their old lives were being rubbished, judged to be worthless – or help feeling resentment at what they saw as attempts to totally re-educate them.

The "identity of defiance" against this state of affairs expressed itself in various ways. First and foremost it gave the political Left a new lease of life. To the annoyance of West German commentators, the PDS received a substantial share of the votes in all the NBL, notably in Berlin (East) and the poorer *Länder* to the north. In the first Federal elections in December 1990 the party scored 18 per cent of the votes in East Germany. Saxony and Thuringia in the south were strongholds of the conservative CDU. The PDS is a purely East German protest party with 90 per cent of their members being former socialist comrades who had to relinquish their positions of power and prestige for early retirement.[9] The overwhelming majority of the PDS (88 per cent) did not think that the GDR had been a dictatorship (*Unrechtsstaat*). Nor did they regard democracy as the best type of state (60 per cent).[10] The party tries to camouflage the average age and political origin of their members by promoting young activists and presenting the image of youthful rebellion in public. Moreover, the PDS goes out of its way to listen to the sorrows expressed at the grassroots and to offer a helping hand. The extreme Right, which is opposed to both communism and democracy, also benefited from this unease and widespread unemployment.[11] East Germany turned out to be a promising playing field for marauding

neo-Nazi gangs, often jobless young men, who continuously attract attention by their notorious xenophobic exploits. They have generally enjoyed
logistical support from the West German NPD, the extreme right-wing party,
which is under constant surveillance by the authorities. These youngsters,
often not highly educated and unskilled, who cultivate a macho-image by
their dress code thrive on the indignation of *bourgeois* society and boost
their ego by taking pride in their German ethnicity and seeking the exclusion
of all foreigners. The PDS cannot, of course, be compared to xenophobic
neo-Nazis. Both phenomena, however, require an in-depth analysis, which
examines the mental make-up of the whole of society, even those strata that
have no sympathy for the extreme Left or Right.

The history of the GDR is full of contradictions between propaganda and
reality. Right from the beginning the Communist régime was determined to
surpass all re-education efforts of the Western Allies by creating the "new
man". Yet most psychologists today are agreed that generally East Germans
have more in common with their compatriots of the late 1940s than
with those moulded by 40 years of public controversy. Since 1933 they were
conditioned by official propaganda promoting an ideological belief-system,
not by a free press upholding the virtues of civic society. Through no fault
of their own, they are characterised by what Theodor Adorno and Max
Horkheimer diagnosed in the late 1940s as "the authoritarian personality"[12]
– something is right or wrong; someone is friend or foe, German or foreign;
truth a matter of belief, not empirical evidence; hard work, cleanliness, thrift,
punctuality are prime "German qualities", not "secondary virtues" (Carl
Amery) which can be employed in the service of an evil system. Joachim
Maaz, a leading East German psychiatrist, thinks that the disposition of East
Germans to obey and to conform to norms and standards laid down by the
authorities have helped them adjust to the Western way of life, but at the
price of growing frustration and social neurosis.[13] Ironically, Maaz himself
entertains the same views, or rather stereotypes, about the West German
"elbow society" as many of his patients: only money matters; competition
comes at the expense of human relations; hierarchical relations in the work
place; democracy as the rule of the manipulated majority, and so forth. Even
critical minds like Maaz who were only too aware of the damage done by
dictatorship could not escape from its pernicious after-effects. We know
from research on the formation of stereotypes that these do not stem from
personal experience. In twentieth century Germany they are often due to
the long lasting effects of propaganda, be it Nazi propaganda against Jews
and Bolsheviks or Marxist propaganda against capitalists and Fascist imperi-
alists. The positive message generated by the two German dictatorships has

proved to be even more effective. Opinion polls after the war in the Western zones and in East Germany in the mid-1990s revealed that a majority of the population believed that National Socialism and Socialism, respectively, were basically good ideas badly carried out.[14] It is still common among East German intellectuals to refer to the GDR's social order as "*real existierender Sozialismus*" (real existing socialism) as distinct from a kind of ideal socialism, modelled on the teaching of Christ, which was given no real chance. Like heaven for religious minds, utopia is the home of idealists which will never close its doors. Among those human rights activists who were in the forefront of the revolution there was no shortage of idealists who were then disappointed by the final outcome of their political dreams. They felt let down by the people who put their trust in Kohl and not in "socialism with a human face".

No doubt many East Germans consider social security, above all security of tenure in both work and housing, more important than political freedom. The fact that social security cannot be guaranteed in a free society is a tough truth, especially to people who have been looked after by a kind of paternalistic dictatorship. Richard Schröder suggests that there was a tacit *contrat social* between the old régime and the people: *Wohlergehen* (provision of basic necessities of life) in exchange for *Wohlverhalten* (good behaviour).[15] Therefore most East Germans would prefer a more caring, less achievement-oriented Federal Republic. Certainly values such as security, equality and solidarity have a higher standing in the East than in the West. Opinion polls carried out by the Allensbach Institute in the mid-1990s suggested that Germany was facing a shift to the left.[16] This forecast proved right in that 1998 saw a Red–Green coalition come to power.

The pendulum may well swing back in the other direction for there are also certain features that point to a more conservative mindset. The authoritarian streak has already been mentioned. What has been said about national-consciousness also needs to be qualified. East Germans are more likely to be proud of Germany than their cousins in the West (although it must be said that since unification, and most noticeably since the World Cup in 2006, the self-image of all Germans is improving).[17] Two reasons come to mind that require further elucidation: first, the sanitised version of German history, including that of Prussia; second, a reserved attitude towards foreigners. After 1945, all Germans were reluctant to face up to the horrors of the Nazi past. But whereas West Germans were slowly coming to terms with what had happened, people in the East were, so to speak "born Anti-fascists" or, as Richard Schröder puts it: "Anti-fascism became the congenital myth of the GDR".[18] Their leaders, who had returned from exile or Nazi prison camps, hastened to absolve their citizens from all responsibility for the Nazi period. Socialism was supposed to have worked as a catharsis. The evil spirit of the Third Reich, meanwhile, was living on in the Federal Republic since Bonn claimed to be the successor state and since its offices were staffed with former members of the Nazi Party. As a result, East German schools and the media did not deal with this topic except as a means of denouncing the West. Youngsters, brought up in the GDR, could feel good about German history. During the last decade of the GDR, historians were permitted to extol the virtues of Prussia, a state that had been officially dissolved by the Allied Control Council as the stronghold of German militarism. Prussia now served as the model of discipline at a time when work ethics were beginning to lapse.[19] Incidentally, because the GDR had adopted certain paraphernalia from Prussia (a belief in blind obedience, the goose-step and the cut of uniforms, etc.), it was quite common in the West to refer to "red Prussia", all the more since Prussia's original lands were in the GDR. But Prussia had its defenders in the West as well, such as Peter Bender, who rejected this comparison saying that it was the "pretence" of Prussia, not its "essence".[20] In fact, in ethnic terms, the GDR was mostly run by Saxons, beginning with its first leader, Walter Ulbricht.

This selective approach to German history helped boost morale at a time when the latter had been shattered, especially during the unification process. Moreover, there had been a strange consensus between the SED, its opponents and the rest of society in relation to West Germany in the sense of saying: "We may be poorer than you but we have not disowned our history and character". East German intellectuals, many of them clergy, were inclined to equate material inferiority with moral superiority – a very common illusion nourished by centuries of Christian teaching. In short, East Germans often thought of themselves as the "better Germans". But the history of the German Question is full of irony, as it was West Germans who were disparagingly referred to as *Besserwessis* (a play on words: the word Besserwisser meaning know-all) because of their alleged arrogance and superior attitude. To be sure some of them behaved as know-alls who felt they had to teach the *Ossis* the Western, and by implication the more sophisticated, way of life. Of the thousands of advisers from the West who invaded the country, many could not resist the temptation to proselytise the unenlightened "natives".

Collective identity in East Germany was also shaped by a different attitude towards neighbouring countries and towards foreigners in general. From 1949 onwards, West Germans began to look upon the occupation forces as their allies who would protect them against Soviet Russia during the Cold War. Not so the East Germans, who saw their country as the protectorate of the Red Army, in spite of all the officially fostered activities of the German–Soviet Friendship Society. While the West Germans of the 1950s and 1960s enjoyed the imports of popular culture from the West, first in the form of Glenn Miller, and later the Beatles, Russia had nothing of the sort to offer the GDR. On the whole, East Germans felt culturally superior to their own neighbours in the East. This changed to some extent with the spring uprising in Prague (1969) and the Polish Trade Union's fight for political self-determination in the early 1980s. But ordinary Germans in Leipzig and Dresden mostly remember the regular invasions of their department stores by Polish and Czeck shoppers. To put it crudely: during the formative decades of the FRG and the GDR the West Germans looked up to their neighbours in the West while the East Germans looked down on theirs in the East. It remains to be said, however, that this is not quite such a new phenomenon since in the past German historians referred to the *west-östliche Kulturgefälle*, an unfortunate term for the observation that Western culture had always found more admirers in the East than vice versa. The most glaring example is perhaps Alsace-Lorraine[21] which, to the annoyance of German nationalists, always looked to Paris rather than to Berlin, regardless of whether it was being ruled by France or Germany.

The GDR was a closed society while the FRG had imported foreign labour, euphemistically called guest-workers, since the 1960s, first South Europeans, then Turks. East Germans had little face-to-face experience of foreigners, with the exception of Russian soldiers. Solidarity with people of a different culture was a matter of ideological correctness, not a human disposition backed up by public opinion. Most of the 160,000 foreigners – 1 per cent of the population as against 8 per cent in the West – lived in separate boarding houses and hostels. Apart from students invited to study socialism at work (for example, from Latin American countries like Chile, or African countries like Ethiopia, Libya, Algeria, or from the Near East like Iraq, Lebanon, Yemen), the largest contingent of labourers came from North Vietnam (53,000), Mozambique (13,000) and Cuba (10,000). They had to conform in every respect to the way of life in the GDR – cultural diversity was not an option. The title of a book *Anders sein gab es nicht* (being different was not on) says it all.[22] Their numbers dwindled rapidly after the fall of the Wall – many were sent home, and many were ordered back home by their own governments. Yet at about the same time the new Germany experienced a sudden growth in the number of refugees and asylum seekers from all over the world. Between 1989 and 1992 the overall number went up from approximately 130,000 to 440,000; that of refugees from Africa grew tenfold to 67,400. After the demise of the Soviet Union, Russians of German background (*Russlanddeutsche*) were invited to emigrate to the FRG. Because of their unwillingness or more often inability to speak German, the local population simply regarded them as "Russians". The German authorities had decided to house asylum seekers as well as *Russlanddeutsche* across the country including the NBL. It now happened that otherwise peaceful East Germans, faced with large-scale redundancies and unprepared for the influx from abroad, vented their frustrations on foreigners who were denounced as spongers. In this atmosphere of simmering xenophobia neo-Nazi skinheads felt encouraged to commit atrocious acts of violence against foreigners.[23] What shocked Western observers most of all was the attitude of onlookers, who seemed indifferent to such crimes, and the sheer incompetence of the police. Up to the present day, incidents of xenophobia, generally acts of violence by marauding neo-Nazi gangs, are a specific problem for the NBL. During the World Cup, teams from Africa were advised not to set up their headquarters in the NBL. Experts are agreed though that this phenomenon must be attributed to the social conditions still prevailing in East Germany, mainly to the large number of young men out of work. They also remind us that neo-Nazi activities were a problem in the early days of the FRG only to evaporate slowly over time. Sub-currents of unreformed nationalism as well as general resentments against the expectations of a liberal society may explain why the NPD, which had had its day in the West, managed to establish itself in Saxony. All right-wing activities in the NBL are closely watched by the Länder offices of the *Bundesverfassungsschutz* (Office for the Protection of the Constitution).

Any attempt to understand the political culture of the NBL must look beyond the usual approach of sniffing out shifts to the Left or to the Right. East Germany remained longer in a kind of historical time-warp. It has been dragged along since 1990 still exhibiting certain characteristics of the past, some amiable, some less so. Not only do people feel more German, even proud to be German – their mentality also reaches further back into Germany's collective psyche. It would, however, be misleading to link the more socialist and the more national mind-set to anything like National Socialism in its historical appearance. A German mentality existed long before the defeat of 1918, the hyper inflation of 1923 and the world depression of the 1930s, all of which combined were indispensable conditions for the rise of Hitler. When people from East Germany say that, psychologically, they lived and survived in a "niche society",[24] the historian is reminded of the small pre-modern world of the *Biedermeier* period in the early nineteenth century, where communities were still more closely knit, under the watchful eyes of the authorities. The essential ingredients of this mentality must now be discussed in order fully to understand the traumatic change after 1990.

The GDR was not only a closed but also a sheltered society in the sense that the state provided a modest living for everyone. Citizens who had no desire to be different did not experience the state as the repressive régime it actually was. Life might have been dull and boring yet it was not a struggle for survival since everybody had access to the basic necessities of life and a fixed world-view. Just like the Church in former centuries, the Party enforced ideological conformity and social discipline through its Marxist belief-system. The East German psychiatrist Irene Misselwitz put it this way:

Father State and Mother Party controlled and determined everything: what was good and what bad, right and wrong, what was to be done and what not, what was to be felt, thought and wished for, who was friend and who foe, what was normal and what abnormal, what was permitted and what not.[25]

The final refusal of further obedience in 1989 has helped to suppress the unpleasant fact that the overwhelming majority of the population had accepted this state of affairs, i.e. the perfect alignment of society in accordance with party instructions, with just occasional grumbling. Political participation, like voting at pseudo-elections, sending children to the FDJ, holding up the portraits of party leaders in the manner of religious icons, etc., was a matter of routine just like Sunday service or taking part in Catholic processions in the West. It has been mentioned that a great many of the dissidents from the ranks of the Protestant Church subscribed to the "idea of socialism" because they were worried about the sudden onset of Western consumer society. Even those who had opposed the government like Heino Falcke, the influential provost of Erfurt, warned against the pitfalls of capitalism as late as mid-November 1989, a week after the Wall had come down. "We cannot just be gobbled up by the West, we need an alternative to capitalism."[26] In other words, large sections of the political opposition saw the GDR as their natural home, which just needed a new warden.

Equality was not only valued, it was also, at least to a much greater extent than in the West, a social reality as far as pay differentials and the spread of wealth were concerned. Naturally, lifestyle was also subject to conformity; elegance or eccentricity were unacceptable or would have been frowned upon. This was, no doubt, also a reflection of the poor quality and choice of consumer goods. The great variety of goods and services after 1990 was wonderful for some, in particular the younger generations, but also bewildering and confusing for others. For most West Germans, social equality and social justice are not quite the same. Not so in (post-1990) East Germany: once the freedom to travel had been guaranteed social equality is being held in higher esteem than political freedom which, now as before, only seems important to a small professional élite.[27] The political conclusion in both societies could not be more different. According to the East German point of view, social justice will not have been established so long as social equality remains a dream. The West German reply would be: what matters to us is that nowadays all citizens in need, especially the unemployed, widows, pensioners and the sick, are being much better provided for than before thanks to a more generous welfare system. Justice in an abstract and ideological sense and justice in a democratic and pragmatic sense are obviously not the same.

In both parts of Germany the notion of money also has a different meaning. Before unification the East German mark was there to be spent or to be saved for a *Trabi*, for hard times or old age. Basically money was there to pay for one's living and perhaps for a little bit of fun, as it is for most people who just have enough to scrape through. In terms of investment capital, money was an evil commodity that yielded interest without work; money as such could not be perceived "as work". Pulpit and Party had the same reservations about a capitalist society that tried to accumulate money for its own sake rather than to satisfy needs, for instance the needs of the Third World. For most working people, productivity and profit were alien concepts. Even East German bank managers, so we are told by a West German adviser, had to be acquainted with the most basic terms and instruments of the world of financial services.[28] The bewilderment of ordinary customers in front of a bank counter was all the greater. If the GDR has often been described as the "Guardian State" (*der vormundschaftliche Staat*) we have to see the meaning and use of money as one of its symptoms. East Germans were kept in a state of innocence and prevented from growing up by making unpleasant discoveries and painful experiences. It should surprise nobody that soon after unification video libraries and *Beate Uhse*'s brand of sex shops (similar to Ann Summers in the UK) were among the most booming service industries.

The GDR referred to itself as the "Workers' and Peasants' State" (*Arbeiter-und-Bauern-Staat*) just as the Nazis had claimed to be a workers' party. SED functionaries made great efforts to prove that they had a working class background. Work as such was canonised – regardless, it could be argued, of its purpose. In a Marxist sense it was seen as a form of existential self-fulfilment, as a "condition humaine". The new socialist man was defined by his contribution to society, not primarily by political self-determination. One is almost reminded of the French saying that the Germans live in order to work and not vice versa. Again the Church raised no objections – the Protestant work ethic as analysed by Max Weber was, after all, receiving a new re-enforcing impetus. In a nationalised economy plans could not be fulfilled if "norms", i.e. certain production targets, were not met in time. That is why the régime also stressed the significance of the *Arbeitskollektiv* and its joint effort, of "team-work" in Western parlance. Viewed from the grassroots, all this might have sounded like pure propaganda. However, the GDR citizen could be assured that his or her workplace was guaranteed, because labour as well as its product were the outcome of a planned economy. Moreover, he experienced the shop floor or the office as a social meeting place of the first order,[29] and that for two reasons. First, at all levels of industry a much higher percentage of women than in the West went to work where they enjoyed the same status as men. Then, the inefficiencies inherent in the system, i.e. the chronic breakdown of machines, the shortage of material and spare parts, etc., always allowed time for chatting, shopping or playing cards during work and office hours. In reality, time was never a precious commodity. Nor was work appreciated in purely monetary terms. As in pre-industrial times a piece of work was to be distinguished by its intrinsic value, the artefact had to satisfy its master. The East German cultural historian Dietrich Mühlberg makes the point that even prostitutes set great store in doing their job "not only" or "primarily" for the money.[30] Everybody would agree that honest living should enjoy more prestige than making a "fast buck"; in East Germany it really did. Business acumen was not a quality to be proud of. Management and workforce were often in cahoots about low production targets which, once fulfilled, were bound to be raised next time without adequate remuneration; official praise yes, but no more money. There were no real incentives to work harder or longer hours. Since virtually the whole working population was employed by the state, it was not surprising that they should all adopt the leisurely working habits of the civil service. Thus the historian is faced with the classical contradiction between ideology and reality that is typical of the GDR in so many ways: work was more highly regarded and at the same time less productive than in the West. It was only after unification that socialist propaganda hit home: it now served as an intellectual excuse for being dissatisfied with the prevailing conditions of life. The transition from "working", as a service to the community, to doing a "job" in order to keep afloat was hard enough. But to be out of work was much worse, it was a shattering blow to one's self-esteem. Often this experience generated a willingness to exploit the system, which evidently did not value honest work. There certainly was no shortage of financial assistance for people out of work whether eligible or not.

In view of the depression that had seized the NBL, the *Besserwessis* referred to East Germans as *Jammerossis* (whinging Easterners) because they were seen to lament their lot without acknowledging that they were better off than before, quite apart from their East European neighbours. On the whole, West Germans had little empathy for the psychological repercussions of the traumatic change with which the East Germans were confronted. Nor were they any longer aware that after the war they, too, were perceived as the *Jammerdeutsche* by the Allies. If we believe the report of British intelligence officers in 1945 then "a sense of impotence . . . mixed with a feeling of self-pity" was "characteristic of many Germans when in distress".[31] Among the innumerable serious attempts to analyse the situation in East Germany, two furiously polemical books about East Germans have been published, both of which sold very well, despite damning reviews.[32] They are of interest here only because of their collection of stereotypes about East Germans, the sort that are usually restricted to pubs or barbershops. Thomas Roethe argues that East Germans would like to work in the way they did under Honecker, while earning and living as they do in Kohl's Germany. He opens up a whole catalogue of West German clichés about "the lazy lot" who have to learn what real and well paid work means. Under Honecker, he maintains, people became accustomed to being looked after, while continuing to cheat on the state, and thus developed a parasitical mentality. Roethe pleads for the withdrawal of financial support for the NBL, and an end to what he regards as the East Germans' long holiday. He exaggerates and generalises individual cases of work-to-rule and pays no attention to the westward migration of more than a million East Germans since reunification, which have greatly benefited the German economy. Roethe clearly does not regard the many industrious shop assistants manning the tills and shop floors of Munich supermarkets as East Germans. He makes the mistake of blaming individuals for social conditions for which they are not responsible – which is, of course, exactly how stereotypes are created. Luise Endlich, the spouse of a West German doctor who settled in the deepest sticks of Brandenburg, provides the perfect example of middle-class snobbery *vis-à-vis* the natives. In her book, she launches a fierce attack on her new neighbours, because they do not know how to behave in civilised society, how to prepare a sophisticated meal (beef in lobster soup) or make conversation, or even what wine to appreciate. And, of course, all the young men are neo-Nazis, and all their parents vote for the PDS. The author's senseless gossip would not merit any mention were it not for the fact that it demonstrates the nature of relations between the two societies. A great many Westerners look down on the East as Germany's "sink estate", a concentration of an uneducated working class systematically proletarianised by their previous masters. What is particularly vexing is that East German attitudes after unification confront the relatively *nouveau riche* West Germans with memories of their own unpleasant past after the war, when they themselves had to be re-educated to fit into Western society. East Germans, meanwhile, feel as though they are being treated as poor relations of whom one is a little ashamed and they reject attempts at re-educating them just as Germans in the Western zones had done after 1945.

The break of 1945 had been largely political and ideological: that of 1990, however, was rather more radical in that it ruptured the whole society and ended an entire way of life. This is unsparingly described in a novel by Ingo Schulze, an East German writer, which has been praised as the first literary effort that came to terms with the fallout of unification.[33] Written in a clinical, matter of fact style, his novel captures East German society through the lives of a group of people living in the small town of Altenburg (Thuringia). Their lives are being turned upside down by the sudden change and its chaotic aftermath: a head teacher is bullied out of office because of his collaboration with the old authorities; his wife moves to the West to seek solace and work; a waitress is seduced by a West German speculator; an arts graduate and university assistant with an unfinished PhD is fired on the arrival of a new professor, meets his biological father in Munich after 30 years and then scrapes through by working at a succession of odd jobs. A *malaise* pervades past and present as though a sinister family history suddenly unravels.

Psychiatrists from all parts of the country are generally agreed that the sudden transition was a huge challenge to the people of East Germany, who were now faced with an immense pressure to succeed. For many, the future seemed bleak and the threat of unemployment loomed heavily. Even school children experienced the change of curriculum and found the sudden expectation that they "think for themselves" as extremely demanding. One psychologist from Leipzig even argues that most East Germans were in a "permanent state of latent or acute stress".[34] It's hardly surprising that the birth-rate dropped dramatically, with young women regarding pregnancy as the surest way to lose their job. Alcoholism also increased – with the low price of Schnapps, drink had long been a problem in the East, but was tolerated by state and society as a means of overcoming boredom. Now, people started relying on it, using it as a crutch to cope with the sudden challenges and stresses.

Experts believe it may take several generations before the people of both German societies are conditioned by their new circumstances to grow into one. In the meantime, the older generation that grew up before 1989 has found solace in a kind of nostalgic appropriation of the past, or rather a reaffirmation of their own collective biography, so to speak "à la recherche des temps perdus", which nevertheless few want to return to. Westerners are often dumbfounded by this phenomenon and have coined the term *Ostalgie* (*Ost*: East). Numerous books about everyday life in the GDR have been published and have found many readers. They cover a wide spectrum of subjects ranging from football, jokes and love life to more sinister areas such as uniforms and border fortifications. Museums now exhibit everyday items like favourite brand-names of the food industry and household goods; restaurants have even opened that offer authentic GDR menus.[35] In the meantime East German television (*Mitteldeutscher Rundfunk*) has broadcast a well documented but by no means uncritical series on "Everyday life in the Workers' and Peasants' State", which has also been published as a book.[36] In the 1950s such reminiscences about the Nazi period would never have been tolerated. The suppression of any nostalgia for the Nazi period cannot be explained only by the criminal record of Hitler's régime. There was also the widespread fear among the new political establishment that a great many Germans might still be under the spell of Nazi ideology. This is not the case in East Germany today. Ulbricht or Honecker were never as evil or as popular as Hitler who had, after all, been the political pop-star of the 1930s. However, *Ostalgie* is coming under increasing criticism with many claiming it represents the commercial exploitation of people's memories, and their naïve attitudes towards the past.[37]

Notes and references

1 Günter Grass, "Don't Reunify Germany" in Harold James and Marla Stone (eds), *When the Wall Came Down. Reactions to German Unification* (London, 1972). See the criticism of this attitude by Rainer Zitelmann (ibid., p. 106) and Jens Hacker, *Deutsche Irrtümer. Schönfärber und Helfershelfer der SED-Diktatur im Westen* (Berlin, 1992) as well as Hans-Peter Schwarz ,"Mit gestopften Trompeten". Die Wiedervereinigung aus der Sicht westdeutscher Historiker, in *Geschichte in Wissenschaft und Unterricht* 1993/44, pp. 683–704.

2 Anne-Marie Le Gloannec, "On German Identity", *Daedalus* 1994/123, p. 133. See also Jan-Werner Müller, *Another Country. German Intellectuals, Unification and National Identity* (London, 2000).

3 Richard Schröder, *Vom Gebrauch der Freiheit. Gedanken uber Deutschland nach der Vereinigung* (Stuttgart, 1996). p. 16.

4 See for instance the collection of essays by Peter Glotz, *Die falsche Normalisierung* (Frankfurt a.M., 1994); also Wilhelm von Sternburg, *Geteilte Ansichten über eine vereinigte Nation* (Frankfurt a.M., 1990).

5 See e.g. the symptomatic title of Heinrich-August Winkler, *Der lange Weg nach Westen* (Munich, 2001).

6 Quoted in *Der Spiegel*, 1992/34 (17.8.1992).

7 See Gerhard A. Ritter, *Über Deutschland. Die Bundesrepublik in der Deutschen Geschichte* (Munich, 1998), pp. 203–06.

8 See the many books by Norbert Frei on this topic, his most recent being: *1945 und Wir. Das Dritte Reich im Bewußtsein der Deutschen* (Munich, 2005).

9 See Ritter, *Über Deutschland*, pp. 237–39.

10 Elisabeth Noelle-Neumann, director of the oldest West German institute for opinion polls, in *Frankfurter Allgemeine Zeitung*, 8.7.1998.

11 See Armin Pfahl-Traughber, *Rechtsextremismus. Eine kritische Bestandsaufnahme nach der Wiedervereinigung* (Bonn, 1995).

12 Theodor W. Adorno *et al.*, *The Authoritarian Personality* (New York, 1950).

13 Hans-Joachim Maaz, *Der Gfeühlsstau. Ein Pychogramm der DDR* (Berlin, 1991), pp. 135–83. See also the West German analysis by Michael Schmitz, *Wendestress. Die psychosozialen Kosten der deutschen Einheit* (Berlin, 1995).

14 See Ritter, *Über Deutschland*, p. 242; also Richard Schröder, p. 36. For the period after 1945, Anna J. Merritt and Richard L. Merritt, *Public Opinion Polls in Occupied Germany. The OMGUS-Survey 1945–1949* (Urbana, IL, 1970), p. 32.

15 Schröder, p. 36.

16 See Elisabeth Noelle-Neumann, "Die linken und rechten Werte: Ein Ringen um das Meinungsklima", in Karl Graf Ballestrem and Henning Ottmann (eds), *Theorie und Praxis. Festschrift für Nikolaus Lobkowitz* (Berlin, 1996), pp. 243–67.

17 Characteristic for this new self-confident national identity: Matthias Mattussek, *Wir Deutschen. Warum die anderen uns gern haben können* (Frankfurt a.M., 2006).

18 Schröder, p. 26 and p. 94.

19 See Alexander Fischer and Günter Heydemann (eds), *Geschichtswissenschaft in der DDR* (2 vols Berlin, 1988–90); also Werner Weidenfeld (ed.), *Deutschland: Eine Nation – doppelte Geschichte* (Cologne, 1993).

20 See the excellent analysis of the GDR legacy by Peter Bender, *Unsere Erbschaft: Was war die DDR – was bleibt von ihr?* (Hamburg, 1992), p. 155.

21 It is on Alsace that the author did his PhD thesis (Lothar Kettenacker, *Nationalsozialistische Volkstumspolitik im Elsass* (Stuttgart, 1973).

22 Marianne Krüger-Potratz, *Anders sein gab es nicht. Ausländer und Minderheiten in der DDR* (Münster, 1991).

23 See Karl-Heinz Heinemann and Wilfried Schubarth (eds), *Der antifaschistische Staat entlässt sein Kinder. Jugend und Rechtsextremismus in Ostdeutschland* (Cologne, 1992).

24 See Mary Fulbrook, *Anatomy of a Dictatorship. Inside the GDR 1949–1989* (Oxford, 1995), pp. 129–50. The term "Nischengeselslchaft" has been introduced by Günther Gaus, *Wo liegt Deutschland. Eine Ortsbestimmung* (Hamburg, 1983). Gaus, the FRG's first "ambassador" to East Berlin, was the typical West German intellectual who tended to transfigure the GDR.

25 Quoted by Schmitz, p. 90 (translation L.K.).

26 Reproduced by Gerhard Rein (ed.), *Die Opposiiton in der DDR. Entwürfe für einen anderen Sozialsimus* (Berlin, 1998), p. 228.

27 See Heiner Meulemann, *Werte und Wertewandel. Zur Identität einer geteilten und wieder vereinten Nation* (Munich, 1998); also Ritter, *Über Deutschland*, pp. 241–45.

28 See the report of a Bavarian bank manager (Arvid Mainz) in Saxony regarding monetary change-over in Grosser, pp. 437–48.

29 See Günther Heydemann and Francesca Weil, "Der Betrieb als sozialer Raum vor und nach 1989", in *Enquete-Kommission, Überwindung der Folgen der SED-Diktatur im Prozess der deustchen Einheit*, Deutscher *Bundestag* (ed.) (Frankfurt a.M., 1999), vol. V, pp. 577–654 (henceforth EKB/2).

30 Dietrich Mühlberg, "'Leben in der DDR' – warum untersuchen und wie darstellen?", in Evemarie Badstübner (ed.), *Befremdlich anders. Leben in der DDR* (Berlin, 2000), pp. 648–95. Perhaps the best summary on the East German mentality. See also EKB/2, vol. 1, pp. 524–28.

31 PID-Report, 24.8.1945, PRO/London: FO 1049/264.

32 Thomas Roethe, *Arbeiten wie bei Honecker, leben wie bei Kohl. Ein Plädoyer für das Ende der Schonfrist* (Frankfurt a.M., 1999). Luise Endlich, *Neuland. Ganz einfache Geschichte* (Berlin, 1999). Due to the sales a follow-up came out in 2000: *Ostwind. Nicht ganz einfache Geschichten*, with equally bad reviews.

33 Ingo Schulze, *Simple Stories. Ein Roman aus der ostdeutschen Provinz* (Berlin, 1998, now 6th edition as paperback /dtv: Munich, 2006).

34 Quoted by Schmitz, p. 126. See his whole chapter, Wendestress', pp. 125–82.

35 See Mühlberg, p. 652. See also the peculiar success of the East German magazine Super Illu described in Süddeutsche Zeitung, 2./3./ 10. 2008 ("Die Couch der Ostdeutschen").

36 Hans-Hermann Hertle and Stefan Wolle, *Damals in der DDR. Der Alltag im Arbeiter- und Bauernstaat* (Berlin, 2006).

37 See chapter 10.

Attempts at explanation

The collapse of the GDR and German unification happened so fast that they left historians and political scientists flabbergasted – out of breath, as it were, and struggling to make sense of these unexpected and overwhelming events. Many had been convinced of the GDR's longevity. It was politicians, rather than academics, who made the first steps towards tackling the recent past. Thanks to the initiative of former dissidents, now elected to political office, the *Bundestag* was transformed into a historical debating society. On 14 May 1992, with the backing of all parties, including the PDS, parliament set up an enquiry into the history of the GDR (*Enquete-Kommission "Aufarbeitung von Geschichte und Folgen der SED-Diktatur"*). The main aim of the exercise was to provide moral support to all citizens, above all to those in the NBL, who had been left in a state of confusion by events. Its aim was to reassure them that they had been right to demonstrate the GDR out of existence and had no reason to regret their actions. Before the Commission, made up of deputies, witnesses and historians began its work, the *Bundestag* debated for an entire day how the topic should be tackled. Many of the speakers in that debate had been actively involved in the decision-making processes of the past years, such as Wolfgang Schäuble, who had negotiated the unity treaty and Markus Meckel, former GDR foreign minister, and their contributions constitute useful source material for the historian. The terms of reference for the Commission were very broad, ranging from the political strategy of the SED, the importance of ideology for social discipline, the role of the churches, the impact of inner-German and international relations, to the question of continuing psychological habits and behaviours, in particular under the influence of the Nazi dictatorship.[1] The end product of two years of intensive deliberations was a massive bundle of paper: 9 volumes (in fact 18 books) covering 15,187 pages altogether, enough material to keep students of history occupied for decades. Yet the chairman and one of the former dissidents, Rainer Eppelmann, claims that it was not their intention to anticipate the verdict of history; all they wished to achieve was to do justice to the victims of dictatorship and to encourage a public debate.[2]

However respectable they might have been, members of the Commission were not entirely free of a certain bias – or of harbouring an ulterior motive. That motive was to remove any remaining notion of the GDR as a legitimate state and can be summarised in one sentence: "Whatever you have been told, the GDR was a repressive dictatorship". Of course, the term *Diktatur* had been used to describe the GDR before, but now it received the stamp of official approval. Kohl and his government felt that the victims and opponents of the régime deserved this effort as a gesture of recognition and reconciliation. The decision to set up a separate, and as it turned out, huge and expensive authority to administer the Stasi archives[3] had the same origins. As a trained historian who took pride in his first profession, Helmut Kohl was perhaps more amenable to such undertakings than other chancellors might have been. He went to university at a time when German historians regarded it as their patriotic duty to examine cases of resistance to Hitler's criminal régime; if history does not repeat itself, historiography sometimes does. Now the same psychological mechanisms were at work, in that those who had opposed the régime were granted a leading role and were in a position to direct further research. Indeed notwithstanding further debates, there was now agreement among most established historians in East and West (except for the former guardians of historical materialism who were made redundant) that the GDR should henceforth be seen as the second German dictatorship of the twentieth century – though in no way of the same criminal calibre as the Nazi régime.

On two days in May 1994, the Commission, following the submission of the summary report, discussed the impact of the two dictatorships in the plenary chamber of the *Reichstag*. The two main speakers, Horst Möller and Jürgen Kocka, leading West German historians from different political backgrounds, were in full agreement that it made sense to compare the Nazi and SED dictatorships.[4] Both proceeded from the assumption that comparing does not mean equating and that this methodological approach highlights both analogies and differences. Nor do comparisons serve to make excuses for one or the other of the two systems, i.e. in this case to play down the inhumane ideology and the criminal energy of Nazism, as is often implied by critics of this procedure. But the analogies between the two systems are all too obvious, the common rejection of liberal democracy and civic society and the techniques of monopolising power through a one-party régime, secret police, personality cult, persecution of minorities and total control of the public sphere, to name just some of the most important aspects. The only disagreement between the two speakers arose on the question of attributes: Should the two dictatorships be defined as "totalitarian" (Möller) or simply "modern" (Kocka)? The next day two heavyweights of an older generation entered the debate and decided the issue in favour of "totalit-arian dictatorships": Karl Dietrich Bracher, the liberal grandee of German contemporary history, and the left-wing philosopher and social scientist Jürgen Habermas.[5] In their different ways, both papers constitute a superb intellectual review of the old FRG's democratic re-education. So why were they able to agree where Möller and Kocka with their flawless command of the facts, of all the analogies and differences, could not? One explanation is that Bracher and Habermas discussed the ideologies and the techniques of power in their historical context, in the ways in which they had affected the German mentality since the nineteenth century. This is, arguably, the key to understanding the two German societies today. While West Germans lived under the spell of a totalitarian régime for 12 years; people in the East were conditioned by such circumstances for more than two generations, having slid from one system of total control into the next. In other words, ordinary people in East Germany were subjected to the same abuse of human rights, the same authoritarian concept of politics for a much longer period. Bracher argues that the SED dictatorship was based on the rejection or ignorance of a liberal political culture by many Germans used to the pre-1918 authoritarian state that had mutated into a totalitarian system, first after 1933, then after 1945. Rather than being moulded by the open expression of public opinion in a free society, their experience fluctuated between resistance, adaptation and collaboration. The debate in the *Reichstag* benefited from the concrete experiences of GDR dissidents called as wit-nesses. Rainer Eppelmann, chairman of the Commission, suggested that the GDR did not encourage serous research into the techniques of the Nazi régime because attention would have been drawn to similar structures in the SED state. Obviously, the *Wende* had produced a change of paradigms. The term "totalitarian" had been intellectually out of favour as a discredited Cold War argument unsuitable for the new period of détente. It now turned out that most human rights activists of the GDR insisted on its rehabilita-tion: Yes, they said, we lived under totalitarian conditions. West German political scientists now had to accept this verdict; Bracher with pleasure, Habermas somewhat more reluctantly.

As could be expected, the PDS did not accept this comparison, which was in such contrast to the SED's anti-Fascist mythology. The reservations about the report,[6] expressed by its committee member Dietmar Keller, which were not uncritical with regard to the SED's record, raised two main objections: first, an evaluation of the GDR could not take the old FRG as a model; second, it was wrong to assume that a majority of the population had always been in opposition to the aims and politics of the government. No plausible answer is given to the failure of socialism except for the admission of economic inefficiency and the claim that Soviet predominance left no leeway for reforms, or for a "German path to socialism", as it were.

No doubt, the most convincing argument for the totalitarian character of the SED-régime was the ceaseless and zealous efforts of the Ministry of State Security (Stasi) that epitomised Orwell's Big Brother like no other institution of the twentieth century. Other secret services in Eastern Europe, notably the KGB with which the Stasi closely cooperated, might have been more brutal: no other service had a more extensive and bureaucratically organised network of spies carefully examining every corner of society and reporting on the most trivial activities of people under suspicion. Again the German penchant for perfectionism produced strange effects. After the threat of Russian tanks rolling again into Berlin as during the uprising of June 1953, the Stasi's omnipresent web of spies was the GDR's most effective means of control and intimidation. Not surprisingly, the Stasi was the first target of popular wrath during the revolution of 1989/90. Following rumours that the Stasi was ordered to destroy compromising material and in view of the reluctance of the last SED government to dissolve the agency altogether, thousands of people stormed Mielke's headquarters in *Normannenstraße* on 15 January 1990, an event that might eventually occupy a similar place in the annals of revolutions as the storming of the Bastille. While the Round Table, in fear of foreign intelligence services, agreed to "physically destroy all electronic material concerning personal data" – a great mistake as it turned out – civic committees across the country tried to save as many files as possible, even those that had already been shredded.[7] It was only thanks to these archives, which still amount to some 180 km of files, that we are able to gain a picture of the staggering scale and nature of the Stasi's activities. Not surprisingly, the *Enquete-Kommission* investigated this aspect of the GDR most thoroughly.[8]

The Ministry of State Security, founded in 1950 with virtually no definition of its real purpose, was a bureaucratic monster employing, at the time of its dissolution, no fewer than 91,000 full time officials and 173,000

so-called *Informelle Mitarbeiter* (IM), i.e. ordinary citizens who had been persuaded to spy on their friends, colleagues and neighbours. In this context it
is important to remember that the Nazi Gestapo managed to control a larger
population with considerably fewer agents, largely because people then
had tended to do its work by denouncing each other without needing to be
first wooed and signed up as informal helpers.[9] There was one Stasi agent
for every 50 people (1:20 among border guards). The previous director of
the Hannah Arendt-Institute (Leipzig) concludes: "In a state, based on an
ideological world-view and a totalitarian system, every citizen is *per se* a
suspect."[10] The Stasi had its own defence force of divisional strength, its own
university, sports club and its own stores and health clinics. Yet it was not a
state within the state but the most loyal organ of the SED, according to its
own motto "the Shield and Sword of the Party".[11] Based on the command
structure of the *Nationale Volksarmee* (NVA)[12] it served the régime as an
efficient machinery for controlling, disciplining and repressing all suspicious
elements of the population. However, Mielke's loyalty was to the Party,
not to its current general-secretary, as proven by his role in everyone of the
Party's sea-changes, from Ulbricht, via Honecker to Krenz, once Moscow
had given its blessing.

Before 1989, fear of the Stasi was pervasive. "There were constant
rumours that this or that friend was working for the Stasi. They provided the
breeding-ground for the general atmosphere of Angst."[13] Nevertheless, people
had no clear idea how far the tentacles of the Stasi had actually reached into
their private lives. The sheer number and the wide-spread activities of the
informal agents, the IMs, came as a great and most shocking surprise after
preliminary evaluations of the archives. The previous anxieties about the
Stasi's unscrupulous actions, tapping phones, reading mails and medical
documents, wiring homes, sabotaging friendships and careers and so forth,
turned out to have been more than justified. Spectacular cases came to light
where brother denounced brother, husband reported on wife, teacher on
pupils and vice versa. Sometimes agents were asked to spy on each other to
prove their "honesty". A total corruption of human decency was the means,
which was justified by the higher end of achieving socialism. As under the
Nazis, an old and dangerous aspect of German political culture reasserted
itself: the dubious distinction between *Privatmoral* and *Staatsmoral*, between
the different moral laws applicable to the private citizen and the state. These
revelations suggest that the term "totalitarian" is indeed the appropriate
attribute to be attached to the SED-dictatorship. Moreover, they also explain
why it seems futile to spend much time and energy exploring reasons for the
relative longevity of the régime. It is typical of unimaginative West Germans

to wonder why people were able to make themselves at home in such a state as the GDR: people simply had no alternative.

Typical targets for *Operative Personenkontrolle* (OPK), i.e. the surveillance of people you know or shadowing those you do not know, and *Operative Vorgänge* (OV), i.e. interfering in, and often destroying the lives of suspects in one way or another, were members of the Protestant Church, dissident artists and human rights activists, such as active pacifists who objected to the growing militarization of society. They were generally referred to as *feindlich-negative Kräfte* (hostile-negative elements). The East German hierarchy was most upset when Gerhard Besier, a West German theologian who had worked on the relationship between Church and State during the Third Reich, revealed how many high ranking church officials, including bishops, had in fact collaborated with the Stasi.[14] Stasi officers who wished to recruit Church informers tended to proceed in a very tactful manner and rarely asked for a signed commitment,[15] which allowed many collaborators to claim subsequently that they had not been aware of what was going on. Most experts agree that money as such was not a crucial motive for conspiring with the Stasi. Loyalty *vis-à-vis* the government and ideological convictions did play a certain role, though not to the extent demanded by the Stasi. More important were the feeling of self-importance, and the promise of personal advantages, career prospects, a higher living standard or the chance to exercise more influence. Recruitment was carefully organised. Potential candidates were persuaded, occasionally blackmailed, but never forced to work for the Stasi. Some were made to believe that they were among the chosen few trusted by the government. Others were found guilty of certain acts of trespassing and were told that now they had a chance to make good. The perverse paternalism that was so characteristic of the GDR in general was the Stasi's guiding model. Controlling officers were supposed, and often indeed felt themselves, to be friends, counsellors or psychotherapists to their charges. Since the SED perceived organised religion as its chief ideological rival, the Stasi tried hard to infiltrate church organisations at all levels. Synods of the Protestant Church were the last platforms of free speech and intellectual opposition. However, since Luther's days, there was also the Protestant tradition of *Staatskirchentum*, of close cooperation with the secular authorities (*Thron und Altar*).[16] Thus it is no contradiction that local vicars like Rainer Eppelmann were sworn enemies of the system while their superiors like Manfred Stolpe secretly collaborated with the Stasi. As a secular religion, socialism abused mental habits and ritual practices instilled by the Protestant and Catholic Churches over centuries for its own ends. The *Jugendweihe*, the equivalent of confirmation and a popular initiation rite in the East up to the present day, is only the most glaring manifestation in this context. The Stasi was not, as mentioned before, a state within a state but it certainly saw itself as a church-like secret society within society that placed great emphasis on conspiratorial methods – secret meetings and messages, code names, etc. – destined to uphold the SED's monopoly on power. Rainer Eppelmann later stated: "One can only fully grasp the moral bankruptcy of the SED-dictatorship if one realizes that the whole of society had been organised by the SED in conspiratorial ways. Everything in the GDR which was of any real importance was secret at the same time."[17] Collaborators of the Stasi were lured into believing that compared with the capitalist Federal Republic, the GDR was the better, though constantly threatened, Germany which needed their watchful eyes. To withstand such brainwashing required a measure of self-confidence and independence of mind that had not been nurtured by German political and religious culture in the past. The courage of dissidents and human rights activists, therefore, deserves all the more admiration.

By the time the proceedings of the *Enquete-Kommission* were published, the *malaise* in East Germany had grown worse. To many politicians the new *Ostalgie* that had seized the NBL seemed to be symptomatic of a kind of collective denial of what the GDR stood for. On 22 June 1995 the thirteenth *Bundestag*, decided therefore, to continue the work of the previous parliament and to investigate the transformation process after 1990.[18] The idea was to show that the problems arising from the transformation process were the direct result of 40 years of neglect, mismanagement and repression. Moreover, the *Bundestag* wished to document what had been achieved since 1990 and what was still to be done. Again the undertaking had the support of all major parties and resulted in no fewer than 14 volumes of papers and debates. This time *Bündnis 90/Die Grünen* joined the governing parties by submitting a joint petition which stated:

The political and moral condemnation of the SED dictatorship does not imply a verdict on the people which had been subjected to it. On the contrary, Germans in the GDR had to carry the heavier burden of Germany's post-war history. With their overthrow of the SED dictatorship in the autumn of 1989 East Germans made an essential contribution to the fact that a widely accepted anti-totalitarian consensus had been established in Germany which belongs to the most important intellectual foundations of democracy.[19]

The Commission clearly recognised that the German nation consisted of two societies that had yet to grow together. This, they felt, could only be achieved if West Germans knew more about life in the GDR, thus acknowledging how privileged they had been, and if East Germans recovered their self-esteem by accepting their individual biographies without condoning the dictatorial system under which they had had to live. East German deputies of the former civil rights movement were fully aware that they were in competition with the PDS, who would tell people that their lives in the GDR had been worthwhile but were about to be rubbished by the new political establishment. Thus Markus Meckel would stress that a full life in a dictatorship was undeniably possible but that at the same time the assessment of the system must be clear and unmistakable.[20]

Ostalgie, the somewhat romantic reappraisal of everyday life in East Germany as a popular phenomenon, came as an unwelcome surprise to the political establishment. It was mainly for two reasons that the second *Bundestag* Commission felt the need to investigate everyday life (*Alltagsleben*): first, in order to understand its essential features and second, to find out how far former expectations and values still determined life and mental habits in the new Federal Republic.[21] In other words, not only the political system but "life from below" was also worth looking at: work and leisure, eating and drinking, interior design and clothing, consumption and sexual behaviour, social and religious habits. As was typical for the West German academic community the attributes that characterised this strange society soon triggered off a kind of social-anthropological debate: was it divided into niches (*Nischengesellschaft*) or socialist estates; was it organised, tragic, nationalised (*verstaatlicht*), sedated or totally dominated (*durchherrscht*)?[22] The Commission confirmed the crisis of identity brought about by the sudden turn of events described in the previous chapter: concern about the new importance of time and money, worries about the loss of employment, anxieties caused by public controversies, and by liberty at the expense of equality, a rising crime rate, a more permissive society, and so forth. The Commission approached this problem by trying to calm high-running emotions: no one had reason to dismiss his or her former life as "lost years". To stress that life experiences of East Germans were generally just different and not worse than those in the West was more of a well-meant psychological prop than a description of reality. Members of the Commission clearly recognised that East Germans were about to reassert their collective ego *vis-à-vis* their West German cousins and to develop a specific mode of self-confidence. They saw no harm in a different East German mentality as long as looking back did not transfigure reality into a blissfully shining past. They were fully aware that the PDS tried to use existing resentments against the better-off West for its own dubious purposes of exculpating the GDR. "Such tendencies should be met with forceful arguments", they declared.[23]

If we are to understand the problems with which the dissidents turned parliamentarians had to cope it is important to recall the different circumstances of the 1950s and 1990s. West German democracy took root at a time of unprecedented economic boom whereas the aftermath of unification was characterised by the fallout of globalisation and a shortage of jobs due to rationalisation and the outsourcing of labour. The shadow of the Nazi past was much darker than that of the GDR so that public nostalgia for the Third Reich was out of the question. Now, former leaders of the SED took their place in the *Bundestag*. The PDS, while distancing itself from the excesses of the SED, chose the former head of the GDR's Lawyers Association, Gregor Gysi, as its chairman who then became something of a media celebrity, by being invited to countless television talk shows. Markus Wolf, deputy of Stasi chief Erich Mielke and head of foreign intelligence, was welcomed to present his new cookery book on television. Egon Krenz and other SED chiefs who were responsible for 900 murders along the Berlin Wall and the fortified border, got away with very light prison sentences. Early post-*Wende* films on the GDR, such as "Go, Trabi, Go", "Sonnenallee" or even the world success "Goodbye, Lenin" portrayed life as a comedy. Dissidents and victims felt that a state founded on the rule of law was out of its depth in dealing with the crimes they had witnessed. Many of them feared that, sooner or later, the GDR would be entirely whitewashed with the West wishing to draw a line under the past, with the result that the perpetrators of East German outrages would have the last word. There can be no doubt that the danger of playing down the past – the German term being *Verharmlosung* – was much more real after 1990 than it ever had been after 1945. This threat provided the background for launching a second investigation into the SED dictatorship and its legacy: the desire to set the record straight as to the true nature of the SED régime and to make sure that people would not forget. The project had the Chancellor's full support. In the meantime, some dissidents whose natural home might have been with the SPD, made their peace with Kohl. This applies in particular to Bärbel Bohley, the most prominent activist of *Neues Forum* who had been referred to as "the mother of the Revolution".[23a]

By the end of the century, making sense of the history of the GDR had evolved into a veritable academic industry: 500 experts, most of them West Germans, 1,000 research projects and a book market that could no longer be quantified (at least 10,000 titles) were dedicated to the task.[24] Memorial sites and archives, generally in the hands of East Germans, also proliferated. But all these efforts at spreading the right message about the true nature of the SED dictatorship evidently did not have the desired impact on the population at large. Ignorance among adults and school children in both parts of

Germany was still widespread. There is an easy explanation for the situation in East Germany. The Commission's report states: "In East German schools a discussion about the GDR period does not take place, nor does it in West German schools."[25] Often the school year ended before there was to time to confront the immediate past. The report concludes that these experiences were the same as those made in West Germany in the 1950s when the treatment of the Nazi period was often skipped for lack of time. Obviously teachers did not wish to be asked uncomfortable questions or to be forced to critically contemplate their own formative years. Margot Honecker, in charge of education during her husband's rule, was an energetic lady and only picked reliable teachers, 70 per cent of them being members of the SED (1988). Her officials knew what they were doing when the times of change approached. By 1992, 155,000 out of 185,000 teachers were still in employment. Teachers, active as ideological instructors or as FDJ officials, who had been made redundant, often took successful legal action to be reinstated. Nonconformist teachers who had been expelled in the past could not return as a matter of course. Nor did teaching methods change with the arrival of unification and the ideal of fostering independent minds. "Striving for discipline, order and the teaching of mere facts still enjoys a high standing."[26] The many theologians among East German parliamentarians had no illusions as to the influence the Church exercised in making up the short-fall in the conveyance of democratic and Christian values (which this generation of young East German pastors believed to be identical). With only 25–30 per cent of the population still members of a parish, religious instruction in school would not remedy the situation, described as extensive *Entchristlichung*. Therefore, the Land Brandenburg introduced the subject *Lebensgestaltung, Ethik und Religion* (LER), which proved to be a controversial decision in Germany though not within the Commission. The latter's recommendations were trenchant and suggested, among other things, that most textbooks would need to be rewritten to offer a "differentiated comparison with the Nazi dictatorship".

The real aim of the Commission was to convince the government of the need to spend more money on memory culture as a means of re-educating the public. The term "re-education" (*Umerziehung*) had, of course, been out of favour in Germany since post-war days. But that was exactly what all the arguments brought forward amounted to: the general ignorance about the GDR was so worrying that a well funded foundation for the purpose of critically reviewing the SED dictatorship was clearly in the public interest of a unified but not yet united Germany. By the end of the Commission's deliberations on 5 June 1998, this aim was finally reached when the *Bundestag* passed a law setting up a public foundation to this end. The idea was not to create another large research institute or anything resembling the huge bureaucracy into which the administration of the Stasi Archives had grown. It was conceived as a centre that would support all sorts of other institutions like memorial sites and projects such as exhibitions destined "to review the causes, the history and the legacy of the dictatorship in the Soviet zone of occupation and in the GDR".[27] Again the emphasis was on an "anti-totalitarian consensus", designed to strengthen democracy and Germany's *innere Einheit* (a society at one with itself). Naturally one could argue that the Commission had, all along, been preparing a job-creation programme for former dissidents and human rights activists who had difficulties in adapting to the harsh climate of the new Germany. But that view would be somewhat too cynical. There were numerous worthwhile institutions, especially memorial sites such as former Stasi prisons now often run by former victims, which received private contributions but could not survive without public funds. By generously financing the two commissions the government had demonstrated its determination to meet the concerns of all those East German politicians and intellectuals, like Rainer Eppelmann, Joachim Gauck, Richard Schröder, Markus Meckel and many others, who had put their heart and soul into the reconciliation of the two German societies now cohabitating under one "roof". Clearly this was not a party political project because government and opposition (except for the PDS) were agreed that this endeavour was in the national interest.

According to the federal constitution, cultural affairs, notably schools and universities, are the responsibility of the *Länder*. As a consequence, the federal government has no influence on school curricula or teacher training, and is restricted to making funds available for certain institutions for which it accepts full responsibility. The Commission therefore attached great importance to the funding and reorientation of memorial sites: "For a democratic memory culture monuments of remembrance to the National Socialist and Communist dictatorships are of central significance."[28] Particular attention was to be paid to "anti-Fascism as a founding myth of the GDR and an ideology legitimizing the SED dictatorship". It acknowledges the federal commitment to all sites and places of national importance (*gesamtstaatliche Bedeutung*).[29] The following is a list of East German memorial sites funded so far by the Federal government for a period of ten years, which should be financed permanently by both the Federal and *Länder* governments: Nazi concentration camps like Sachsenhausen, Buchenwald and Ravensbrück, which served the Gestapo as well as the NKWD after 1945, and GDR prisons such as Hohenschönhausen, Bautzen and Torgau, which started off as Soviet special camps before they were taken over by the Stasi.

Members of the Commission felt strongly that the anti-Fascist myth could best be exposed by drawing attention to Nazi concentration camps being transformed into Soviet special camps, a fact systematically suppressed by the SED. A further list of memorial sites, which should also be permanently maintained, are: Münchner Platz, Dresden (hardly known in the West) where Nazi courts and Soviet tribunals sentenced thousands of people to death; Marienborn, the most prominent checkpoint along the border; and Normannenstrasse, Berlin, the Stasi headquarters. Two institutions were not specifically mentioned because they were financially secure: *Gedenkstätte Berliner Mauer* (the Museum remembering the Berlin Wall at Bernauer Strasse) and the administration of the Stasi Archives. Maintaining the latter, with a budget of 100 million Euro, probably costs more money than all the other memorial sites of the GDR put together. No wonder members of the Commission wished to spread public funds more evenly. The whole concept of memorial sites was well suited to stress the crucial assumptions underlying the new agreed approach to Germany's terrible twentieth century: the common legacy of two totalitarian dictatorships.

The Commission had the East as well as the West German population in mind when it suggested extending the number of remembrance days beyond those already established: 27 January (Holocaust), 17 June (East German uprising), 3 October (Germany Unity, official red letter day); 18 March (revolution of 1848 which for the East Germans gained a particular significance in relation to 1989); 8 May (Germany's capitulation or, more precisely, unconditional surrender); 23 May (promulgation of the Basic Law); 20 July (German resistance against Hitler); 13 August (erection of the Berlin Wall); 9 October (crucial Monday demonstrations in Leipzig and elsewhere); 9 November (proclamation of the German Republic 1919, destruction of the synagogues in 1938, fall of the Berlin Wall 1989), and *Volkstrauertag* (national remembrance day, penultimate Sunday before first Sunday in Advent – not in remembrance of the "war heroes" but remembering the victims of despotism, war and expulsion). Of course, nobody has suggested that Germany should commemorate all those historical dates in terms of holidays. It would suffice if schools were asked to draw special attention to their significance. A foreigner looking at this sombre calendar might pity the Germans for being asked to remember more national catastrophes than uplifting events. If he has a background in psychiatry he might conclude that this cannot be doing the German psyche much good. Indeed most Germans, especially East Germans, would be tempted to agree with Richard Schröder who wrote: "A democracy cannot only be legitimized by the sad memories of dictatorships."[30] But then they might remember that

Germany has more religious holidays than most of her neighbours which, while belief in their literal truth has receded, are enjoyed as religious folklore. Invented traditions, like the feast of Corpus Christi (1264), are cherished as much as if not more than those emanating from real and often tragic events. Few Germans would wish to swap the holiday in honour of Mary's Assumption, based on the last Catholic dogma (1950), for the 20 July plot against Hitler.

Some seven years later not much had changed. No coherent concept of how the GDR should be publicly remembered had emerged. In spite of a growing bulk of literature, the general ignorance about the second German dictatorship was still widespread. An opinion poll among 2,000 Berlin school children revealed that two-thirds were unaware that everyday life in the GDR was marked, at least for many citizens, by constant surveillance and repression; in fact, a majority believed that elections had been more or less democratic.[31] The degree of knowledge among West German pupils was not much better inasmuch as they did not regard the GDR as part of German history. In the NBL the trivialisation of life in the GDR made further progress. Thus the federal government, now run by a "Red–Green" coalition under Chancellor Gerhard Schröder, appointed a new Commission of experts in close co-operation with Rainer Eppelmann (CDU), chairman of the Federal Foundation instituted in 1998, and Marianne Birthler, now in charge of the Stasi Archives. A year later, on 15 May 2006, Professor Martin Sabrow, director of the Potsdam Centre for Contemporary History, presented the Commision's recommendation to the public. This report sparked an immediate and passionate public debate on how to remember the GDR, not least because of a distancing vote from Freya Klier, a member of the Commission and one of the GDR's most prominent dissidents. Klier criticised the approach being taken to the subject, which she described as excessively academic.[32] She demanded a more down-to-earth approach towards state repression and a greater focus on the day-to-day cruelty of which people were capable during the dictatorship – as exemplified by the Stasi prison at *Hohenschönhausen*. That memorial site, run by Hubertus Knabe,[33] worried some of the Commission members who objected to its "unprofessional" (i.e. over-emotional), representation of the GDR. It could be argued that this debate boils down to a fundamental confusion as to the purpose of memorial sites: should they convey a sophisticated historical perception of the past or should they have a clear political message. The controversy was not so much between academics and museum experts as between conservative historians, who favoured a clear message with due attention to the instruments of repression, and more liberal and left-wing academics who pleaded for historical empathy focused on everyday life. Richard Schröder was right to suggest that academic rivalry between West German academics and research institutes vying with each other for public funds should not be overlooked.[34] The antagonism between the Munich *Institut für Zeitgschichte*, with its singular record on Nazi and post-war German history, and the Potsdam *Zentrum für Zeithistorische Forschung* specialising on the GDR, is no secret in the academic community. Franziska Augstein referred to an "unpleasant competition" among experts for the prize of being "the most anti-dictatorial".

Finally, the Commission recommended focusing remembrance on three interlinked centres situated at sites across Berlin:

1   a new central forum dealing with everyday life under the heading "Political Control, Society, Resistance";

2   "Surveillance and Persecution" under the auspices of the Stasi Archives (BStU) with the Stasi headquarters at Normannenstraße and its main prison at Hohenschönhausen as memorial sites;

3   "Division and Border" linking various memorial sites devoted to the Wall and important border check-points.

The Commission's recommendations were discussed at a public hearing in early June 2006. The chief criticism against the three-pillars-concept came from Horst Möller, director of the Munich Institute, who felt that important aspects were missing, such as the establishment of the SED dictatorship by the Soviet Military Administration, which then remained under Moscow's tutelage for the rest of its existence. Moreover, he objected to memorial culture being split up into three different themes since these were intrinsic aspects of one and the same régime that should not be separated. He also felt uneasy about the statement of the Commission that hitherto the methods of repression and surveillance had been given too much attention at the expense of everyday life under a dictatorial régime oscillating between conformity and resistance. Putting his objections into a nutshell Möller said: "In my eyes the Stasi was more characteristic of the GDR than the nurseries."[35] In his view, repression and surveillance were the significant features of the SED dictatorship to which attention should be drawn in the first place and, if at all possible, in one permanent exhibition within a reasonable space. There is much to be said for this "no-nonsense approach" in view of the limited time and intellectual capacity of any ordinary visitor. However, one can also argue that this is a typical view from outside the walled-in society of the GDR, which demonstrates a lack of empathy for those who had to cope with an unpleasant reality. This point of view has been taken up by Richard Schröder and Joachim Gauck who were, as they saying goes, *gelernte DDR-Bürger* (socialised GDR citizens), and who now came to the rescue of the Commission. Schröder had the impression that many West German experts, who had already come to terms with the past of their fathers and now felt the urge to do the same with their East German compatriots, had no real idea what life in a dictatorship really meant.[36] There was, he said, a partial identification with the reality of the GDR that must be depicted, embarrassing as it might be. It was in fact a plea for more empathy for those ordinary GDR citizens who just tried to get along with each other, including the ruling party. Two days later, he said in an interview: "A dictorship does not consist of heroes, victims and opportunists. Whoever believes that is clueless. There were many shades of grey."[37] Joachim Gauck, the first federal commissioner for the Stasi Archives, came to his assistance and rejected all insinuations that a look at everyday life meant to play down the evil aspects of dictatorship.[38] The argument between *Alltagsverwaltern* (everyday-administrators) and *Repressionsspezialisten* (experts on Stasi and repression), he explained, was a silly dispute if one knew how people really were conditioned to become political puppets. In his lectures to West German audiences he would tell people "how to become an Ossi"; not by imagining being a polical prisoner, but by growing up in a small town as a child of six years. The mechanisms of producing conformist citizens, he argued, were much more subtle than people in the West might think. The GDR was a state on the wrong track even without the Stasi. It is indeed true to say that West German historians approaching their sixties had no first hand experience of how their parents had been brainwashed during the Nazi period. In this sense a closer look at everyday life in the GDR could sharpen the perception of the pitfalls during the Nazi period and thus contribute to a common understanding of the past. There was a tendency after the war to look upon the 12 years of Nazi rule as an accident, a freak of nature as it were, due to the Great Depression, not really part of Germany history. Gauck felt that West Germans were inclined to look upon the GDR in the same way, as just a misbegotten creature of the Soviet occupation force in bed with the German Communists.[39] Gauck argued that Germans would grow together to such an extent that they would integrate the East German experience into their sense of national identity. Even though the debate lingered on in the press for the next two months the intervention of Schröder and Gauck had in fact settled the issue of how important the display of everyday life actually was for a true understanding of the second

German dictatorship. How to reorganise the memorial culture so that the various aspects of the GDR would not get lost in a vast array of different sites, is of course, a slightly different matter. However, this question still awaits an answer because here we are confronted with a struggle for financial survival and independence among the various memorial sites. A lot will depend on what will become of the Stasi Archives, by far the most expensive institution employing a staff of no fewer than 2,000 people. There is general agreement that sooner or later it will have to be attached to the Federal Archives, which only has a third of that number on their pay-roll.

Both Schröder and Gauck, the two honest brokers between East and West, were much impressed by the Oscar winning film *Das Leben der anderen* and felt that films like these are probably more suitable to interpret everyday life in the GDR than some of the memorial sites – though they are, of course, in favour of maintaining every single one of the sites. Since then a few more films of that kind, if not of the same calibre, have been shown on German television.[40] Perhaps novels and films are now the most appropriate and effective media through which to keep the collective memory alive, especially to a new generation which finds it hard to grasp the unbelievable follies and crimes of which their forefathers were capable.

Academic in-fighting is a hallmark of historical controversies in Germany. In spite of a professional distrust in mono-causal explanations, the historian's mindset is not unlike that of a theologian who longs for a final answer. I am no exception. Common sense suggests that there are clear criteria for a definite verdict on the GDR which are often lost in a battle of words and terms. The GDR was the illegitimate child of the Cold War. Its German state builders were agents of the Soviet Military Administration. Throughout its history the SED had the backing of its protectors. When support was withdrawn at the end of the Cold War the régime collapsed because of people's resolve to be free. The beginning and the end of the GDR define its essential nature though not every aspect of its character. The most significant German input was the Stasi or rather the sheer extent and the bureaucratic performance of its spying activities. All other aspects of life in the GDR are reminiscent of the first German dictatorship despite all due emphasis on the ideological differences and their consequences. Life under the eyes of a repressively watchful régime was bound to have affected people's mentality over a period of 40 years, and longer in the case of the older generation. There is no better re-education than the rule of law and the environment of a functioning democracy. With the arrival of new generations, the two societies will grow together again as Willy Brandt predicted in 1989. In

50 or 100 years' time, it is likely that Nazi and SED régimes will be remembered as the "Holocaust State" and the "Stasi State" while school books will continue to refer to the two "totalitarian dictatorships".

Notes and references

1 Deutscher *Bundestag* (ed.), *Die Enquete-Kommission, Aufarbeitung von Geschichte und Folgen der SED-Diktatur im Deutschen Bundestag*, 9 (18) vols (Frankfurt a.M., Baden-Baden, 1995), vol. 1, pp. 154–56 (henceforth: EKB/1).

2 Ibid., vol. 1, pp. VII–X.

3 Because of its long-winded name the authority *Der Bundesbeauftragte für die Unterlagen des Staatssicherheitsdienstes der ehemaligen DDR* is usually being referred to by its present chief executive, first Gauck, now Birthler. It has at present a staff of nearly 2,000.

4 Protokoll der 75. Sitzung, 3.5.1994, EKB/1, vol. IX, pp. 575–675. As to the methodological problems involved, see e.g. Günther Heydemann and Heinrich Oberreuter (eds), *Dikaturen in Deutschland. Vergleichsaspekte: Strukturen, Institutionen und Verhaltensweisen* (Bonn, 2003); also Günther Heydemann and Lothar Kettenacker (eds), *Kirchen in der Diktatur* (Göttingen, 1993).

5 Protokoll der 76. Sitzung, 4.5.1994, ibid., pp. 676–777.

6 EKB/1, vol. I, pp. 680–738.

7 See Klaus Schroeder, *Der SED-Staat. Partei, Staat und Gesellschaft 1949–1990* (Munich, 1998), p. 343. See also Anna Funder, *Stasiland. Stories From Behind the Berlin Wall* (London, 2003).

8 EKB/1, vol. VIII: *Das Ministerium für Staatssicherheit. Seilschaften, Altkader, Regierungs- und Vereinigungskriminalität.*

9 See Robert Gellately, *The Gestapo and German Society. Enforcing Racial Policy 1933–1945* (Oxford, 1990).

10 Klaus-Dietmar Henke in Werner Weidenfeld and Karl-Rufolf Korte (eds), *Handbuch zur deutschen Einheit 1949–1989–1999* (Frankfurt a.M., 1999), p. 723.

11 See evidence by Karl Wilhelm Fricke, the foremost West German expert who as a journalist had been kidnapped by the Stasi in the late 1950s, in EKB/1, vol. VIII, pp. 7–19. As to Fricke's numerous works on the Stasi and the repressive nature of the GDR see bibliography in Schröder, pp. 739–40.

12 Fricke (ibid., p. 42), "Generally a cleaning lady had the rank of a sergeant", a remark for which he gained a laugh from members of the enquiry.

13 Hans-Hermann Hertle and Stefan Wolle, *Damals in der DDR. Der Alltag im Arbeiter und Bauernstaat* (Munich, 2006), p. 319 (translation L.K.).

14 Gerhard Besier, *Der SED-Staat und die Kirchen* (Munich, 1993). See also his article, "Aus der Resistenz in die Kooperation. Der 'Thüringer Weg' zur 'Kirche im Sozialismus'", in Heydemann and Kettenacker (eds), pp. 182–212.

15 Evidence by Prof. Hans-Joachim Memmler, EKB/1, vol. VIII, p. 55.

16 See Ulrich Kühn, "Die theologische Rechtfertigung der 'Obrigkeit'", in Heydemann and Kettenacker (eds), pp. 259–81.

17 Rainer Eppelmann, in EKB/2, vol. I, p. 27 (translation L.K.)

18 Deutscher *Bundestag* (ed.), *Die Enquete-Kommission "Überwindung der Folgen der SED-Diktatur im Prezess der Deutschen Einheit" im Deutschen Bundestag* (Frankfurt a.M., Baden-Baden, 1999), 8 (14) vols (henceforth: EKB/2).

19 Ibid., p. 5 (translation L.K.).

20 Ibid., p, 82.

21 "Alltagsleben in der DDR und in den neuen Ländern", ibid., pp. 522–52.

22 A new term which seems to some historians more acceptable than "totalitarian".

23 Ibid., p. 528.

23a See her interview in Süddeutsche Zeitung (10./11.1.2009) where she says of herself: "I have been enemy of the state, Jeanne d'Arc, and later the cry-baby".

24 See Beate Ihme-Tuchel, *Die DDR* (Darmstadt, 2002), p. 2. See also e.g. the bibliography in Hermann Weber, *Die DDR 1945–1990* (Munich, 1993) who lists no fewer than 1,420 books on the GDR (pp. 191–299).

25 EKB/2, vol. I, p. 429 (translation L.K.)

26 Ibid., p. 420 (altogether pp: 411–36 of the Final Report).

27 Gesetz über die Errichtung einer Stiftung zur Aufarbeitung der SED-Diktatur, 5.6.1998, ibid. pp. 137–41.

28 Ibid., p. 588.

29 This terminology proves the fear of contact with the word "national" which is still politically not correct.

30 Richard Schröder, *Die Zeit*, 29.6.2006.

31 Klaus Schroeder, *Deutschland-Radio Kultur*, 21.5.2006, reproduced in: Martin Sabrow et al. (eds), *Wohin treibt die DDR-Erinnerung? Dokumentation einer Debatte* (Göttingen, 2007), pp. 279–81 (henceforth: Sabrow).

32 Sondervotum by Freya Klier, in Sabrow , pp. 44–45.

33 Hubertus Knabe (ed.), *Aufbruch in eine andere DDR* (Hamburg, 1990). His contributions to the Stasi debate since then in Schroeder (p. 750).

34 Richard Schröeder, *Die Tageszeitung*, 8.6.2006, in Sabrow, pp. 306–08. Siee also Franziska Augstein, "Knast und Alltag. Wie soll der DDR gedacht werden?", *Süddeutsche Zeitung*, 8.6.2006, in Sabrow, pp. 304–06.

35 Sabrow, p. 56.

36 Ibid., pp. 70–76.

37 See n. 34. See also his contribtion in *Die Zeit* ("Auch wir hatten glückliche Tage"), 29.6.2006, ibid., pp. 339–43.

38 The invention of new terms is typical for any polemical debate in German. In this case the reproach is *Entsorgung* (waste disposal, i.e. of the unpleasant features of the GDR) or *Weichspülung* (adding fabric conditioner to the washing process). The equivalent term for the Nazi period is *Verharmlosung* (playing down).

39 As a West German historian the author admits this to have been – and to some extent still to be – his own view of the GDR.

40 Within one week in September 2007, for instance, two documentaries were shown on German Television, one about the "Prague Embassy" drama, the other about a mother fighting for her two daughters, forced into adoption after her failed escape ("The Lady at Checkpoint Charlie").

Epilogue

In September 2008, the Federal Government published its latest annual report on the economic state of affairs in East Germany since unification.[1] Like many official documents, it is fulsome in its praise of past achievements and lists a variety of future initiatives, but does not necessarily paint an accurate and realistic picture of the present. With its emphasis on economic data, the report may nevertheless serve as a useful summary of nearly 20 years of *Aufbau Ost* – the gigantic project to rebuild the East German economy after 40 years of socialism. In it, the Federal Government concedes that, since 1989. East Germans have been exposed to a variety of bewildering experiences, which have left many feeling as strangers in the united country, not least owing to lower levels of individual prosperity. Moreover, the *Datenreport 2008*,[2] compiled by the Federal Statistical Office in cooperation with other institutions, shows that between 2001 and 2006 the poverty rate in the East has gone up from 15.3 per cent to 22.7 per cent (in Germany as a whole from 11.4 per cent to 13.9 per cent). Throughout the country, the gap between rich and poor has widened thus leading to a shrinking of the middle classes.

In the early 1990s, the impression prevailed that the government in Bonn did not think it right that the state, discredited as it had been in the whole of Eastern Europe, should shoulder the burden of reconstruction, beyond extending its political and economic system and keeping the new *Länder* financially afloat. Since then, that initial restraint has ebbed away, resulting in what has been a huge, systematic attempt to develop East Germany's infrastructure and economy. This change of direction is in part due to a steep rise in unemployment, resulting from large-scale de-industrialisation. The government decided to invest heavily in the neglected infrastructure such as public transport, health, education, communal services, and telecommunications. It also tried to provide financial incentives for investors, especially those interested in modernising the dilapidated housing stock. To give but one example: nearly 10 billion Euros were spent between 1991 and 2006 on military installations for the *Bundeswehr* (the military forces) in East Germany. The result of this massive state investment is that, as far as public services are concerned, conditions in the two parts of the country are now on a fairly even keel. Indeed, certain city centres in the West's old industrial heartland now appear shabbier than those of many towns in the East, which have been expensively refurbished, such as the Renaissance town of Görlitz close to the Polish border. However, due to ongoing migration to the more prosperous West and a declining birth rate, the housing market in particular has failed to stimulate the economy as was hoped. Nevertheless, over the years East German unemployment figures, the most sensitive of statistics in political terms, have declined in line with those in the West reaching the lowest level since the early 1990s (June 2008: 12.7 per cent or 506,000 fewer than 2005, still twice as high as in the old Federal Republic). This is the result of steady growth and the reform of social services introduced by Gerhard Schröder's government between 1998 and 2005.

Financial support for East Germany is based on the so-called *Solidarpakt II*, which will have provided 156 billion Euros by 2019, by which time it is hoped that the East German economy will be self-sufficient. Due to a variety of investment programmes initiated by the Federal Government, as well as low local government trade taxes compared to the West, industrial development in the East has gained new momentum. In the 1990s central government was accused of being indiscriminate in its financial aid, i.e. following the principle of equal "shares for all". Here, too, lessons have been learnt and there is now a new emphasis on developing industrial growth clusters (*Wachstumskerne*), especially as regards innovative technologies. Industry now has a share of 19 per cent (compared to 24.7 per cent in the old *Länder*) of the overall GDP in the East. Compared with other national economies (France: 16 per cent, UK: 19 per cent, USA: 18 per cent, Japan: 24 per cent) this is no bad record, demonstrating that East Germany is well on the way to regaining its old industrial strength. Traditional economic centres such as the motor and chemical industries have resurfaced while at the same time modern technologies in the field of microelectronics and renewable energy have also managed to establish themselves. Trade with the new EU countries in Eastern Europe, meanwhile, has intensified – but so too has competition for investment, with many German businesses investing in the low-wage economies of Poland and the Czech Republic. Thus, growth and productivity in the new *Länder* have not yet caught up with West Germany (GDP being 70 per cent). Except for the domain of public servants, salaries and wages are not yet on a par with those in the West (on average in 2006 5,000

Euros per annum less) and East Germany still has relatively few small to medium sized enterprises, which are the backbone of the Federal Republic's economy. It is important to note, however, that Berlin, which has the highest rate of people on social benefits of all German *Länder*, distorts these figures by dragging down the East's performance.

One problem highlighted in the government report is unlikely to be solved soon: the new *Länder* are more severely affected by Germany's overall demographic decline than the West. It is estimated that between 2005 and 2025 the East German population will have declined by 11.2 per cent, compared to an estimated 2 per cent for Germany as a whole. What worries the authorities above all is the ongoing westward migration of younger people (i.e. those aged between 18 and 30), who leave their hometowns mainly in search of jobs and higher salaries. Of the 50,000 East Germans who moved to the West in 2006, 33,000 were below the age of 30. The number of vacant properties in towns and cities also worries the government. In 2002, when the number of unoccupied flats reached the staggering figure of one million, the government began its programme of demolition known as *Umbau Ost* in an attempt to revitalise and repopulate urban centres. This project made one billion Euros available to reduce the volume of unused housing. By 2007 220,000 flats had been dismantled, mainly unattractive prefabricated blocks in modern suburbs. Historic buildings predating 1919 were left untouched. Indeed, many historic town centres have been placed under preservation orders and have been carefully restored so as to make them attractive as residential areas. Some local governments have even tried to attract pensioners from the West by promising cheaper rents in newly refurbished period blocs.

For a variety of reasons Berlin is the Federal Government's problem child. It is Germany's most heavily indebted *Land* and it has the highest percentage of citizens on social benefits. The Federal Government tries to make up for these deficiencies by generously supporting all kinds of cultural institutions: museums such as those old gems assembled on the famous *Museumsinsel* (adopted by UNESCO as a world heritage monument) as well as the German Historical Museum and the Jewish Museum, the Academy of Arts, a number of opera houses, and memorial sites recalling the horrors of the two German dictatorships. Apart from strengthening the appeal of the capital, known all over the world for its role during the Cold War, the government's largess is also designed to create jobs and appease the many retired stalwarts of the old régime who have not come to terms with the new political order. Of course, the government is rather more concerned for the victims of the old régime than its perpetrators. In 2007, the government introduced a compensation scheme for those imprisoned for six months or more because of their political views. Almost 42,000 people now receive 250 Euros as a result of the scheme.

It must be noted that East Germans are, of course, better off than their neighbours to the east, as indeed they always had been. However, East Germans compare their living standard with that of people living in the West, rather than those of Poles, Czechs or Hungarians. For this reason, many East Germans are not aware of how greatly they have benefited from unification in material terms. Their real income has risen from approximately 6,500 Euros to more than 14,000 (in 2006), while in percentage terms, they have reached about 80 per cent of the German average. The initiatives of the Federal Government, currently, of course, led by a chancellor from the East, demonstrate that no efforts are being spared to remove the last vestiges of inequality. However, it may well take another 40 years to undo the damage done to the economy of Germany's East between 1949 and 1989.

Notes

1 Jahresbericht der Bundesregierung zurn Stand der deutschen Einheit 2008. *Die neuen Länder – für ein modernes und soziales Deutschland*, published by: Bundesministerium für Verkebr, Bau und Stadtentwicklung (24 September 2008, 127 pp. plus 42 pp. statistical evidence).

2 See article in *Süddeutsche Zeitung*, 19.11.2006: "Germany's middle class is shrinking".

Select bibliography

I. The German Question during the Cold War period (1945–1989)

Amos, Heike, *Die Westpolitik der SED 1948/49–1961* (Berlin, 1999)

Badstüber, Evemarie (ed.), *Befremdlich anders. Leben in der DDR* (Berlin, 2000)

Bahr, Egon, *Zu meiner Zeit* (Berlin, 1999)

Brandt, Willy, *Erinnerungen* (special edition for the GDR: Berlin and Frankfurt a.M., February 1990).

Besier, Gerhard, *Der SED-Staat und die Kirche. Der Weg in die Anpassung* (Munich, 1993)

Buchheim, Hans, *Deutschlandpolitik 1949–1972. Der politisch-diplomatische Prozeß* (Stuttgart, 1984)

Dannenberg, Julie von, *The Foundations of Ostpolitik. The Making of the Moscow Treaty between West Germany and the USSR* (Oxford, 2008)

Deutscher *Bundestag*/12. Wahlperiode (ed.), *Enquete-Kommission, Aufarbeitung von Geschichte und Folgen der SED-Diktatur in Deutschland,* (Frankfurt a.M. and Baden-Baden, 1995), 9 vols

Foschepoth, Josef (ed.), *Adenauer und die deutsche Frage* (Göttingen, 1988)

Fricke, Karl Wilhelm, *MfS intern: Macht, Strukturen, Auflösung der DDR-Staatssicherheit* (Cologne, 1991)

Fulbrook, Mary, *Anatomy of a Dictatorship. Inside the GDR 1949–1989* (Oxford, 1995)

Garton Ash, Timothy, *In Europe's Name: Germany and the Divided Continent* (London, 1993)

Geisel, Christof, *Auf der Suche nach einem Dritten Weg. Das politische Selbstverständnis der DDR-Opposition in den 80er Jahren* (Berlin, 2005)

Genscher, Hans-Dietrich, *Erinnerungen* (Berlin, 1995)

Goeckel, Robert F., *The Lutheran Church and the East German State* (Ithaca, NY, 1990)

Grünberg, Andreas, *Der eingemauerte Staat. Die DDR vor der Wende* (Stuttgart, 1999)

Hacke, Christian, *Die Außenpolitik der Bundesrepublik Deutschland. Weltmacht wider Willen?* (new edn Berlin, 1997)

Hacker, Jens, *Deutsche Irrtümer. Schönfärber und Helfershelfer der SED-Diktatur im Westen* (Frankfurt a.M., 1992)

Haftendorn, Helga, *Deutsche Außenpolitik zwischen Selbstbeschränkung und Selbstbehauptung, 1945–2000* (Stuttgart, 2001)

Henke, Klaus-Dietmar *et al.* (eds), *Widerstand und Opposition in der DDR* (Cologne and Vienna, 1999)

Hoffmann, Dirk *et al.* (eds), *Die DDR vor dem Mauerbau. Dokumente zur Geschichte des anderen deutschen Staates 1949–1961* (Munich, 1993)

Ihme-Tuchel, Beate, *Die DDR* (series: Kontroversen um die Geschichte, Darmstadt, 2002)

Kettenacker, Lothar, *Germany Since 1945* (Oxford, 1997)

Kleßmann, Christoph, *Die doppelte Staatsgründung. Deutsche Geschichte 1945–1955* (Göttingen, 1982)

Kohl, Helmut, *Erinnerungen 1982–1990* (Munich, 2005)

Korte, Karl-Rudolf, *Deutschlandpolitik in Helmut Kohls Kanzlerschaft. Regierungsstil und Entscheidungen 1982–1989* (Stuttgart, 1998)

Kotschemassow, Wjatscheslaw, *Meine letzte Mission. Fakten* (Berlin, 1994)

Kowalczuk, Ilko-Sascha *et al.* (eds), *Der Tag X – 17. Juni 1953. Die, innere Staatsgründung' der DDR als Ergebnis der Krise 1952/54* (Berlin, 1995)

Lemke, Michael, *Einheit oder Sozialismus? Die Deutschlandpolitik der SED 1949–1961* (Cologne, 2001)

Loth, Wilfried, *Stalins ungeliebtes Kind: Warum Moskau die DDR nicht wollte* (Berlin, 1994)

McAdams, James A., *Germany Divided: From the Wall to Reunification* (Princeton, NJ, 1993)

McElvoy, Anne, *The Saddled Cow. East Germany's Life and Legacy* (London, 1992)

Mittag, Günter, *Um jeden Preis. Im Spannungsfeld zweier Systeme* (Berlin, 1991)

Mitter, Arnim and Stefan Wolle, *Untergang auf Raten. Unbekannte Kapitel der DDR-Geschichte* (Munich, 1993)

Neubert, Erhart, *Geschichte der Opposition in der DDR 1949–1989* (Berlin, 1998)

Ostermann, Christian F. (ed.), *Uprising in East Germany 1953* (New York, 2001).

Plock, Ernest D., *East German–West German Relations and the Fall of the GDR* (Boulder, CO and Oxford, 1993)

Ploetz, Michael, *Wie die Sowjetunion den Kalten Krieg verlor. Von der Nachrüstung zum Mauerfall* (Munich, 2000)

Poppe, Ullrike *et al.* (eds), *Zwischen Selbstbehauptung und Anpassung. Formen des Widerstandes und der Opposition in der DDR* (Berlin, 1995)

Potthoff, Heinrich, *Im Schatten der Mauer. Deutschlandpolitik 1961 bis 1990* (Berlin, 1999)

Press and Information Office of the FRG, *Documentation Relating to the Federal Government's Policy of Détente* (Bonn, 1978).

Ritter, Gerhard A., *Über Deutschland. Die Bundesrepublik in der deutschen Geschichte* (Munich, 1998)

Rolf Steininger, *Deutsche Geschichte seit 1945. Darstellung und Dokumente* (new edn, Frankfurt a.M., 1996)

Ruggenthaler, Peter (ed.), *Stalins großer Bluff. Die Geschichte der Stalin-Note in Dokumenten der sowjetischen Führung* (Munich, 2007)

Schroeder, Klaus, *Der SED-Staat. Partei, Staat und Gesellschaft 1949–1990* (Munich, 2000)

Schwarz, Hans-Peter, *Die Legende von der verpassten Gelegenheit. Die Stalin-Note vom 10. März 1952* (Stuttgart, 19982)

Siebenmorgen, Peter, *Gezeitenwechsel. Aufbruch zur Entspannungspolitik* (Bonn, 1990)

Smyser, William R., *From Yalta to Berlin. The Cold War Struggle over Germany* (Basingstoke, 1999)

Taylor, Frederick, *The Wall. A World Divided, 1961–1989* (New York, 2007).

Vogtmeier, Andreas, *Egon Bahr und die deutsche Frage. Zur Entwicklung der sozialdemokratischen Ost- und Deutschlandpolitik vom Kriegsende bis zur Vereinigung* (Bonn, 1996)

Weber, Hermann, *Die DDR 1945–1990* (Munich, 1993)

Weidenfeld, Werner and Karl-Rudolf Korte (eds), *Handbuch zur deutschen Einheit, 1949–1989–1999* (Frankfurt a.M., 1999)

Wentker, Hermann, Außenpolitik in engen Grenzen. Die DDR im internationalen System 1949–1989 (Munich, 2007).

Wettig, Gerhard, *Bereitschaft zur Einheit in Freiheit? Die sowjetische Deutschland-Politik 1945–1955* (Munich, 1999)

Zimmer, Matthias, *Nationales Interesse und Staatsräson. Zur Deutschlandpolitik der Regierung Kohl 1982–1989* (Paderborn, 1992)

II. German unification and its aftermath (1990–2006)

Albrecht, Ulrich, *Die Abwicklung der DDR. Die, 2 plus 4 – Verhandlungen. Ein Insider-Bericht* (Opladen, 1992)

Baker, James A., *The Politics of Diplomacy* (New York, 1995)

Bender, Peter, *Unsere Erbschaft: Was war die DDR – was bleibt von ihr?* (Hamburg, 1993)

Berlin-Institut für Bevölkerung und Entwicklung (ed.), *Die Demografische Lage der Nation. Wie zukunftsfähig sind Deutschlands Regionen* (Munich, 2006)

Biermann, Rafael, *Zwischen Kreml und Kanzleramt. Wie Moskau mit der deutschen Einheit rang* (Paderborn, 1997)

Childs, David, *The Fall of the GDR. Germany's Road to Unity* (Harlow, 2001)

Deutscher *Bundestag*/13. Wahlperiode (ed.), *Enquete-Kommission, Überwindung der Folgen der SED-Diktatur im Prozeß der deutschen Einheit'*, (Frankfurt a.M. and Baden-Baden, 1999), 8 vols

Falin, Valentin, *Politische Erinnerungen* (Munich, 1993)

Gedmin, Jeffrey, *The Hidden Hand. Gorbachev and the Collapse of East Germany* (Washington, DC, 1992)

Glässner, Gerd-Joachim, *The Unification Process in Germany: From Dictatorship to Democracy* (London, 1992)

Görtemaker, Manfred, *Unifying Germany, 1989–1990* (New York, 1994)

Grix, Jonathan, *The Role of the Masses in the Collapse of the GDR* (London, 2000)

Grosser, Dieter, *Das Wagnis der Währungs-, Wirtschafts- und Sozialunion. Politische Zwänge im Konflikt mit ökonomischen Regeln* (Stuttgart, 1998)

Grünberg, Andreas, *Wir sind das Volk! Der Weg der DDR zur deutschen Einheit* (Stuttgart, 1994)

Hertle, Hans-Hermann and Stefan Wolle, *Damals in der DDR. Der Alltag im Arbeiter- und Bauernstaat* (Munich, 2006)

Heydemann, Günther *et al.* (eds), *Revolution und Transformation in der DDR 1989/90* (Berlin, 1999)

Jäger, Wolfgang, *Die Überwindung der Teilung. Der innerdeutsche Prozeß der Vereinigung* (Stuttgart, 1998).

James, Harold and Marla Stone (eds), *Uniting Germany. When the Wall Came Down: Reactions to German Unification* (London, 1992)

Jarausch, Konrad and Volker Gransow (eds), *Uniting Germany: Documents and Debates, 1944–1993* (Providence, RI, 1994)

Jarausch, Konrad, *The Rush to German Unity* (Oxford, 1994)

Jesse, Eckhard and Armin Mitter (eds), *Die Gestaltung der deutschen Einheit* (Bonn, 1992)

Kaiser, Karl, *Deutschlands Vereinigung: Die internationalen Aspekte* (Bergisch-Gladbach, 1991)

Kiessler, Richard and Frank Elbe, *Ein runder Tisch mit scharfen Ecken. Der diplomatische Weg zur deutschen Einheit* (Baden-Baden, 1993)

Kohl, Helmut, *Erinnerungen 1990–1994*, vol. 2 (Munich, 2007)

Krenz, Egon, *Wenn Mauern fallen. Die friedliche Revolution* (Vienna, 1990).

Kuhn, Ekkehard, *Der Tag der Entscheidung: Leipzig, 9. Oktober 1989* (Berlin, 1992).

Küsters, Hanns Jürgen and Daniel Hofmann (eds), *Dokumente zur Deutschlandpolitik. Deutsche Einheit. Sonderedition aus den Akten des Bundeskanzleramtes 1989/90* (Munich, 1998)

Kwizinskij, Julij, *Vor dem Sturm. Erinnerungen eines Diplomaten* (Berlin, 1993)

Langguth, Gerd, *In Search of Security. A Socio-Psychological Portrait of Today's Germany* (Westport, CT, 1995)

Leiby, Richard A., *The Unification of Germany, 1989–1990* (London, 1999)

Leonhard, Jörn and Lothar Funk (eds), *Ten Years of German Unification: Transfer, Transformation, Incorporation?* (Birmingham, 2002)

Lewis, Derek and John R.P. McKenzie, *The New Germany: Social, Political and Cultural Challenges of Unification* (Exeter, 1995)

Maaz, Hans-Joachim, *Der Gefühlsstau: Ein Psychogramm der DDR* (Berlin, 1991)

Maier, Charles S., *Dissolution. The Crisis of Communism and the End of East Germany* (Princeton, 1997)

Maier, Gerhard, *Die Wende in der DDR* (Bonn, 1991).

Mitter, Armin and Stefan Wolle (eds), *Ich liebe Euch doch alle! Befehle und Lageberichte des MfS, Januar-November 1989* (Berlin, 1990)

Müller, Jan-Werner, *Another Country. German Intellectuals, Unification and National Identity* (New Haven and London, 2000)

Müller, Uwe, *Supergau Deutsche Einheit* (Berlin, 2005)

Noelle-Neumann, *Demoskopische Geschichtsstunde. Im Wartesaal der Geschichte zur deutschen Einheit* (Zurich, 1991)

Pawlow, Nikolai, *Die deutsche Vereinigung aus sowjetischer Perspektive* (Frankfurt a.M., 1996)

Philipsen, Dirk, *We are the People. Voices from East Germany's Revolutionary Autumn of 1989* (Durham, NC, 1993)

Pond, Elizabeth, *Beyond the Wall. Germany's Road to Unification* (Washington, DC, 1993)

Rein, Gerhard (ed.), *Die Opposition in der DDR. Entwürfe für einen anderen Sozialismus* (Berlin, 1989)

Ritter, Gerhard A., *Der Preis der deutschen Einheit. Die Wiedervereinigung und die Krise des Sozialstaates* (Munich, 2006).

Sabrow, Martin *et al.*, *Wohin treibt die DDR-Erinnerung? Dokumentation einer Debatte* (Göttingen, 2007)

Schabowski, Günter, *Das Politbüro. Ende eines Mythos* (Hamburg, 1991)

Schäuble, Wolfgang, *Der Vertrag. Wie ich über die deutsche Einheit verhandelte* (Stuttgart, 1991)

Schmitz, Michael, *Wendestress. Die psychosozialen Kosten der deutschen Einheit* (Berlin, 1995)

Schneider, Wolfgang, *Leipziger Demontagebuch* (Leipzig and Weimar, 1990)

Schönbohm, Jörg, *Two Armies and One Fatherland. The End of the Nationale Volksarmee* (Providence, RI, 1996)

Schröder, Richard, Vom *Gebrauch der Freiheit. Gedanken über Deutschland nach der Vereinigung* (Stuttgart, 1996)

Stöss, Richard, *Rechtsextremismus im vereinten Deutschland* (Bonn, 1999)

Sturm, Daniel Friedrich, *Uneinig in die Einheit. Die Sozialdemokratie und die Vereinigung Deutschlands 1989/90* (Bonn, 2006)

Szabo, Stephen F., *The Diplomacy of German Unification* (New York, 1992)

Teltschik, Horst, *329 Tage* (Berlin, 1991)

Weidenfeld, Werner, *Außenpolitik für die deutsche Einheit* (Stuttgart, 1998)

Zelikow, Philip and Condoleezza Rice, *Germany Unified and Europe Transformed* (Cambridge, MA, 1996)

Zwahr, Hartmut, *Ende einer Selbstzerstörung. Leipzig und die Revolution in der DDR* (Göttingen, 1993)

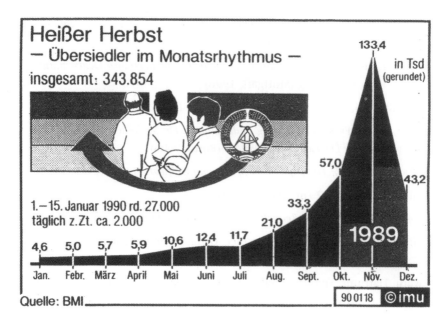

Heißer Herbst
— Übersiedler im Monatsrhythmus —
insgesamt: 343.854

133,4

in Tsd
(gerundet)

57,0

43,2

1.–15. Januar 1990 rd. 27.000
täglich z.Zt. ca. 2.000

33,3

21,0

1989

4,6   5,0   5,7   5,9   10,6   12,4   11,7

Jan.   Febr.   März   April   Mai   Juni   Juli   Aug.   Sept.   Okt.   Nov.   Dez.

Quelle: BMI

90 0118   ©imu

1 Steep rise of migrants in 1989.

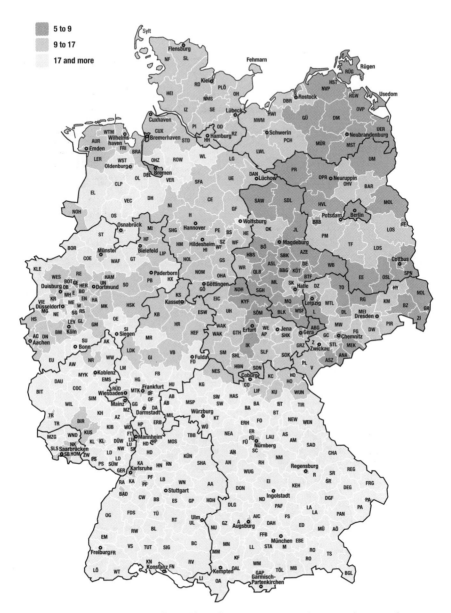

2 Unemployed and recipients of social benefits per 100 citizens between the ages of 18 and 65 in 2003.

Source: Federal Statistical Office.

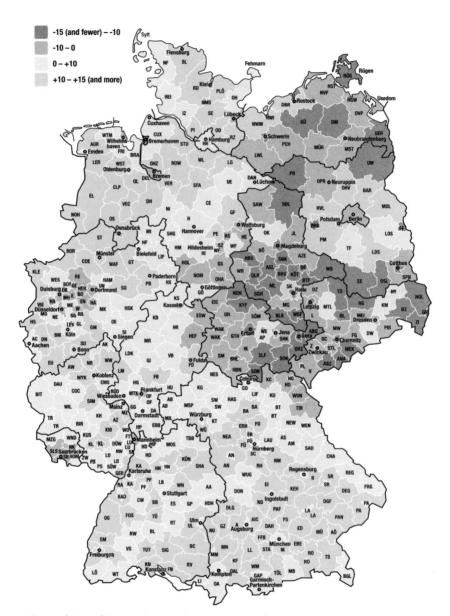

3 Depopulation of Eastern Germany between 1990 and 2004.

Source: Federal Statistical Office.

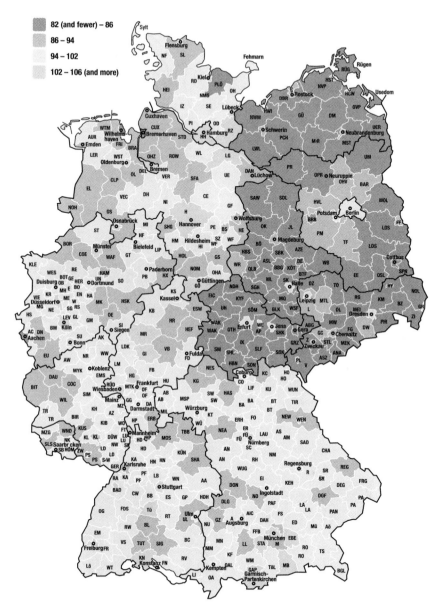

4 Westward migration of women. Percentage of women aged between 18 and 29 in 2003; 63% of all persons moving from East to West Germany were women.

Source: Federal Statistical Office.

Wie holen wir ihn da herunter?

Zeichnung: Walter Hanel

1 How could we get them down to earth?

„ Es ist die Wiepervereinigung "

2 Mitterand to Maggie et al.: "It is the Reunification . . . " (November).

„Glaubst du auch an die Geschichte vom Sozialismus mit menschlichem Antlitz?"

3 Do you also believe in that story about Socialism with a human face?

Ängste

4 *"Ängste"* (anxieties).

5 SPD leader/chancellor candidate Oskar Lafontaine posing as champion of both the Socialist would-be reformers in the East and the hedonistic West. Placards: "What about our prosperity?", "What will become of our achievements?" (In the past the SED kept stressing their *Sozialistische Errungenschaften* (January/February).

Der Spiegel, 51/1989, S. 89

Hält das soziale Netz?

Hanel, Bergisch-Gladbach

6 "Will the social net hold?" (*soziale Netz* is the German term for benefits of the welfare state).

7 Fill it up please! (Meeting in February).

8 Modrow insisting United Germany to be neutral, on orders from Gorbachev (reconnecting with Stalin's policies in the early 50s). (January-May).

9 Confused Germany between the demands of Bush and Gorbachev not knowing where to go.

10 Are you for or against the free market economy?" (man with life-belt is Adenauer who has introduced the market economy). (February-May).

11 We are ready, roofer hurry up!

12 Big Fish Federal Republic of Germany (BRD) swallowing the little Fish GDR (DDR): No Thank You!" Students in Leipzig were the last defenders of the GDR because their professional future, guaranteed on the basis of political loyalty, suddenly seemed to be in jeopardy.

Index